MARY
RENAULT

BY THE SAME AUTHOR

Van Gogh: His Life and His Art

DAVID SWEETMAN

MARY RENAULT

A BIOGRAPHY

HARCOURT BRACE & COMPANY
NEW YORK   SAN DIEGO   LONDON

Library of Congress Cataloging-in-Publication Data
Sweetman, David.
Mary Renault: a biography/by David Sweetman.—1st ed.
p. cm.
Originally published: England: Chatto and Windus.
ISBN 0-15-193110-0
1. Renault, Mary—Biography.
2. Homosexuality and literature—History—20th century.
3. Women novelists, English—20th century—Biography.
4. Lesbians—Great Britain—Biography.
5. Lesbians—South Africa—Biography. I. Title.
PR6035.E55Z87   1993
823'.912—dc20   93-16391

Printed in the United States of America

First U.S. edition

A B C D E

FOR

VATCHARIN BHUMICHITIR

I feel sure that had such a competitor appeared
at the court of Alexander, it would have given Bagaos
some very anxious moments. . . .

—*Mary Renault to the author, May 1982*

Contents

List of Illustrations

Words

Because this book deals with two controversial topics – homosexuality and South Africa – and because it covers the years of transition, from the turn of the century to the present day, a few words about words are essential.

When Mary Renault was young, to have called an African a 'Black' would have risked violence, while to have called a homosexual 'gay' would have provoked incomprehension. A mere thirty years ago it was not uncommon for homosexuals to refer to themselves as 'queers' or 'homos' in self-defence against the homophobic use of such epithets by the 'straight' world. 'Gay' has predominated for twenty years, but, as I write, 'queer' is being used again. Today Blacks are proud to be so, though the use of the word 'Coloured', which lingers in South Africa, seems particularly offensive where once it was considered refined (itself a much diminished word). To complete the circle, in America many Blacks now ask to be called African-Americans.

But, however debased, all words have a historical existence which ought not to be suppressed, and for this book I have employed them in the manner of another time. Where this book covers a period of transition, I have tried to make clear that a particular usage was slipping from favour.

Ancient Greece must be added to the mix, for Mary Renault had her own preference for the transcription of Greek into Latin script, preferring the *k* form of names such as Sokrates for her books, while using the more common Socrates in her correspondence. I have left such things as I found them, despite the irritating inconsistencies.

Foreword

We Speculate about You

'Nobody reads Mary Renault in public,' says the homosexual bank clerk in Tubstrip *to the homosexual steam bath attendant. 'It's a dead giveaway.'*

This one-liner comes from what the theatre critic of the *Oakland Tribune* of 29 August 1974 called 'a gay comic melodrama designed to amuse a gay audience'. He was not amused. Nor would Mary Renault have been: she was never best pleased by what she considered a misuse of the old French *'gai'*, a word she stoically employed in its original sense, no matter what suppressed amusement this provoked. Nor did she want her books to belong to any particular sexual grouping – and a glance at her sales figures shows that here at least she succeeded handsomely.

When she died in 1983, Mary Renault was one of the most popular historical novelists in the English language, with her books translated into every major tongue, yet there was always something odd about this success. She told a good story, with enough adventure to satisfy the common reader, and her fastidious attention to historical detail made classical scholars some of her greatest fans, but it was also true that several of her leading characters were unashamedly homosexual at a time when many of those same readers would, under other circumstances, have considered the subject repellent.

A great deal about her life and work seems contradictory. While she is famous for books set in the ancient world, few remember that her earliest reputation came from a series of contemporary novels, published before and during World War II, which touched on the then forbidden subject of lesbianism. Few of her readers were aware that she lived in South Africa for a large part of her life and that while she was recognized as an apostle of sexual revolution in Europe and America, within her adopted country she was best known as the president of the Cape Town centre of PEN International (Poets, Playwrights, Editors, Essayists, Novelists), a position which left her open to attack by those who considered her lukewarm in the struggle for African rights. Even more astonishing is the fact that while she wrote about Greece with unsurpassed knowledge and sympathy, she visited the country only twice.

How a bookish, suburban girl became a key figure in the sexual revolution of the twentieth century is surely the most intriguing aspect of all. *The Charioteer*, the last of her six contemporary novels, was the first to deal openly with deviant sexuality, and the following eight novels, set in ancient Greece, made her the first author to reach a worldwide audience with books whose principal characters might be – though they were not always – male homosexuals.

Between her first historical novel and her death in 1983, the Western world underwent a revolution in thinking about human sexuality and an equally extraordinary revolution in sexual behaviour. During this period Mary Renault's novels helped millions of people come to terms with their sexuality, people who had never 'come out' or protested in public, but who, without her work, would have considered themselves alone and unnatural. One of her greatest achievements was to give homosexuals a place in history while offering non-homosexuals a sympathetic world where heterosexuality was neither the only nor the dominant sexual type.

Given such loyal and grateful readers, it is all the more surprising that so few knew anything about her. Living in South Africa, she was able to isolate herself from inquisitive journalists and only twice allowed herself to be interviewed for British radio – and then only because the broadcaster was Sue MacGregor, the daughter of an old friend. Thus it was all the more surprising when she agreed that I should go to South Africa in 1982 to film an interview with her for BBC television. That millions watched the programme was evidence of her popularity and an indication that there were now many who believed she had said something crucially important about the diversity of human sexuality. It was a message many people needed then and still need today, and I believe that in her own life she exemplified a substantial number of the things about which she wrote. Hers was not always an easy life and she may not always have made the right choices, but she never wavered from her profound belief that all personal and political decisions should be built on strong ethical foundations, and that those with a sexually variant nature had the same duty to exemplify this morality as anyone else. As she put it in our interview:

> Politics like sex is only a by-product of what the essential person is. If you are mean and selfish and cruel it will come out in your sex-life and it will come out in your politics when what really matters is that you are the sort of person who won't behave like that. Which is why I think the writer has no other duty than to address himself to the individual and to display to that individual the standards he thinks he ought to have.

It is worth highlighting that in *her* avowal, Mary thought that *he*, the writer, should address *himself* to the matter, a choice of personal pronouns that was no mere slip of the pen. Indeed, it is hardly surprising that the question most people ask about Mary Renault is whether *she* was really a man. A letter from a vicar in Bath, written after the publication of *The Last of the Wine*, neatly reveals the confusion many of her readers felt: 'Both my friend and I think it would be a mistake to buy your other books for we do not think they could be half as good. We speculate about you and I have hazarded a guess that you are a man writing under a "nom de plume"!'

This would not have displeased her. She would have preferred to have been a man because, as she put it, 'Men have more fun,' and she *was* using a *nom de plume*. She was born Mary Challans, but had adopted the name Renault on the publication of *Purposes of Love*, her first hospital novel, a story which daringly hinted at lesbian love. She was working as a nurse at the time and was aware that any scandal might mean her dismissal. She was also conscious of the fact that her family, especially her mother, would not have approved of their name being associated with such matters.

PART ONE

ENGLAND
1905–1948

I

Mothers and Daughters

As she grew older, Mary Renault became increasingly self-conscious about her appearance. How could she not, when her mother had always warned her that, if she kept her nose in a book, no man would ever look at her twice. And told her again and again. Clementine Challans was not a woman to be sparing with advice. Her most frequently repeated word was 'nice' – nice girls liked to please their mothers, nice girls liked sewing and knitting, and knew how to attract nice young men in steady careers. Being brainy was *not* nice.

When she was young, this meant little to Mary, who was far too vivacious and outgoing to be bothered by her mother's nagging, but in time the endless repetition of her faults preyed on her mind. Had she not become a well-known author, it might have mattered less, but after her books had made her famous, the thought of people staring at her, judging her by her appearance, became intolerable. Clothes were chosen, then discarded. This or that blouse and slacks – her preferred day-time ensemble – would be tried on, then rejected. Spending the royalties from her books on clothes was little help. She liked well-made things – a good silk scarf, a hand-made leather belt, an exotic kaftan for evening wear – and her wardrobe held sufficient alternatives for her to agonize over, trying one coloured blouse against another, matching it to this belt or that, then rejecting them all and starting again.

Only the reassuring presence of Julie Mullard, the friend with whom she shared her life, could help end the indecision. Calmly but firmly, Julie would stand by the mirror in their bedroom insisting that she looked fine, that what she was trying on was what she looked best in, that there was nothing to get fussed about, until finally, if still reluctantly, Mary would agree to go out.

By the time they arrived at their destination, the crisis would be over. If the occasion was in any way official then, as the celebrated author, Mary would be the inevitable, though always unwilling, centre of attention. Both women, however, preferred the company of friends, preferably actors, with whom Mary, drink in hand, could relax and enjoy herself. Only Julie knew what it had taken to get her there. To their friends Mary was known for her sense of humour, matched by occasional hilarious flickers of absent-mindedness. Her actor friends all described her as a strong personality, someone on whom they could lean in time of trouble. They were all a little wary of her superior intellect, but unanimous in insisting that she never flaunted it and, indeed, that her most charming attribute was the way she encouraged them to prattle on about theatrical nonsense, for which she appeared to have an insatiable appetite. The most durable of her youthful ambitions was to go on the stage as an actor – she never thought of herself as an *actress*, a word she pronounced witheringly. Her great friend, the dancer and choreographer David Poole, thought that her ideal role would have been Tamburlaine.

Mary was far from unattractive. There were moments when, for instance, fired by something akin to anger over an error of historical fact discovered during her reading, her passion brought a kind of stern beauty to her features. Had she submitted to a great photographer or even to one who could have put her at her ease, such a moment might have been captured and she would have seen it for herself. As it was, she remained exceptionally wary of her own image and very particular about which prints her agents and publishers might use. It is revealing to study the few that she authorized: what they offer is a smiling, well-coiffed, middle-aged lady in a chunky cardigan, the epitome of cosy English femininity. On the strength of such images alone, one would be left thinking of a thatched cottage with climbing roses somewhere in the Cotswolds, of tea with the vicar and an interest in moderately teasing detective fiction. It is little wonder, therefore, that her readers were puzzled by the photograph on the dust jackets of her books and preferred to imagine the whole thing was a glorious hoax, that behind those tough stories of battle and male love lay the unseen hand of a man who almost certainly lived in Greece and who probably had a Greek lover. Mary Renault had inadvertently obscured the author from the reader far more successfully than many writers who go to extraordinary lengths to disguise their persona. It is hardly surprising: hiding was something she had been doing since childhood, when she would climb into the loft of the ramshackle wooden stable at the side of her parents' home in the East End of London so that she could read in peace, far from the sound of her mother's voice telling her yet again that this was the very thing that would make her unattractive to a nice young man.

*

Everyone agreed that Mary Renault's mother was attractive. Mary Clementine Newsome Baxter was the eldest of four daughters of a Yorkshire dentist who had moved to London and established his practice in Kensington High Street. He was strong and hearty, but his wife was frail. She died shortly after the birth of her fourth daughter, whereupon the father came to rely more and more on the girls, until he seems to have assumed that they would always be there to take care of him. Not surprisingly, they came to regard marriage as their sole means of escape. Only one of them, Bertha, managed to acquire an education, going on to London University, a rare thing at the time, but even she chose marriage in the end.

The eligible young men available to the sisters were drawn from their father's colleagues in the dental and medical professions, and when, in 1899, Clementine met the twenty-four-year-old doctor, Frank Challans, two years her senior, he must have seemed an ideal catch. He was tall, elegantly dressed, with a sharply pointed moustache which gave him a raffish military air. What is less understandable is how they contrived to be engaged for five years without discovering the least thing about each other.

Frank Challans had been brought up in Boston, Lincolnshire, the home of his father William's Huguenot ancestors. As the youngest child and only son, Frank might have been spoiled, but was subjected to a certain amount of stiffening by his father – being thrown in the water to make him swim was a recurring memory. When he was nine, he had the appalling experience of seeing his father suddenly lurch forward and fall into the blazing hearth, dead from a stroke. Now there was no one to stop his mother and sisters indulging him. His mother sacrificed everything for his future, working – at what is not now known – in order to pay for his education. Happily, the boy was bright and soon decided that he wanted to become a doctor. He passed his school matriculation at fifteen and was then obliged to idle away several years until eligible to begin his training at the London Hospital in Whitechapel, at the time one of the largest general hospitals in the country.

By 1901 Frank had taken his MB and two years later his MD. He wanted to specialize, but junior surgeons were barely paid and only the exceptionally rich could hope to become consultants – for the rest there was general practice. His education had been a great drain on his mother's limited income. While she might have been able to pay for the years of training had he remained a bachelor, the costs of an Edwardian household would far exceed the meagre stipend of a hospital registrar. If he insisted on marrying, the only solution would be to buy a partnership in a general practice, but even for that he would need the help of his mother. Indeed the circumstances of his marriage remain something of a mystery and were certainly a puzzle to Mary in later life. Few doctors married before their late thirties. A long, secret engagement was just possible, yet here he was plunging into wedlock at twenty-nine.

From Clementine's point of view it was the perfect match: he came from the same social background as she did and he had apparently excellent prospects – in a word, he was 'nice'. They were married on 17 November 1904 at St Paul's Church, Hammersmith, and honeymooned on the Isle of Wight, where it is probable that Mary was conceived. From the start, however, Clementine's ideal marriage began to unravel. Frank was undoubtedly an excellent physician who might have made a successful consultant, but in general practice he was merely another young doctor of limited means. His mother was in no position to buy him a wealthy or fashionable West End practice. Not for Frank the luxuries of Harley Street; what he got was an East End practice in a moderately large Edwardian house on Plashet Road, Forest Gate.

The house, blessed with the rather grand title of Dacre Lodge, was double fronted and, although it did not look large when viewed from the street, it stretched back some distance and had four bedrooms, a reception room and dining room. It also had a consulting room and small dispensary, though in the absence of a proper waiting room patients sat in the dining room until called. Forest Gate was an area of respectable modest folk, many of them retired, living in neat, terraced houses bordering tree-lined roads, though behind this façade was another reality of meaner streets which housed the poor Jewish immigrants who eked out a living in the East End rag trade. A Dr Duffie had the neighbouring practice, and a little farther away was Dr Dayus, two colleagues who would be the kernel of the newlyweds' social circle.

In common with others of her class, Clementine was not expected to do much beyond supervising her household: a 'cook general', a housemaid, a tweeny (between stairs maid) for fetching and carrying, and a young boy who worked in the dispensary washing bottles and delivering prescriptions. As Mary's birth approached, a nanny was hired who would share the night nursery with the child. Once again Frank Challans found himself surrounded by women.

To the side of the house was a wooden stable, but as they could not afford a horse and carriage it was always empty and quickly became dilapidated. Dr Challans walked everywhere, visiting his patients on his daily rounds and finding his way home through impenetrable London fogs by clacking the ferrule of his umbrella along the iron railings.

He was undoubtedly a good doctor, proud of the fact that in all his years he 'never lost a mother', no mean feat at the time. Despite his skills, he had, of course, no hand in the delivery of his own child. The family was always treated by Dr Dayus, the neighbouring practitioner.

*

The baby was delivered at Dacre Lodge on 4 September 1905 and was christened Eileen Mary. As Clementine was often called Mary within the family, she decided that since the baby's soft bubble curls gave her an Irish look, she should be known as Molly.

Clementine's sister Bertha was godmother. Little Molly kept her intense blue eyes and was always told that the first word she uttered was 'pretty', repeating it after an aunt had said it of her and reinforcing it by adding, 'That's right.' She remembered sucking on something metal protruding from the hood of the rather grand bassinet in which she was pushed by her elderly nanny down streets strangely literary for so modest a borough – Shakespeare Crescent, Coleridge Avenue, Byron Road – though opposite the house was an ironmonger who used to set out his goods on the pavement, ladders and buckets and chamber-pots, which always distressed her mother. If the weather was fine, she was allowed to play in Upton Park with its splendid rhododendrons; if not, she spent hours at the nursery window watching the horse-drawn trams rattle down Plashet Road towards the City or trundle back to the Stratford Depot. Sometimes there was the pungent smell of the manure cart heading towards Aldgate, its driver dozing over the reins, his horse sure of the route. More pleasant was the scent of the elder tree in the back garden, so that ever afterwards the smell of elder blossom brought back memories of childhood.

It was a brief idyll, soon marred by the sounds of arguing behind closed doors. Although she could not understand why, Molly was quickly aware of a poisonous tension between her parents, barely held in check when she was brought in to see them. In later life she had only to look at one of those large glass marbles with a beautiful coloured spiral down the centre to recall how she had put one under her pillow for comfort, often waking to find that it had rolled down into the bed beside her and was caught in the fold of her body like a rare jewel.

It is easy to lay the blame for the collapsing marriage entirely at Clementine's door: her nagging appears unattractive, and beside her the bookish doctor seems long-suffering and put-upon. But he must share a good deal of any criticism. Used to being indulged by women, he believed that once they had given him what he required, they should keep to their place. A woman like Clementine had little in life except husband and family, while he saw himself as a man's man, unwilling to meet her on her own terms. Of course her social pretensions were foolish and her attempt to mould her eldest daughter in her own image was wrong, but he ought to have taken account of such matters before his early marriage. Worst of all, he seems to have had a knack for irritating his wife, as when he told stories about his student days, describing how he loved to eat at Lockarts, where cab drivers got their 'nosh', sitting on wooden benches scooping up tripe and onions with a tin fork. This was not by any stretch of the imagination 'nice', and its effect on Clementine was predictable.

Despite such differences, their conjugal life was active, and Clementine became pregnant again. Well into her term she miscarried and they lost a boy. Had he lived, there is little doubt he would have been their darling; Clementine would have indulged a son where she was unbending with a daughter. The couple were briefly united in grief, and their only thought was to try again in the hope that they might yet have a son.

Molly was oblivious to all this. Her favourite toy was Jumbo, a plump soft elephant whose legs stuck out, which she hugged and teased until it eventually fell apart. Conventional dolls held no attraction for her, especially since her mother bought only expensive and fragile porcelain dolls, quite useless as toys, meant for nice girls to hold and look pretty with. Molly once stripped one of these sacred objects to dress up Stalkey, the back yard tabby. Strong-willed from the start, she always remembered learning to walk on her own and refusing to take the afternoon nap her nanny considered essential. The only time she did curl up and sleep in an armchair was on an afternoon in April 1911 when her sister was born – an instinct for self-preservation having prompted Molly to hide away in this manner while the traumas of a difficult delivery were taking place upstairs.

The birth of Frances Joyce (always known by her second name) marked the effective end of Frank and Clementine's marriage. They had been denied the longed-for son, and there would be no further children. Divorce was unthinkable, for it would have put an end to Dr Challans's career and reduced Clementine to penury. The only solution, which was to reach a civilized *modus vivendi*, did not occur to Mrs Challans, who seems to have decided to wage war on her husband by nagging him, constantly and creatively. His one refuge was the tiny study that housed his books – a modest collection of first editions, all of Dickens and Kipling, and the works of Austin Dobson, a favourite.

To the outside world, however, the Challanses put on a respectable enough face, going together to St Peter's, Upton Manor, for Sunday services. But once back home, such pretence ended at the front door. Worse for Molly was the obvious fact that her mother's affections were now exclusively reserved for Joyce with her pretty auburn hair, so different from the Irish looks of the elder daughter. These, though, were not to last. Having the poorer patients waiting in the dining room had always been a risk, so no one was overly surprised when Molly caught ringworm and had to have her head shaved. When her hair grew back, it was thick and tightly curled; the soft bubble curls and thus the Irish looks were gone forever.

In later life Mary Renault would be haunted by the memory of her mother's aimless existence. Having nothing to occupy her except trivialities destroyed Clementine Challans. Idleness was forced on her, as it was on all her class, but she did little to resist it, taking no interest in running the house beyond filling out the order books for the tradesmen, who would then deliver the required goods, which the cook would prepare and the housemaid serve. Her days drifted by, filled only with embroidery and gardening. She was 'at home' on Thursdays, and the vicar came to tea on Tuesdays. She occasionally played the piano. If asked, she would have said her days were full. In consequence, the annual holidays in rented houses at minor coastal resorts were a sore trial as she was obliged to take charge of buying the food, which had to be brought back for the landlady to cook for them. Clementine was always relieved when the day came for their return to London, yet every winter the ritual would be repeated with her making a number of brief journeys to find suitable lodgings before the holiday season arrived. Joyce remembers going one year to Broadstairs, where she and Molly watched the 'Nigger Minstrels' performing on the beach. Another year they spent a pleasant week at Shanklin on the Isle of Wight.

Any hurt her mother's rejection may have caused was eased for Molly when she began to attend a local school just before Joyce was born. This had come none too soon: the precocious Molly had been bombarding her poor nanny with questions on everything that passed her way, but had quickly realized that the simple, good-hearted woman was merely making up the answers.

Molly was sent to a dame school run by the Misses Levick in their mother's house about a mile from Dacre Lodge. Mrs Levick senior took morning prayers and hymn singing, while her elder daughter Edith and the younger Maude supervised the classes with some help from a French lady always known as 'Mad*aa*m', who gave elementary French lessons. The neighbouring doctors also sent their children there, and Molly was friendly with Dorothy, the daughter of Dr Dayus, and another Dorothy, the daughter of a Dr Reid. In the school, social graces and health were as important as formal education; the children were drilled by running up and down the large staircase, and had lessons in dancing, especially the polka, at which Molly proved awkward.

Much to her mother's chagrin, it was already clear that reading was all Molly cared for. Mrs Challans's own interest in books went no further than the occasional work of popular romantic fiction hired from Mudie's Postal Library. That her elder daughter seemed as intent on reading as her husband only inclined Clementine even more towards Joyce with her girlish preference for nice porcelain dolls. At the time, Molly's taste in reading ran to nothing more serious than stories of cowboys and Indians, but it was her obsessive interest, so like her father's, which irritated her mother. Molly had discovered that the loft above the dilapidated old stable provided the perfect refuge in which to hide with a book. When the rickety stairs collapsed, she was not deterred but clambered up the remaining spars to her hidden sanctuary as often as she could.

So successful was she at keeping out of everyone's way that no one noticed when her front teeth began to protrude. With a dentist grandfather it would have taken little to rectify the problem, but by the time it was identified the damage had been done. When she was finally sent to his surgery, her grandfather proved very entertaining and showed her how to fire his pistol. From then on, she was forever drawing from the hip in imaginary Wild West shoot-outs. It is scant wonder that the few friends she had were all boys, and this despite her mother's ceaseless warnings that no male would ever befriend her unless she became more ladylike.

Even her posture provoked her mother's criticism: she stood badly and her feet were far too big, though what she was expected to do about the latter was never made clear.

*

The outbreak of war in August 1914 liberated Frank Challans from the battlefield of his marriage. At first a problem with his eyes delayed his call-up, but by 1915 the need for men was so acute that he was enrolled in the Royal Army Medical Corps and posted to India, where he remained for the duration of the conflict. His practice was put into the hands of Dr Duffie, which reduced the family's income substantially. Until the war ended Molly had to continue at the Levicks' school, even when she had absorbed everything they had to teach, and she was forced to sit through it all again in the company of her younger sister. She never resented her mother's attachment to Joyce, but, with a difference of six years between them, they were never close. While Molly was a studious tomboy, Joyce adopted the girlish looks and behaviour her mother demanded of her – each being held up as a lesson to the other.

Clementine Challans's one great pleasure was her constant communications with her sisters. Known in the family as the 'Baxter Exchange', this involved a continuous round of letters passing between the four of them, giving full details of all family doings so that everyone knew precisely what had been said and done, or what was about to be done, and what everyone thought about it. Little wonder that later Mary Renault always loathed telling people exactly what she was up to. She had a massive correspondence, but would never give a clue as to the subject of any book she was working on. If asked at parties, she never lied but dissembled carefully. With the memory of the secrets of her childhood being bandied about and speculated over on the Baxter Exchange, she maintained a lifelong loathing of female tittle-tattle.

There were occasional visits from the Baxters: Bertha, the university-educated sister, Cathy, the third child, and Rosalind, the youngest. Bertha had no children, but Cathy, having looked after their father for some years, married a clergyman and emigrated first to Australia, where her son Alan was born in 1919, and then to New Zealand. The fourth sister, Rosalind, had three children.

Molly's closest friends were two of the three children of Dr Dayus, Dorothy and Eric. But as they were not near neighbours, they could be seen only when visits were arranged. Eric Dayus, who went on to become a doctor himself, still recalls a curiously grown-up little girl who was capable of holding a very adult conversation with his father. On one occasion Molly noticed a spider in the room where they were having tea. 'Do you cultivate spiders?' she enquired of her host. But with the grown-ups safely out of the way, the other Molly resurfaced, and Eric would be called upon to play cowboys and Indians – a game for which he felt slightly too old, but in which he would agree to take part just to please her.

Sometimes Eric would ride her back to Plashet Road on the crossbar of his bicycle, and his memories of Mrs Challans are of a rather merry woman, willing to go along with his practical jokes.

Molly was quite accustomed to other people seeing a side to her mother rarely on display when they were alone. Clementine Challans loved a mild flirtation over the teacups, and it is possible that her greatest grievance with her elder daughter was that she was never likely to bring home the sort of nice young man with whom such innocent coquettishness would be possible. It was a side to her mother Molly dreaded, since it made friendship difficult. How to explain what you really felt about your mother, when she had just proved herself such a good sport?

With Dr Challans in India, Dr Dayus occasionally took on the role of father to the Challans girls, escorting them and other local children to the Stratford Empire for the pantomime and thus launching Molly's lifelong passion for the theatre. Dr Dayus would take the entire front row of the dress circle so that they could all see perfectly, and Eric remembers Molly being absolutely thrilled one year when they went to *Aladdin*.

At some point during the war years, Molly added to her love of the Wild West an interest in the Middle Ages, in castles and knights in armour, in a world of troubadours and chivalric battles. Her earliest surviving composition is a poem entitled 'Sir Eglamour', copied out in a spidery child's hand, liberally blotted with ink. Two verses suffice to show her skills:

> Sir Eglamour drew his be-jewelled sword
> And galloped along as the dragon roared
> And with his feet the hard ground pawed
> Preparing for the fray.
>
> He struck at the knight with his seven tails
> Then fell to the earth with many wails
> Which were heard in all the hills and dales
> As the knight's sword ran him through.

One can wax too lyrical about children's creative efforts, but this is an ambitious rhyme scheme, which offers enough evidence of a 'good ear' to merit a moment's attention. The knights were for poetry, however, and when she decided to write her first novel just before the end of the war, at the age of eight, she returned to cowboys and Indians. That tale has been lost, but she always remembered having finished it. When she somewhat imprudently told her mother what she had been doing, she was promptly informed that wishing to be a cowboy was foolish: as a girl, she would simply be made to wash the other cowboys' socks.

Until 31 May 1915 the war was scarcely more than a distant excitement, but on that day the first Zeppelin raid terrorized the East End, and others followed whenever there was a moonless night. The children were entranced: while Boy Scouts were driven round the neighbourhood blowing trumpets to warn of a raid, they would be rushed across the road from the school to the basement of the local bakery. Once they saw a German Zeppelin go up in flames, and everyone cheered and clapped. Molly's passionate interest in everything to do with flying seems to date from these events and while Joyce liked the raids because she could play with the baker's kittens, her elder sister dreamed of becoming a pilot. Despite the disruptions, Molly came first in the class examinations in 1916 and was presented with a copy of *Kingsley's Heroes* on the school's prize-giving day. What neither donor nor recipient could have known was that these simple tales from history and legend would permeate Mary's thinking throughout her life.

The 'Zepps', as they were popularly known, caused little damage and most crashed while attempting to return to Germany. By 1917, however, Gotha aeroplane bombers were in operation, and by mid-June a large part of East Ham, including nearby Sebert Road in Forest Gate, had suffered extensive damage. It was becoming increasingly clear to the adults that the situation was growing ever more dangerous. Now there were daylight bombing raids, mostly without advance warning. One was so unexpected that the children could be hurried only as far as the Levicks' basement before the bombs started raining down, after which it was decided evacuation was essential.

Molly and Joyce were sent to the Buckinghamshire village of Whiteleaf Cross, far from the air raids, where they remained for just under a year. Molly never referred to this period, and all Joyce can remember is the pony and trap which came to take them to school in a house in Great Missenden.

When they returned to London, life went on much as before except that there was even less reason for Molly to continue at the Levicks' school. Everything they could teach her had already been taught twice, yet until the war ended and Dr Challans returned, there was little hope of change. Worst of all there was now rationing and, when Clementine insisted on taking Molly shopping with her, the poor girl was consumed with boredom, trailing around Sainsbury's while her mother counted out coupons and nattered with acquaintances. It is not surprising that she looked forward to the return of her father as the one thing that might transform her life.

*

The armistice of 11 November 1918 came and went, but Frank Challans did not reappear. It was not until early 1919 that he was shipped back from India, by then a captain and a much changed man. He was nearly bald and smoked constantly. It was also clear that he had withdrawn into himself: the discovery that his practice was much reduced was accepted with the comment that he might give it up and go back to India. Molly's hopes that his return would transform her life were swiftly dashed. Her father showed no more concern over her education than her mother had done. He preferred to pass his free time reading in his study at the front of the house while Mary was doing the same in the deserted loft above the stable.

It was Molly's godmother, Aunt Bertha, who resolved the problem. With the war over, it was possible to travel again and Clementine took the girls to stay with her sister and her husband, the Reverend Richard O'Reilly, at his rectory near Colchester. Having been to university and having no children of her own, Aunt Bertha was keen to help Molly develop her talents and she began to press for her god-daughter to be sent to a proper secondary school. She succeeded in getting Clementine to agree. Dr Challans was indifferent, but saw no reason to interfere. Molly was never told why they chose Clifton Girls' School, a boarding school in Bristol. It had a good reputation, but there were others of equal standard nearer home, and it is interesting that, when Joyce's turn came, Clementine insisted she attend a day school in nearby Blackfriars.

Molly was no doubt glad to get away. She was fifteen when term began in 1919 and far too old to be starting her secondary education, but she had always been a voracious reader and did what she could to catch up, though subjects like mathematics and Latin were beyond her.

For her first year she was a boarder and found the disciplined life strange, missing the rough and tumble of the Levicks', where she had mixed with boys on equal terms. But she soon made friends with a group of six girls her own age and found a 'best friend' in Beryl Lewis, a day pupil whose family lived near the school. Beryl was the first truly close companion Molly had had, and her gentle, concerned nature was the counter-balance she needed. When Molly became a senior in her second year, she was allowed to lodge with the Lewises in Clifton. They were a comfortable middle-class couple of solid Welsh stock who did not spend their time quarrelling with each other, and she was happy to be there. Her only dread was her mother's occasional letter full of complaints about her life, and she was nervous when Beryl accepted an invitation to spend the holidays at Dacre Lodge.

Happily, Clementine did not try to charm her new friend, having concluded that Beryl was another bookworm to be ignored.

As her first real friend, Beryl was crucial to Molly's emotional development. Very slim with silvery fair hair, calm and quiet where Molly was boisterous, she complemented her perfectly and let her take the lead in their games. Molly encouraged Beryl to read Malory's *Morte d'Arthur* and came up with the idea that they should write a musical comedy based on the story of Dido and Aeneas. *As the Gods Decree – a musical tragedy of the South* by E. M. Challans and B. M. Lewis, 1924, is preserved in a small green exercise book with the title in red ink and the text in blue. The larger, rounder hand is Beryl's, the smaller Molly's. At one point Dido and Aeneas serenade each other to the tune of 'If you were the only girl in the world'.

DIDO: If I were the only Queen in the world,
And you were the only King,

AENEAS: I should not be chased around the world like this:

DIDO: There would be no Juno here to mar our bliss.

BOTH: A palace in Carthage, just made for two;
No Gods to spoil everything!

DIDO: There would be suche [*sic*] plenty and peace in store –

AENEAS: I should never have to be seasick more –

DIDO:
AENEAS: If { I / you } were the only Queen in the world

DIDO:
AENEAS: And { you / I } were the only King!

After forty-three pages it ends with 'Aeneas kept on walking' to the tune of 'Felix kept on walking' – proof that Molly and Beryl were devotees of the cinema, going to the Saturday morning matinée, where Molly followed avidly the adventures of her current hero Tom Mix.

Not that life at school was always fun. Molly's principal recollection of her time at Clifton was of how bored she was – literally to tears on one awful occasion when an insensitive teacher insisted

17

on knowing why she was so moody and was rewarded by the sight of Molly weeping with frustration. As for work, she was good at English and history, but already preferred the former, while Latin actually terrified her, and her failure at Greek was to cast a long shadow. The lessons were hard, and she and Beryl formed a union to protest about the long hours schoolchildren were obliged to work, and spent much time yearning for the school to burn down.

This was the point in her adolescence when she had most need of an understanding parent. At home for the holidays, she longed to talk with her father, but his sole concession to his daughter was to allow her to use his library provided she handle the books with exceptional care. Worse than his indifference were the obvious signs that he found her less than adequate. When Eric Dayus's father died after a bus accident in 1921, the Challanses invited his widow and two children to join them for Christmas and, when lunch was over, Molly was obliged to leave the room with the other women, while her father, who had barely spoken to her, asked Eric to stay and play chess with him. By then Eric was studying medicine at St Mary's and must have seemed like Frank Challans's ideal son. That his daughter had passed her School Certificate and was about to pass her Higher School Certificate meant little to him.

For Molly these successes brought a blessed relief from lessons. She was now nineteen and, with the exams behind her, was considered mature enough to spend as much time as she wished in the school library reading whatever caught her fancy. This provided the seminal experience of her schooldays and one which would condition much of her subsequent thinking. Years later, in 1982, she described it vividly:

We had a rather good library at my school because, I think, somebody had given them a whole lot of books which we weren't actually taught at all. They were just sort of sitting there, and when you got more senior, you could riffle about in this library and I found Plato's *Dialogues* and I was entranced by them. By the time I left school I had read all of Plato, in translation, on my own.

Miss Phillips, the headmistress, had been at St Hugh's College, Oxford, and she suggested that Molly consider applying for a place there. When she was accepted, her father was not best pleased. Although she would be entitled to one of the new state scholarships, expense would be involved, expense Frank Challans considered utterly wasted on a daughter. He was prepared to offer her £20 a year, the allowance he thought fitting for an unmarried girl, but beyond that he would not go. By Molly's calculation she would need a further £60 to see her through the three-year English course. Her father refused.

Once again Aunt Bertha came to the rescue, lending her the money, which Molly could repay after she qualified and had found a job of some sort. Everyone imagined she would become a school-teacher, the most likely career for an educated girl at the time. What none of them knew was that Molly was already determined to avoid such an outcome at all costs. She was also determined that everything about her former existence should be changed. Firstly, she would no longer be called Molly, for that had been her mother's response to her Irish looks. In her new life, she would be Mary.

Needless to say, Mrs Challans was not impressed with her daughter's success in getting to Oxford. Women students, she declared, were unfeminine, they lacked sex appeal – a new line of attack. It was not until many years afterwards that Mary was able to reveal how much these remarks had hurt her and only later still that she could admit the extent to which she had longed, throughout her childhood, for her mother's approval.

2

Oxford Made Me

Michaelmas Term, Oxford, 1925, began in the second week of October, a month after Mary's twentieth birthday. Along with the forty-eight other first-year students at St Hugh's, her initial task was to find the room allocated to her in the main college building. A blend of country house Queen Anne and banker's Georgian, St Hugh's was new by Oxford standards, having been completed in 1911, and was some way out of town along the Banbury Road, at its junction with St Margaret's Road. While the older members of college were happy to have a purpose-built establishment after years in converted houses, the under-graduates found it inconvenient and disappointing to be shut off from the main life of the university. It certainly seemed so to Mary, whose first complaints were over the difficulties they all encountered in working out where everything was. Even finding the library took time when no one appeared to be in charge of guiding them. Then there were the rules. Having to travel back to St Hugh's by eleven meant that many evening activities within the main university were impossible. It is not surprising that in later years she would say, 'Oxford made me,' then immediately complain that having been in a women's college had spoiled it because she had felt so out of things. In a sense both judgements were valid. Mary's generation occupied a curious interregnum between the first slow campaign for women's education and the liberation which followed World War II when most of the remaining restrictions on female students were swept away. Today St Hugh's is a co-educational college, while all but one of the formerly exclusively male colleges have opened their doors to women.

Mary went up a mere five years after women were granted full membership of the university in 1920, an event which for many of the older generation concluded years of struggle. To have their new building with the status of a full college within the university was an end in itself to those who remembered when women had had to be hidden behind pillars in the lecture halls lest a disapproving male don change his mind about allowing them to attend. That someone like Mary, who had not lived through those years, felt less grateful and more irritated about being stuck out on the Banbury Road was inevitable.

If she had imagined that the rather fierce-looking lady dons, staring so mournfully out of their official college portraits, were solid, sober creatures, dedicated to the emancipation of their sex and single-mindedly bent on advancing the cause of women's education, she was to be quickly disabused. The reputation of St Hugh's was at its lowest since its beginnings thirty-nine years earlier. Most of the women dons had been at the college barely a year. Even the Principal, Miss Barbara Dwyer, had been at her post only a matter of months, and ill health would keep her away for a large part of that academic year. Mary's first tutor, Miss Mary Ethel Seaton, had come straight from finishing her own studies at London University, and her French and history tutors were equally inexperienced. Although it was mentioned only in half-whispers, the reason behind all these new faces was what was known as 'the Row'.

The origins of the Row lay in the publication in 1911 of a book which excited enormous popular interest and academic controversy for nearly fifty years. Entitled *An Adventure*, it told of a visit to Versailles in August 1901 by two English ladies, one of whom claimed to have been confronted by a vision of Marie Antoinette seated outside the Petit Trianon. The book was published pseudonymously and generated widespread curiosity, for the ladies, whoever they might be, were clearly educated and of good family. Much press speculation was followed by support and rebuttal from many quarters, religious, scientific and esoteric, until the authors, carried away by the attention, reissued the book under their own names. It was then that a bemused public learned these ladies of good family were none other than Miss Charlotte Moberly, Principal of St Hugh's, and her deputy, Miss Eleanor Frances Jourdain. That the daughter of an Anglican bishop, along with a leading female academic, should have been involved in such bizarre goings-on was scandalous, if revealing of the limited world of women academics when such beings were relatively new. Neither Miss Moberly nor Miss Jourdain was truly acquainted with research in any sense: their training had been literary, and their attitude was romantic. In subsequent years they persisted in taking students on visits to Versailles to continue their investigations into this supernatural experience, yet saw nothing contradictory in continuing to hold conventional Anglican beliefs and in obliging their students to attend long rambling sermons on any aspect of theology which happened to preoccupy them at the time.

Women like Miss Moberly and Miss Jourdain, while nominal supporters of women's education, were themselves poor examples of it. Even Miss Jourdain's sister Margaret, the distinguished antiquarian and companion of Ivy Compton-Burnett, could barely disguise her disdain for Eleanor's and Miss Moberly's 'visions', and noted how even a potential supporter such as the investigating officer for the Society for Psychical Research had dismissed Miss Moberly's evidence with the damning word 'fishy'. The reputation of St Hugh's sank ever lower with each new edition of *An Adventure*, but the Principal and her deputy were not alone in pursuing unorthodox areas of research. One of the English tutors, a Miss Wardle, wrote a book on how to tell character from people's ears, while peculiarities of dress and speech seem to have been commonplace among the female dons.

Thus the opportunities available to a St Hugh's student in the first quarter of the century were fairly limited. A clutch of eccentric, if kindly, women dons formed the first line of teaching, beyond which lay a patchwork of male dons more or less willing to admit the young women to their lectures. As a result, courses had to be juggled to fit these constraints, with girls pursuing, say, zoology purely because they had managed to find a suitable tutor. To fill any gaps the college employed part-time male tutors – usually younger, impecunious dons keen to supplement their incomes. In the years following World War I the young J. R. R. Tolkien took on pupils from St Hugh's to augment his meagre salary while working on the *Oxford English Dictionary*. A married man, Tolkien was ideal for St Hugh's, as the young women did not have to be chaperoned when visiting his house.

The college was often referred to as 'the School' and the Principal ran the place like an all-powerful headmistress, directing her underlings as if they were staff rather than independent-minded dons. Had she distanced herself from them, her approach might just have worked, but, like many closed institutions, St Hugh's was prone to the sort of intimate friendships that inevitably complicated matters. Miss Moberly and Miss Jourdain were a case in point. When the former retired in 1915, her protégée succeeded her. In quick succession Miss Jourdain had Miss Cecilia Ady, *her* favourite, appointed tutor in history – '*cara mia* Cecilia', as Miss Jourdain sometimes addressed her in unconscious mimicry of E. F. Benson's flamboyant character Lucia. But while Miss Jourdain had been prepared to spend years in her predecessor's shadow, Miss Ady was ambitious and determined to see that tutors at St Hugh's obtained the same rights as those taken for granted in the men's colleges. During the years of waiting for recognition, such demands could be held down; after the triumph of 1920, agitation was inevitable.

Miss Ady's demands were ostensibly for such reasonable things as pension rights, though her real motivation may have been personal. Certainly Miss Jourdain's reactions showed all the signs of thwarted affection, and in 1923 she used a loophole in Miss Ady's contract to dismiss her and thus precipitated the Row.

In support of Miss Ady the entire tutorial staff of St Hugh's resigned. Pushed into a corner, Miss Jourdain fought with all the obstinacy of a determined woman who had spent a good part of her life defending a bizarre vision seen in the gardens of a royal palace on a hot summer's afternoon. Rashly, she decided to replace the protesting staff, but could draw only on the limited pool of women graduates, most of whom were schoolteachers and hardly likely to improve the college's academic standards. Worse, this move finally provoked those male dons who had formerly acted as tutors into withdrawing their labour in support of the now-dismissed women. There was nothing to be done except appeal to the Chancellor, Lord Curzon, to resolve the impasse and, though the subsequent inquiry delicately avoided unqualified support for either side, this silent rebuke was too much for the proud Miss Jourdain. Four days after publication of the inquiry's findings she collapsed and died from a heart attack, leaving the college without anything resembling a faculty. Only after a decent interval had elapsed could Miss Dwyer be appointed principal and the task of reconstruction begin.

It was at this point that Mary arrived. Everything she encountered reinforced the notion that she had simply passed from Clifton into another girls' boarding school. Each year's new group of undergraduates kept to itself, with its own tables in the dining hall. There was little mixing of the years at the cocoa parties which were almost the only evening entertainment permitted. There was even a form of schoolgirl slang – you were 'scalped' if someone dropped the Miss and addressed you by your Christian name. Chaperonage was still in force, male visitors were strictly regulated, and while other rules – no ballooning, if you please – were inexplicable, even the most ordinary aspects of daily life were governed by an attitude to women that was already outdated. The students were obliged to wear hats when moving between college buildings, a spare one being left on the hall table for those who forgot their own. At evening meals it was obligatory to wear a long evening dress, so that Mary, in common with other 'freshers', had had to have something serviceable run up. Alone of her year, Margaret Lane, daughter of the famous journalist Hugh Lane, and thus someone from a smarter, more metropolitan background, had turned up for their first college dinner in a couture creation – a fact recalled with telling clarity sixty-five years later by her surviving contemporaries.

For Mary, worse than these petty restrictions was the growing awareness that the quality of education open to her would not be of the highest. Her tutor, Mary Seaton, belonged to what had become a St Hugh's tradition of lecture-hall eccentrics. She had a propensity to illustrate a talk on the Elizabethan lyric by bursting into song, and her antiquated full-length skirts and outsize carpet bag were unlikely to attract the admiration of young women longing to break free from fusty Victorian traditions.

Beyond St Hugh's, the male dons, in what was then known as the Faculty of Medieval and Modern Languages, were hardly more stimulating. Within the faculty there was a rift between those who taught Anglo-Saxon and those who taught Literature, with each side inflicting its discipline on the students of the other. Neither faction was truly concerned with any sort of literature, the great preoccupation being the completion of the *Oxford English Dictionary*, which meant that most faculty members were primarily lexicographers and grammarians, dry stuff for someone like Mary whose head was full of poetry.

Much of the Oxford cultural life open to Mary was middle brow. To study the pages of *Fritillary*, the magazine of the Oxford women's colleges (price 6d), is to enter a jolly world of hockey and lacrosse matches and meetings where the House might debate the existence of ghosts. College plays, on which St Hugh's was very keen, were frequently lightweight pieces: *Thirty Minutes in a Street, Friar Bacon and Friar Bungay, Two Gentlemen of Soho*. Only rarely does a Shaw or a Shakespeare occur, and certainly nothing more adventurous. Serious drama was left to the productions of the Oxford University Dramatic Society, which were forbidden to women students. The first issue of *Fritillary* after Mary's arrival announced that the freshers were 'engaged in weeding the terrace'!

Mary knew there was more to Oxford than this. She had heard about the clashes between the Aesthetes and the Hearties. Evelyn Waugh had gone down from Hertford College only two years earlier, but already the antics of his generation, with its heady suggestion of *louche* sexuality allied to avant-garde writing, would colour impressions of Oxford down to the present day. How exciting such things must have seemed when set against the stuffy mediocrity of St Hugh's, and yet how distant – somewhere over the high, impenetrable walls of the men's colleges in meetings, discussions and parties to which she could never be invited.

Mary was an exact contemporary of W. H. Auden, then at Christ Church, and attended the same lectures, but while he was writing 'The Letter' and 'The Secret Agent', she was still composing mock medieval verses. A fellow fresher, Kasia Abbott, was interested in fine calligraphy and asked if she might have one of these, 'The Lamp and the Sword', to practise on, thus preserving what Mary might well have discarded. Ink blots aside, however, there is little progress since 'Sir Eglamour':

> A Sword there was, that turned the war.
> Men praised the sword and wiped the blade,
> Sheathed it in silver fair inlaid,
> Nor thought upon it any more.

It is, however, strange to note that Mary's quaint tale of a sword forgotten once it has served its purpose is not so far removed in spirit from Auden's harsh anecdote about the abandoned secret agent whom they would 'shoot of course, / Parting easily two that were never joined.'

A large part of the problem was that while St Hugh's was isolated within Oxford, it was even more shut off from events in the world outside. When the General Strike began during the second term in May 1926, *Fritillary* recorded that, although some male students had gone off to 'do things', the women had taken no part whatsoever.

Mary contributed nothing to *Fritillary* in her first year. Her fellow fresher (and another future novelist) Margaret Lane published a poem and a book review, and by the final edition in June had been elected to the editorial committee. Sixty years later Mary recalled that 'women in Oxford were only tagging along', a fair description of her first year, though there were better things to come.

At the end of term Mary took Kasia home for part of the holidays, hoping perhaps that her father would be impressed with her friend and more kindly disposed to her new life. Kasia's father was a civil engineer who collected books and was a keen amateur artist. But while the visit passed without anything untoward occurring, it provoked no especial interest from Dr Challans.

The holiday was Mary's last stay at Dacre Lodge; her father was giving up general practice for a less demanding job as Deputy Health Inspector in Bristol, presumably having grown to like the place during his occasional visits to Mary's school. Mary was unmoved. She had never cared for London beyond its theatres, and most of her friends were now in Bristol or Oxford, so her father's announcement, close to her twenty-first birthday, only added to a growing sense of independence.

*

Returning to Oxford in October 1926, Mary found that second-year students were treated slightly more like adults and were allowed to live outside the main building, even if only in nearby college houses, which backed directly on to the gardens of St Hugh's. This was a considerable advance. On the first day of term the students were paired off in reverse alphabetical order, leaving Mary Challans and Kasia Abbott last. They were allotted two rooms on the top floor of a house which had just been donated to the college by Joan Evans, one of its former students and future Fellows. Miss Evans was half-sister to Sir Arthur Evans, who that same year would present the British School of Archaeology in Athens with the great palace complex at Knossos, which he had excavated so spectacularly and so controversially restored.

One of the first things Mary did when she arrived in Oxford was to visit the Ashmolean Museum, whose Keeper Evans had been until he retired in 1908 to devote himself to Knossos. He had then been made an Honorary Keeper of the Ashmolean and during the 1920s he sent the museum replicas of his major discoveries, including the Cretan Bull-leaper, which Mary adored. Again and again she returned to study the slim-waisted boy finely balanced on the curving horns of the great beast he is so delicately vaulting. In the 1920s the Ashmolean gave pride of place to its extensive cast collection, which provided Mary with her first experience of classical art. The copies of the Blond Ephebe and the Acropolis Head of Alexander were like real people to her: 'I fell in love with them,' she told Kasia, and they remained all her life the exemplars of physical beauty beside which all else would be judged.

In matters of taste, Sir Arthur Evans was Mary's unwitting tutor. His half-sister Joan was another protégée of Miss Jourdain's, who had brought her to St Hugh's in 1914, where Joan developed a lifelong interest in the history of jewellery. She was a member of the college during the move to its permanent home and, after graduating, became its librarian. Although she had left St Hugh's in 1922 to devote herself to writing, her connections were close and the substantial redbrick house at 82 Woodstock Road was only the most visible of her many gifts to the college. Mary was given a large room at the front of the house, overlooking the street; Kasia a smaller one at the back. This latter room they nicknamed 'the Ark' because of its sloping ceiling, though Kasia was happy with it because it was quaint. There was a resident don, a French tutor, Miss Elizabeth Francis, another recent Jourdain appointment in the aftermath of the Row, who breakfasted with the women and acted as personal tutor. Everyone liked her and, while the centenary history of St Hugh's describes her as 'wreathed in a cloud of vagueness . . . scattering hairpins, oblivious to time', she was no fool and was quickly made a Fellow.

With a room of her own, Mary had her first real chance to express her new-found taste, decorating it with considerable gusto. Her style leant heavily on the Middle Ages. She had acquired a tapestry with a chivalric theme and had been collecting old swords and daggers to hang on the walls – hence her poem. These weapons were to be a cause for concern to the less boisterous Kasia when Mary took to practising dagger-throwing against the door of the room, making it hazardous for friends to enter. Eventually she was persuaded to confine this activity to the college gardens, usually after dinner when it was dark and there was no one about. It was only some years later that Kasia learned that the younger dons had been spying on them from behind the curtains of their common room, much amused at their unconventional antics.

Such happenings would have been quickly suppressed a few years earlier, and there were other signs that the rules were no longer as strictly enforced as once they had been. Chaperonage was still insisted upon, but providing no outrageous behaviour was suspected, the rule about being back early was fairly loosely applied. Undergraduates returning late could climb the walls, and the punishment for being caught was no more than having their names published on the college notice board, which could be seen as a source of pride as much as of shame.

The college was strictest over boating since there had been accidents: anyone wishing to take out a punt had to prove she could swim fifty yards and could be barred from the river if there was a suggestion of bad weather. This seems to have provoked Mary, who had punted at Clifton and saw no reason to be restrained at Oxford, and Kasia recalls a stormy day when they found themselves scudding down the river virtually out of control, with Mary thrilled at the danger of it all. Nemesis struck when they tried to get back and found themselves in for a long, exhausting struggle against the current. It is obvious from her recollections that Kasia admired Mary's spirit and found her romantic looking in a pre-Raphaelite way, an intriguing mix of opposites, at once high-spirited and ethereal.

As the effects of the Row began to recede, attempts were made to revive the college's cultural programme. Joan Evans returned to give a lecture on the history of jewellery. She was well known as a fashionable dresser and already possessed an impressive collection of gems, which she wore with great style, representing an enviable mix of scholarship and sophistication to her attentive audience. Mary became a lifelong admirer and an avid reader of her many books as they appeared.

Outside St Hugh's, Mary loved the Oxford theatres where she could see the young John Gielgud, whose curious ambivalence was as entrancing as the near-feminine beauty of the Blond Ephebe and the epicene Bull-leaper in the Ashmolean.

In December 1926 it was decided that an English Club should be formed with Miss Seaton as President. The other English tutor, Miss Buckhurst, gave the inaugural lecture, which *Fritillary* described as 'an amusing paper on Icelandic folklore', a subject very much of the moment in Oxford English circles since Tolkien had returned that term as the new Rawlinson and Bosworth Professor of Anglo-Saxon. Although he would no longer be giving home tutoring to the women of St Hugh's, they still had every reason to be grateful for his return. He was a conscientious lecturer, offering almost double the statutory hours in order to ensure that his students, female as well as male, covered the entire subject. Indeed, he was unusual in being notably sympathetic to women undergraduates. And, of course, 'darling Tolkien', as Kasia still refers to him, fitted neatly into Mary's medieval dream-world, though not because of his own writing. Thus far none of his fictions had been published – he had been working privately on the *Silmarillion* and was only at the first stages of drafting *The Hobbit* – so that for Mary and Kasia his reputation rested on his brilliance as a scholar, allied to his ability to make the somewhat dry study of philology come alive as literature. Auden later wrote to tell Tolkien that his reading of *Beowulf* was 'an unforgettable experience . . . the voice was the voice of Gandalf'. According to his closest friend, C. S. Lewis, what distinguished Tolkien from all other philologists was that 'he had been inside language.'

No one doubts it was the influence of Tolkien which began the transformation of the somewhat dusty and faction-ridden English faculty, though there is less agreement as to the value of the changes he initiated. Until his intervention there had been the acrimonious rift between Language and Literature with both sides opposed to the draining of energy from their speciality. Tolkien found this division artificial and refused to accept the idea that philology should be a theoretical study, preferring to bring it within the realm of literature by emphasizing the living poetry of the old texts. In this he must have enjoyed the intense gratitude of his students, who were suddenly liberated from the somewhat dead Anglo-Saxon they had been taught until then.

There was, however, another side to Tolkien's reforms which was less favourably received by some. While he loved the literature of the past, he had little time for the modern. Evelyn Waugh referred to C. S. Lewis, Tolkien, and their friends as the 'grim, pipe-smoking *intelligentsia* who . . . despised almost everything'. By this he no doubt meant the avant-garde as represented then by such diverse figures as T. S. Eliot, Edith Sitwell and Gertrude Stein, figures guaranteed to cause apoplexy amongst the Inklings and the Coalbiters, the sort of intimate clubs dedicated to the study of Icelandic and Middle English to which Tolkien and his friends subscribed.

The main result of the Tolkien/Lewis opposition to modernism was that the study of literature at Oxford stopped at the opening of the Victorian age. The effects of this on undergraduates such as Mary are obvious: at no point does she seem to have considered formal experimentation in literature as of any relevance to her. While Waugh and Acton had been opposed to what they called 'olde worlde' obsessions, she was delighted by them. In the books she kept from her Oxford years one sees that the contemporary writers she favoured were firmly in the mainstream and, though Eliot is there, he is conspicuous as the sole experimentalist among more popular authors such as Huxley, de la Mare, Wodehouse, Buchan, Graves, Priestley, Maugham and Galsworthy. She long recalled that the greatest treat of her Oxford literary life was the chance to attend parties in North Oxford, where John Masefield would read his poems. Although not yet Poet Laureate, Masefield was already the most famous poet of his day, possibly the last to have so wide a popular following. Now that he is almost forgotten except for 'Cargoes' and 'I must down to the seas again', it is hard to believe that, when he gave public readings, huge audiences thrilled to his high, quavering, yet commanding voice. But it was this voice, not that of the younger avant-garde writers, which first attracted Mary and which at this stage found its echoes in her own poems, one of which appeared in *Fritillary* in May 1927; it is firmly in the Masefield mould.

Sonnet

If all the Beauty we have ever loved
Of sight and sound were stripped at last away,
And we, from all earth's gallant laughter, moved
To some dead wilderness of primal clay,
Still we could send a fearless valediction
After romance great-hearted and dim of eye,
Nor bind our sight with veils of lovely fiction,
But stand erect in our sheer you and I:
We two alone, unhelped and undefended,
Could reach the substance, whence like shadows fall
Music and moon-kissed trees and flowers splendid,
And merge our being, and be Beauty all,
And from God's heart be shed again to earth
To make new dawns, new flowers, new lovers' mirth.

The publication of her poems in the two undergraduate magazines *Fritillary* and *The Imp*, at the end of her second year, heralds Mary's debut into the public life of St Hugh's. She had already taken a small part in the second year's production of A. A. Milne's

Make Believe and had been singled out for praise. It was then decided that she should direct the college's annual play in the next academic year and, as she left for the summer holidays, the question of what this should be was much on her mind.

She and Kasia had been invited to stay with a Miss Verney, the aunt of a friend, a visit which helped clarify some of their thoughts about the future. Miss Verney had studied at Royal Holloway College, a pioneering establishment in the early years of the women's education movement, but while she was a keen advocate of further advances, she was in many ways typical of what a female graduate was expected to become: a dedicated teacher helping to educate more girls who would themselves become teachers.

It was a future which already appealed to Kasia, but to Mary looked worryingly like an end to literary ambition. She was more and more convinced that she should try to be a writer, but was equally aware that she needed something to write about. As a teacher, she would continue within the same closed world she had known since her days with the Misses Levick, and where was the adventure in that?

*

Michaelmas Term 1927 opened with all Mary's thoughts directed towards her forthcoming production. It is clear from the recollections of her surviving contemporaries that Mary intended to be completely in charge from the start. The somewhat retiring fresher, struggling to find her way round Oxford, privately jotting down verses, was to emerge as a natural leader. Her first move was to track down an obscure play which combined several virtues: a huge cast so that a large number of willing applicants could take part; a subject which appealed to Mary's unchanging obsession with the Middle Ages; and last, but definitely not least, a thumping good leading role, which she was unashamedly determined to have for herself.

The play, *If I Were King*, had been written a quarter of a century earlier by one Justin Huntly McCarthy, who had adapted it from his own novel. It enjoyed a short season at the St James's Theatre, London, in 1902, since when it had languished. Its subject was the French medieval poet François Villon, but despite so flamboyant and fascinating a hero McCarthy had run up no more than a slight melodrama, liberally sprinkled with popinjays, chanticleers, flagons and pipkins. It is, however, easy to see why Mary was attracted to it. Kasia recalls her interest in Villon, which had probably been stimulated by their house tutor Miss Francis and reinforced by lectures in French literature, given in English, by Henry Berthion, one of the Taylorian Lecturers in French, which both women attended.

It was decided that Margaret Lane would play the heroine Katherine to Mary's Villon. There was only one performance, but over sixty years later it is still remembered as a glorious occasion. Kasia has kept two photographs of the play. One shows Mary in wig, doublet and hose clasping Margaret Lane in a passionate embrace at the foot of the gallows with the entire cast looking on. The second shows the tavern with Mary/Villon in the background addressing the crowd, arm thrown out in a flamboyant gesture. Even allowing for the artificial nature of such posed shots, one is left with the impression that the melodrama of the piece had won through.

Reviews were mixed; in fact there were only two. *Fritillary*'s reviewer took a decidedly sniffy tone, criticizing the direction of the crowd scenes, though admitting that much of this was due to the limited size of St Hugh's stage. Mary, too, came in for a sharp prod: 'Miss Challans as François Villon had a suitable appearance and usually moved well, but her voice was so obviously feminine that she never seemed entirely inside her part.'

It seems unlikely that this sniping by a fellow student did much to dampen the fun the performance generated. In any case a second review in one of the magazines of the men's colleges was entirely laudatory. Now untraceable, it is still recalled in detail by Kasia for its remark that 'an extremely beautiful girl took the part of Villon', which caused them both much amusement. It cannot have escaped Mary's notice that on the first occasion on which her looks were praised in print she had been dressed as a man.

She was not especially concerned about her looks. She was young, healthy, vivacious and clearly great fun to be with. In common with Kasia and the other St Hugh's women, she always had escorts to accompany her to theatres and concerts, and there were male undergraduates who could be invited to chaperoned tea parties at St Hugh's, and who in turn would invite her to dances. It was all quite innocent, and if her bicycle had to be tossed over the wall of number 82 by her companion, who would then give her a leg up to get back unseen, it was only because the play had run on and the gates were locked so ridiculously early. To a young woman just growing out of a childhood prolonged by the war and now attending an institution which was scarcely more than a school for grown-up girls, these men were no more than necessary, hopefully amusing companions. The St Hugh's centenary volume tackles the subject of undergraduate sexuality and lesbianism quite frankly in one of its articles and concludes that the attitudes of the women at St Hugh's evolved with those of the rest of society: there were those who did and those who didn't; but it hardly seems to have been a prime preoccupation among Mary's group in the late 1920s. Romantic love, as expressed by Villon in the play, was more common, and Mary was certainly in love, though not with any of her undergraduate companions. The object of her affection – and it was emphatically a great passion – was Edward, Prince of Wales, the golden boy of the period. When this began, during her last years at school, it was no more than a conventional schoolgirl crush. That it should have continued and blossomed at St Hugh's says much about her delayed adolescence. She would go to extraordinary lengths to catch a glimpse of her hero, travelling to wherever he was expected, standing in the rain to see him pass, returning to dream of the 'glow' which seemed to surround him. She discovered her prince during his golden years, when he was dutifully carrying out the arduous functions of an heir apparent: the state visits to the colonies, the endless tours around Britain. His life as a socialite lay ahead of him, and if the devotion of millions of young women like Mary suggests the idolatry offered to pop stars today, at least the object of their passion did seem at the time to be kind-hearted and worthy.

It would be wrong, however, to imagine that the women of St Hugh's were strangers to physical attraction. Reading *An Adventure*, one is struck by Miss Moberly's constant preoccupation with the appearance of the people she met and whether or not she found them 'attractive'. Miss Jourdain and Miss Ady had clearly been drawn to each other before the Row, as the former's references to her 'Baby Don' make clear. But these were only the rather childish intimacies of an over-intense friendship, the expression of unrequited passion, and in such an atmosphere it is hardly surprising that Mary was more concerned with deep friendship and romantic love than with sexual gratification. For the moment there was the Prince of Wales, at a safe distance.

With her play over, Mary could concentrate on her writing. She contributed a short story to *Fritillary*, a charming tale in which the author fantasizes that the women researchers in the Reading Room of the British Museum are in fact witches. The tone is light and brisk, and already shows a talent for detailed visual observation that would later become one of the most notable features of her writing style:

> She wears black velvet with point-lace collar, and her grey hair and fine-drawn profile bear, as novelists say, the unmistakable stamp of breeding. She bends over her ancient tomes of evil with a ladylike concentration, but sometimes the stoop is a shade too eager, and when she reaches a particularly stimulating passage she mouths it over, furtively, as she copies it down.

By the end of the story the author has vowed to stop visiting the place, as she fears she, too, is becoming a witch. Told with considerable wit and observation, it demonstrates the qualities of simplicity and directness that were to be the hallmarks of Mary's literary style. If Oxford made her then, in terms of writing, it had wrought someone who would choose the accessible above the experimental, and this leaning towards the popular was reinforced from another source during her last year, one which would have the most enduring influence on her future. She and Kasia began attending lectures given by the Regius Professor of Greek, Gilbert Murray. Murray lectured in English and had since his days as Professor at Glasgow attempted to bring Greek drama to a wider audience. His success in filling an East End theatre for a performance of Euripides was already legendary and part of that success was due to the contemporary feel of his 'free' translations. Murray had founded the League of Nations Union, and this link between present and past was to have an abiding effect on Mary's thinking. She was much taken with the emphasis Murray placed on the barbaric and tribal elements underlying Hellenic civilization, a revolutionary view at a time when the ancient world was most often depicted as classically Aryan. In this Murray had much in common with Sir Arthur Evans, whose highly coloured reconstructions at Knossos had already incurred the wrath of those conditioned to a purer classical vision of the ancient world.

Auden, who attended the same lectures, described Murray as a 'mythopoeic' character, and he was undoubtedly the greatest single influence on Mary's thought from her Oxford years. She would even come to share a similar reaction to modern Greece – Murray was fascinated by the ancient world, but found little joy in visiting its modern counterpart.

Murray's lectures reawoke Mary's schoolgirl interest in Plato, which grew into a search for moral guidance. Apart from her confirmation as an Anglican, her religious beliefs were fairly conventional and not particularly profound. She enjoyed the beauty of the Church's ceremonial and attended services if called upon to do so, but that was as far as it went. She was certainly not drawn to the Oxford Movement and the belief in Moral Rearmament, which appealed to many undergraduates at the time. She had a horror of being subsumed into any form of organization and was equally repelled by that other great fashion of the day, the Communist Party. It was Plato's belief in the individual which caught her imagination and which furnished her with an ethical code that she attempted to maintain throughout her life. Plato's views on politics seemed equally valid: a good state would be produced only by good people; first educate the few to a knowledge of the good, then permit them to rule. Systems alone could not create the ideal state, only individuals could.

Such beliefs were wildly at variance with the collectivist theories, both Right and Left, which dominated Oxford thought, and Mary's contemporaries still recall how she stood out in any discussion. She had accepted totally Plato's dictum that men are unequal and must strive towards the achievement of their *arete*, their personal excellence. But Plato aside, Mary shared the student fads of her day: Eastern mysticism had its moment, and she remained devoted to the *Bhagavad Gita* and Murasaki's *Tale of Genji*. In common with almost all her contemporaries, she absorbed a good deal of second-hand Freudianism. Little of Freud's work was available yet, but journalistic notions about the Oedipus Complex and the Subconscious had passed into general speech and were often referred to with little understanding of what lay behind them. Freudianism propped up an odd assortment of liberal attitudes. The notion that childhood experiences conditioned adult behaviour was widely accepted, especially in the area of sexual orientation. Here, at least, Mary was a product of her generation, as full of the jargon of the psychiatrist's couch as any other Oxford student at the time.

*

In the spring of 1928, during her last term at Oxford, Mary decided to attempt a novel. It would be set in the Middle Ages. Plato was for the spirit; for adventure she still turned to knights and troubadours. She bought an antiquated typewriter from Margaret Lane – a piece of felt soaked in ink popped up when a letter was pressed – and taught herself to type. When final examinations loomed, however, this had to be set aside for the weary business of revising. In the end she obtained a Class Three degree (along with Auden). Kasia and Margaret Lane both managed a Class Two, but as Mary had no intention of taking up an academic career this hardly mattered. Kasia would stay on to take a teaching diploma, but Mary's concern was to continue with the novel while seeing something of life. As she packed the small trunk that would dictate the limit of her material possessions for the next twenty rootless years, there was not much to sustain her hopes of succeeding as a writer except for one small incident during her last term. While she was at a party in North Oxford, she was introduced to Arthur Waugh, father of Evelyn and a senior partner in the publishing firm of Chapman & Hall. When he asked what she was planning to do, she answered, 'Be a writer.' Waugh was a gentle person, sympathetic to youthful ambition; he made a few encouraging remarks and told her that when she finished her first book, she was to send it to him to read. He then gave her his card, which became a much cherished object. While she must have known that he was simply being kind, such encouragement by one of London's leading publishers was something precious to cling to.

*

For all her ambiguous feelings about the place, leaving Oxford was painful. She had to go to her parents' house in Bristol until something turned up, but she knew this could be only a temporary measure. Her mother gave her the spare room to sleep in, but, when Mary asked if she might use the slip-room – the empty narrow cell above the entrance hall previously used by a maid – as a study to write in, her mother said it was needed for her sewing.

It was Mary's bad luck that as a doctor her father was financially secure. With the Depression, many middle-class families were coming to accept the idea of working daughters, placing less emphasis on marriage. Dr Challans, however, would not modify his attitude. If Mary refused to teach or to apply herself to being attractive to men, he saw no reason to encourage her in foolish day dreams. He would continue her allowance of £20 a year, an ample sum were she to remain at home, as was expected of an unmarried daughter, but barely enough on which to survive, should she choose to be independent.

It seemed to Mary that she no longer had a choice. How could she write in the midst of her squabbling parents without a room of her own? It says much about their attitude towards her that, when she announced that she was going to move out, they made no effort to dissuade her, despite knowing that she would not have enough money to live on.

She decided to stay in Bristol and managed to get cheap lodgings in a council house until she found a basement flat in Charlotte Street. The rent took most of her money and the only way to cut costs was on food, making soup out of tuppenny beef cubes on the single gas ring. Despite such economies, it was clear that her father's allowance would quickly disappear and she would have to find work of some sort.

She had a number of temporary jobs: working first in Clark's boot and shoe factory, later as a counter clerk in a branch of the

Civil Service, but the only job which interested her was in the laboratory of a chocolate factory, where she had carefully to weigh samples of silver wrapping paper to ensure that there were no new additives in the foil which might affect the quality of the sweets. She long remembered that it was the one task she felt good at. Where another might have been slapdash, she was careful and exact, pleased by the delicate platinum scales she had to work with and finding a certain satisfaction in the meticulous record-keeping involved.

For entertainment she had Citizens' House, a youth-club-cum-cultural-centre attached to the Town Hall, where, along with others of her own age, she could continue her passion for amateur dramatics.

A photograph of the time shows a tall young woman, her slim figure emphasized by a fitted skirt and the way she hugs a cardigan tight around her. There is something typically 1920s about the way she stands with her shoulders stooped forward in a pose adopted from the cinema where young starlets, pencil-thin and boyish, were much in vogue. But if she had her admirers, there was no possibility of anything beyond friendship; whatever the Bright Young Things might get up to, they were a sophisticated metropolitan elite, while Mary, despite her refusal to conform to her parents' wishes, remained a product of their class and social background. Beyond holding hands and, at most, a kiss – nothing.

Her rare comments on this period in her life show that Mary was most concerned to try to gain a writer's insight into character, studying those she befriended, attempting to understand what made them tick. One such was Winnie Iles, a lively creature, who gradually became more sombre as she developed an interest in Eastern mysticism. Closest of all was a young man called Caesar, presumably his surname, to whom Mary was greatly attached and with whom she maintained a correspondence after she left Bristol. Caesar lived with his mother, was unemployed and spent much of his time tinkering with an old car, of which he was inordinately fond. Mary was clearly delighted to have a friend of the opposite sex on whom she could practise her investigative skills, and he unwittingly provided her with a great deal of material for later use.

Apart from her escorts at St Hugh's, Caesar was Mary's first close male friend and anything he could tell her about himself, his thoughts and ambitions, was fascinating. The difficulty was that learning about real people made her fictional characters seem much less satisfying. She continued to work diligently on her novel, but it did little more than grow longer. She had called her protagonist Renault after a character in Otway's *Venice Preserv'd*, a much-loved work, and he and his companions were followed from break-fast to bed with their every action described in the minutest detail and every conversation running its full course. Only later did she learn the technique she would refer to as 'bound', a reference to the well-worn phrase from adventure stories – 'With a tremendous bound Jack was free' – by which she meant the use of the cinematic cut, the ability to jump ahead, to précis talk and action where necessary. At the time she had no one to explain such things to her and all she could do was plod on, watching the novel swell, unaware of how to remedy matters.

Mary and her group were photographed on a hill-walking tour. The obvious pleasure on their faces says much about the days when people made their own fun and had no notion of bought entertainment beyond the occasional visit to a theatre or cinema. But, in the end, the tuppenny beef cubes proved a poor substitute for real food. Her troubles began with a sore throat, which would not clear up, and, when this was followed by pain in her joints, she thought she had flu and went to see a local doctor who told her not to worry, simply to take more care of herself. The sore throat and aching joints continued, however, and were followed by a rash that covered her skin with red blotches. On a rare visit home the cause was discovered. Her father listened to an account of her symptoms and realized she had rheumatic fever, a direct result of malnutrition and at that time a serious complaint. The general weakening of the patient could place a fatal strain on the heart, and the sole known remedy was total rest for up to two years. It was a double calamity. The only possible place she could get such care was at home, and her father, having completed his diagnosis, insisted she go straight to bed and stay there.

It was Mary's worst nightmare, compounded by being forbidden to read, and it instilled in her a lifelong horror of being helpless or in any way physically dependent on others.

For once Clementine Challans tried to ease her daughter's suffering, but she had so little rapport with 'Molly' that even her noblest intentions fell flat. When Mary was allowed to read from time to time, her mother went in search of library books, but her choices were hardly those her daughter would have made, and Mary long remembered a gloomy tale of Russian serfs chained together and forced to drag their weary bodies across the endless steppe in a freezing winter.

She was bedridden for much of 1931 and part of 1932, but she avoided the full two-year convalescence prescribed in severe cases. She had had endless hours to ruminate on the obvious fact that things had not worked out. She had failed to earn enough to provide herself with the minimum required for a healthy diet, and her novel refused to resolve itself to her satisfaction. Aside from three dead-end jobs and her friends in Citizens' House, she had not penetrated 'real life' in a way that might have given her something of value for her future writing. She had been treading water, and she still had no idea what she might do to improve matters.

*

In mid-1932 Dr Challans obtained a new post in Stoke-on-Trent, a move guaranteed to displease his wife. To Clementine the region was perpetually covered in a blanket of soot, while ribbon developments of 1930s semi-detached villas stretched along the main roads, blocking off the countryside. It was an unappealing prospect until they discovered the village of Barlaston, a short walk from the hills, on a ridge overlooking the Five Towns, where at night the glow of the furnaces lit up the view below. At least at that height the air was clean and fresh, and they were able to buy the Old Vicarage, a curious maze of a house set in a large garden. The front of the building was fairly recent, but the rear was built of stone and considerably older, the two halves sitting oddly together with the upstairs corridors going up two steps, then down two. There were four bedrooms, a sewing room and endless rooms stretching behind the rear kitchen – scullery, outhouses, garden sheds – which ought to have provided Mary with a place to work at last. However, it was not to be: her mother would have a bedroom of her own, her father would have his, Joyce hers, but that left only the spare room for Mary, and as for the sewing room Clementine again claimed that she needed it, not that she had ever been known to sew anything. As a result Mary had to write in the dining room at the rear of the house, a dark place with heavy Victorian furniture and a stone-flagged floor, which made it desperately cold in winter. There was only a small anthracite stove for heating, and she was forced to clear away her papers as each mealtime approached and the table was set.

There was by this time only a solitary housemaid, but no willingness on Clementine's part to comprehend that she could not be expected to do the work of four. As Clementine still disliked cooking, her one employee was supposed to prepare meals and serve them as well as doing all the cleaning and washing. Predictably, there was a procession of aggrieved young women, none staying longer than a month or two. The living room at the front of the house quickly became Clementine's battle ground, its spaciousness considerably restricted by precarious side tables loaded with her collection of ornaments. While the chairs and sofas were theoretically plumped up and comfortable, only Clementine seemed able to sit back and relax; visitors tended to perch on the edge of their seats. Clementine's new theme was to point out that she had her 'own' bedroom. 'Do come up and see *my* room,' she would announce. Or: 'I've just decorated my *own* bedroom.' Mary came to dread these remarks, so clearly were they intended to humiliate her father. Clementine had also taken to giving tea parties for women of a similar social position. The repast was always good with sandwiches and cakes served on fine local Wedgwood china. Indeed, some of the visitors were Wedgwoods. These receptions brought a temporary halt to the bickering, though the '*my* bedroom' remarks continued unabated and there was always the certainty that, when the last guest left, the arguing would instantly recommence.

Dr Challans had his library across the corridor, but it was a poor refuge, and Mary could not understand why he did not engineer some way to absent himself; even with divorce out of the question, he could have found a post that would have kept him away from home more often.

Mary was now twenty-eight, effectively her father's pensioner, with only her annual £20 allowance for income and none of her Bristol friends for company. Her only distraction was two tiny mice who came out to feast on the fallen crumbs after breakfast and whom she cultivated for their company, storing up titbits and playing with them to pass the time, for it had quickly become evident to her that her writing was drying up. Stoically, she forced herself to finish the novel, though she knew in her heart that it had not worked. She was not depressed, but it took all her resources of hope to confront the fact that her attempt to be a writer had floundered and she had precious little to look forward to.

In the summer of 1933, she decided to make a solitary walking tour. In jodhpurs and a cotton shirt, wearing a riding hat – the only headgear she could tolerate – and with a rucksack on her back, she set off through the Cotswolds. It was her favourite landscape: dry-stone walls, hedgerows, unspoiled villages, but this time it was not enough to lift her spirits. Oxford was close and it had been too long since she was there. As she made her way down Woodstock Road, she saw St Hugh's for the first time in five years. Next came the Radcliffe Infirmary, where she paused for breath. She had wanted some real experience of life to write about and behind the classical façade of the Infirmary there was real life to spare, a perpetual drama of life and death. It was her road to Damascus.

Had she known how impossible it was to walk in and see the Matron, she might have hesitated. Appointments were always arranged by letter, but, in her ignorance, Mary simply went to the office and said she wished to become a nurse. Such an unconventional approach must have intrigued the Matron, and she was granted an audience.

Her plan had much to recommend it. As a nurse, she would see human beings at their most vulnerable and, at the same time, she would be paid. On the minus side were the long hours and a punishing regime which could mean that whatever she learned about people might never see the light of day. Her responses to the Matron's questions were startlingly honest. It was considered essential for applicants to avow a total, lifelong commitment to nursing, yet when the Matron asked her if she had always wanted to be a nurse, she replied, 'Oh goodness, no. My father is a doctor, and I always said I'd never have anything to do with it.'

She ought to have been shown the door, but she had inadvertently said the right thing. Nurses then were much more deferential to doctors than they are today and she was the daughter of a doctor and an Oxford BA, two qualifications guaranteed to overawe the Matron. The rest could be overlooked, including her age and her weak heart. She was even excused a medical examination.

It was agreed that she would join the preliminary training scheme that August. During her preliminary training she would not be paid and would be expected to buy three uniforms and a dozen aprons. After finishing, she would complete three years' training in the main infirmary, being paid no more than £30 a year, and only if she were successful in her examinations would she become a fully-fledged nurse able to apply for permanent posts in other hospitals. The work would be hard, the hours long, the discipline strict; from the moment she entered the profession much of her life would be out of her control. Any free time she might have would be more a concession than a right, and during such time there would still be immutable rules about dress, comportment and behaviour. She would move from relative freedom to an almost total lack of it. Why, aged twenty-eight, she should have decided to pursue such an unappealing plan is not easy to explain, but, whatever her reasons, it was the single most important decision of her life.

3

Challans – Mullard

Mary began preliminary training in mid-August at Heading-ton, a beautiful Georgian manor house on a hill overlooking Oxford. For seven weeks she applied herself to the basics of nursing, though in her case the mental adjustment to so spartan a regime was probably as important as the skills she was learning. The trainee nurses did everything, including all forms of domestic work with the single exception of scrubbing floors. Almost as many hours were spent washing and polishing surfaces which had already been cleaned and shined as were used learning to care for patients. Free time was negligible, and any there might be was spent studying for the final examination. The mystery of why she had chosen such a life palls beside the even greater question of why she continued with such a regime once she had realized just how hard it really was.

Part of the answer has to lie in the satisfaction to be had from simply winning through. For someone who had rejected both the marriage game and the teaching lifeboat, there were not many responsible outlets for a woman in the 1930s and nursing certainly offered all the challenges she could require. It is easy enough to list the hardships: the long hours, the physical exhaustion (especially after a sequence of night duty), the finicky and often petty discipline which governed a nurse's waking life. Yet there was also the satisfaction of doing something so evidently worth-while and the pleasure of friendship with like-minded women, her 'set' as each intake was called, united in their determination to see it through.

After the seven weeks she passed her examination and was rewarded with four days off before starting work at the main Radcliffe Infirmary. She was so near to St Hugh's, she might almost have returned. Indeed, the Radcliffe was more a part of Oxford than her college, dating back some 200 years. Of course, once past the Georgian facade, she was confronted by a harsher reality of bare wards with scrubbed floors and lines of precisely made beds with cradles, splints and pulley lines. It was the details Mary noticed: the piles of dirty enamelware in the sluice, the orange peel the patients left on top of the bedside tables. Even in daylight the wards seemed gloomy, while at night they were sepulchral in the yellow glimmer of the corridor lights or the glow from the red shades above the beds. One of her most telling memories was of a young nurse snatching a moment's rest in a chair, sewing a shroud, hoping to be left in peace for a time before the ward sister did her rounds. Such things Mary noted, and filed away.

Despite the hardships, she enjoyed the life. The contrasts were so acute: one minute she was using technical skills for which she never dreamed she had any aptitude, the next she was on her way to Matron to be ticked off for breaking a thermometer. She might have to summon up her resources of sympathy to find the right words to comfort the dying; a moment later she would figuratively hold her nose as she washed an old man's dirty feet. The religious symbolism was not lost on her and she would later write about the pleasure she found in the 'monastic rhythm' of hospital life. Although she lacked any special commitment to church or faith, the obligatory morning chapel, with its prayer for the profession, held her imagination: '. . . To the physicians, surgeons and nurses wisdom, skill, sympathy and patience . . . and shed Thy blessing on all those who strive to do Thy will and forward Thy purposes of love. For the sake of Jesus Christ our Lord. Amen.'

The contrasts were as much about the nurses themselves: fit, often beautiful young women strapped into their archaic uniform, the thick twill dress worn winter and summer so that they were always too hot or too cold, the servile bib and the complicated 'Sister Dora' cap, which Mary never succeeded in pinning up correctly. Mostly they were high spirited and longing for fun, yet were often under the thumb of an overbearing, mean-spirited sister who had failed in the central marriage quest of grabbing a doctor. For, of course, behind those starched exteriors were longings which would have shocked Matron. Like St Hugh's, the nurses' home had windows to be climbed out of, and within the institution there were events going on which never crossed the patients' minds. How could it have been otherwise with so many healthy young women shut in together for so much of the time? As at St Hugh's, each year's set tended to stick together, though affairs were known to happen between years. They might begin at the parties held in the cell-like bedrooms in the nurses' wing overlooking Radcliffe Observatory, parties that sometimes ended in a close embrace and perhaps a lasting passion, but which had to be conducted *sotto voce* lest the Home Sister storm in and break up the fun.

Throughout 1934, her first year at the Radcliffe proper, Mary fell in with the routine and enjoyed such pleasures as she and the others were able to snatch in the all too short intervals between long stretches of duty. Inevitably, as a university graduate a little older than the others in her set, she was the subject of speculation. It soon became common knowledge that she was 'bookish'. Indeed, while she was still at Headington, one of the more sympathetic sisters had noticed Mary's interest in plays and poetry, and pointed this out to Nurse Mullard, who was also thought to be interested in cultural matters. Mullard found the idea of this 'literary nurse' off-putting. Monica Dickens was in vogue at the time, and Mullard thought that Challans would last a year and then write a half-baked book about her hospital experiences.

To Mullard nursing was a serious business, not to be treated as a writer's plaything. She had come to nursing as a means of making her own way in the world and as an escape from an unsatisfactory family background. She had been brought up in Hampstead, a smarter part of London than the Challanses' Forest Gate. The Mullards were middle-class business people, but none of this had been of much use to the young Julie, who had quickly learned that it was best to be secretive about her family circumstances. Her mother was unmarried and there was no father in evidence, a difficult situation at a time when illegitimacy was considered a social stigma. It was a point on which Mullard was understandably touchy. Had her mother showered her with love, she might have borne it; as it was, her childhood had been similar to Mary's, perhaps worse – on occasions her mother's harshness had been cruel. Nursing had been her escape, but the effects of her upbringing were still visible. Her thinness emphasized large eyes which gave her a sharp nervous look. She was unsure about her appearance and thought she 'looked like a penguin' in her starched uniform with its stiff white pinafore. Usually diffident, she could be over-quick to react when she felt threatened, especially if anyone used the word 'bastard' within her hearing.

When she first encountered Challans, Mullard was a senior and, by her own admission, riding high and rather full of herself, a state not likely to recommend her to her superiors, who required a degree of humility from their underlings. Indeed, the one impediment between Julie Mullard and her progress up the nursing ladder was a tendency to defend her rights no matter what and to dash in and speak her mind when she felt they were being challenged – an unheard of 'liberty' at the time.

Mullard was twenty-two and 'on top of the world' when, quite unexpectedly, the junior she had so far dismissed as a dilettante broke through the barrier between the years and approached her. It was shortly before Christmas 1934. There was a tradition of the nurses putting on a show, a short play and a concert, though the organization of this was usually left to the seniors. Challans volunteered to write and direct the play, and one day, as Mullard was pouring herself a cup of tea from the huge two-handled blue enamel teapot, she heard a voice over her right shoulder saying: 'Excuse me, Nurse Mullard, but I've written a play for the Christmas concert and wondered if you'd be playing a part.'

Mullard was not pleased – it had always been the seniors who asked the juniors, and she put down the teapot with deliberate slowness before answering.

'As a matter of fact,' she said, turning to face her questioner, whereupon she dismissed what she had been going to say and murmured, 'I would love to.'

'Thank you,' said Challans. 'I'll put your part in your cubbyhole.'

Still smiling, she departed, leaving Mullard to consume several slices of bread and marmalade while reflecting on how much things had changed since she had been a junior.

Later that day Mullard collected her script, a Victorian melodrama in which a young apothecary falls in love with the beautiful daughter of a rich merchant only to find that there is a rival for her hand, the rich and evil surgeon Sir Jasper Ruthless, who is preferred by the girl's father. All of this might have been thought a bit near the mark, given the godlike status of surgeons at the time; still, it was Christmas and all in fun. Mary would play the apothecary, while Julie, first cast as the nurse who aids the villain, found herself, as rehearsals progressed, promoted to playing Sir Jasper himself, though how Mary managed this Julie cannot recall.

Rehearsals were from six to seven in the mornings, before breakfast at 7.15, or from nine to ten at night before lights out at 10.30. There would be two evening performances of the entire show between Christmas and New Year, with an afternoon preview for the domestic staff attended by Matron, who could thus vet the proceedings. It went well, but during the course of a ward round that evening Matron took the opportunity to warn Mullard against getting 'carried away' in her performance and exaggerating too much, though this was probably more a comment on her recent displays of independence than on her performance in the play.

Determined not to be inhibited by this, Mullard threw herself into the two evening performances with gusto. They were a triumph, with everyone from floor cleaners to surgeons cheering them on. Even the 'horrid, hard-faced ward sister' who usually gave the younger nurses hell on duty could be seen clapping like mad.

It was not until after the final performance that reality crept back. Mullard and Challans had really spoken only during rehearsals and now had no further reason to do so. Even allowing for the limited off-duty time during the Christmas period, the two-year difference between their sets made meeting well nigh impossible. Their sleeping quarters were on different floors in the nurses' wing, so there was no chance of passing in the corridor. They might sometimes find their mealtimes coincided, but they would still be sitting at different ends of the room. They did see each other in chapel every morning, where Mary inevitably arrived last, walking nonchalantly to her proper place near the front, while Mullard, as a senior, sat at the back. Mary's way of strolling into chapel, her 'Sister Dora' inevitably awry, had once irritated Mullard intensely; but no longer. Now that this morning glimpse was the only way of seeing her, Mullard was more forgiving. In fact, she was fascinated and all she could think of during prayers was how she could contrive an encounter.

The sole possible excuse was the annual Christmas party on Twelfth Night, which Mullard's set always gave and which she quickly offered to host in her room. Having been in Challans's play, it was just about all right for Mullard to invite her. She wrote out invitations to nine nurses. All accepted.

Cakes, biscuits and champagne cider were the expected fare, and in previous years two or more of the set had shared the expense. That year Nurse Green said she would go fifty-fifty with Mullard, but pulled out at the last minute, almost scuppering the event, and only Mullard's single-minded determination to see Challans again kept it afloat.

There was a strict convention about such parties. They started at 9 p.m., and the guests wore their best pyjamas with a modest decoration, ribbons or flowers in the hair, plus liberal use of scented talc from recent Christmas presents. Everyone brought a toothbrush mug for the cider and sat on cushions on the floor. As hostess, Mullard stood by the chest of drawers dispensing the food. She wore black pyjama trousers with a short kimono top known as a 'happi-coat' and had a chrysanthemum over each ear, held in place by a new satin ribbon. Her room was not the ideal location, being next door to that of the Home Sister, who would certainly insist on lights out by 10.30 p.m. Nevertheless, she was determined to make the best of it. Two guests had had to drop out and six had already arrived when Challans appeared in what Mullard remembers as a rather charming dressing gown.

The evening was going swimmingly when the door burst open and in came the Home Sister. There was nothing to be done except insist she have a glass of cider in the hope of softening her up. She eventually agreed to leave them to it with nothing more than a mild warning not to be too late, which was taken to mean lights out at 11 p.m., a special concession. Things now looked fine. The greatest fun of the evening was provided by another nurse called Mary whom everyone considered a 'Burne-Jones type', slender and ethereal, but with a risqué reputation. She dressed beautifully and was known to sleep with dons and undergraduates, though everyone agreed there was nothing sordid about her. That night she brought a Christmas present sent to her from Paris, a large and expensive-looking box of chocolates, which turned out, rather shockingly, to be foil-wrapped contraceptives.

At eleven the lights were put out and everyone settled down to tell jokes and ghost stories. On the narrow bed were Mullard, Challans and the other Mary. Everything was cosy and pleasant, but as the evening wore on the others began to slip away without goodbyes, for by then silence was essential. Eventually, only the three on the bed were left. Legs were intertwined, no one was sure whose hand was whose, and Mullard fervently wished that Mary number two would go; she willed her away. And at last she went.

*

Mary Challans and Julie Mullard were to be friends for the next forty-eight years, sharing their lives until Mary's death in 1983. They seem to have known this would be the case from that very first night together, though neither had any experience of such a relationship that could have helped predict this outcome. Although her senior as a nurse, Julie was seven years younger than Mary. That night marked Julie's sexual awakening, but she never asked what Mary's prior experience might have been. It is likely that, of the two of them, it was Mary who took the lead. The following morning they left separately in time for breakfast and were on duty by eight, though not, of course, together. Pursuing their relationship was now almost impossible, so infrequently did they even pass each other in the corridor, while any off-duty periods which coincided were rarer still.

They did, however, manage a brief encounter on Sunday, 6 January, when Mary told Julie about her writing, and of the fateful meeting with Arthur Waugh and his interest in what she was doing. When they discovered that they would both have the next evening off, they decided to see *Aladdin* at the New Theatre and managed to get seats in the front row stalls, where they found themselves the butt of a comedian's jokes, which amused them hugely. More often Julie's only reliable glimpse of Mary was in morning chapel. She was still arriving late, but Julie had now shown her how to pin up her 'Sister Dora'. Occasionally there was a free moment when they could both get out of the hospital and go for a stroll in Port Meadow or a drink in the nearby Gardener's Arms. There was always so much to talk about, starting with their mothers.

While they believed in their hearts that they would stay together, there was little thought that this might be possible in any physical sense. The ease with which couples today move into a flat was quite beyond young people then. They often speculated on what it might be like to live in one of the pretty Georgian houses near the pub, but this was day-dreaming. Sharing an evening out was as much as they could hope for.

Mary was nothing if not adventurous, however, and one evening when Julie was in bed prior to going on night duty, she crept into her room with what was laughingly referred to as 'Radcliffe coffee', a drink consisting of nothing but boiled milk. Unfortunately Mary was so cautious that Julie slept through her entrance and, when she did wake, it was with such a start that she knocked over the searingly hot drink, which spilled on her chest and burned her badly. They were both desperate. The burn looked so red and inflamed that a blister was bound to develop, but what could they do? Julie had to get to her ward, where the work that night was sure to mean lifting patients, a task which always involved pressing them against you as you hauled them up. Panic-stricken, Mary went to get help, dashing from the nurses' home on to one of the wards, fully aware of the risks she was running were a sister to find her there out of uniform. She discovered a sympathetic friend, who quickly smeared a piece of lint with Vaseline and ran back to clamp it on Julie's chest. With the pad concealed beneath her uniform, Julie managed to get through the night, though not without considerable pain.

About three weeks after the party there was an even worse scare. Julie was summoned to Matron's office. After the inevitable terrifying wait, she was shown in and told that it had come to Matron's ears that she had been leading Nurse Challans astray. Every conceivable horror passed through Julie's mind: who had discovered them, who had sneaked on them? It appeared, Matron continued, that they had been seen leaving the hospital *'without wearing hats!'* Julie stammered that they had been going to the theatre, then immediately regretted the *faux pas*. What theatre at 5.30 p.m.? was the inevitable rejoinder, while the answer that it was the first house of a variety show hardly pacified her interrogator. 'I am,' said Matron, 'disgusted with you.' And that was the end of it, though Mary had been sick with worry the whole time Julie was away.

As if to compensate for this ordeal they found themselves scheduled for night duty together. Being the senior nurse, Julie was in the role of teacher, passing on the folklore of the nurse's craft. Mary was astonished when Julie told her that one old lady would die after they had eased her position. To an experienced nurse knowing such things becomes second nature but always shocks the novice. Indeed, dealing with death, laying out corpses, washing them, plaiting their hair, the 'last offices' as they were known, occupied a good deal of the nurses' time and made a lasting impression on Mary.

Working the same shift increased the chances of time off together and, when they heard that they were to get two consecutive nights free, Mary invited Julie home to Barlaston to meet her parents. Every relationship has its testing point and perhaps for Mary this was theirs. They set off on an appropriately gloomy morning, cold and wet, travelling by bus for nearly four hours to Stoke-on-Trent, and after a long wait took a second bus to Barlaston. The new houses stretching along the roadside looked uninviting in the dim light and it was only as they walked to the Old Vicarage that things improved.

As Julie perched on the edge of her seat, listening to Clementine Challans holding forth, she understood the underlying reason for their journey. Fortunately, Mrs Challans seemed to approve of Julie, but it was more significant that, while recognizing this, Julie failed to be charmed. She found the drawing room uninviting, the clusters of objects on their fragile tables worrying, the atmosphere excessively edgy. She noted Mrs Challans's remarks about *her* bedroom, caught all the references to things being 'nice' and remained unimpressed. Dr Challans she felt sorry for, but most of her sympathy was reserved for Mary. She resented Clementine's all-too-obvious preference for her younger daughter. By the time they left, Julie had had the best possible insight into the difficulties of Mary's childhood.

So much did they now trust each other that Mary brought out her novel and gave it to her friend to read. She did not, however, expect her to like it and, without waiting for a judgement, proceeded to point out its faults: no research had been done, it was simply a throwing together of a half-imagined past with no attempt at truth; it was 'presumptuous', and the only thing to do with it was to destroy it. Julie was honest and agreed with her, though she insisted that there was considerable merit in much of the writing. But into the flames it went, an even surer sign that a new life had begun.

*

Having passed her State Finals in the spring of 1935, Julie was offered a post at the Osler Pavilion, the tuberculosis sanatorium out at Headington. At least she would remain in Oxford with Mary, though less close than either would have wished. Still there was some cause for rejoicing and they managed to snatch a celebratory stroll, arm in arm through the foggy park, talking of what lay ahead. It was then that Mary told her about her absolute determination to be a writer, and from that moment Julie never doubted her; she saw it as her given role to help in any way she could. As they strolled back through the traffic, impervious to the cars and bikes, they paused on a traffic island. Mary said that after the next year and nine months of nursing which still stretched ahead of her, she would start to write again.

Headington was a fourpenny bus ride away, and Julie would have six months of day duty followed by six months of nights. She was now a charge nurse, a senior staff grade, but the extra duties meant less free time. No visitors were allowed at Manor House where the nurses lived, so meetings were doubly difficult. An evening at the theatre was all too rare, though they did see Gielgud in *Hamlet* and Anton Dolin in *Giselle*, followed by dinner at Fuller's, for which they had to wear long dresses. If they had a night off together and there was any money left, they could stay in a nearby boarding house for 3s 6d, but such treats were the rare exception and it was more a case of 'sitting in cafés drinking coffee you didn't want'.

One of them was bound to grow careless. One morning, after finishing night shift, Julie made her way to the Radcliffe nurses' home, got past the door and into Mary's room, where she climbed into bed beside her. They were no sooner together than they heard the pass key in the lock. Julie scrambled under the sheets just as the Home Sister burst in, demanding to know why Nurse Challans was still in bed. Was she sick? It was useless for Mary to protest, the Sister insisted on examining her chest – chest infection being a principal cause of illness among nurses – while Julie tried not to breathe. The sheets were pulled down and the examination undertaken. Mary could only be grateful that, in the half light, the two piles of crumpled clothes were barely visible. The examination over, the Sister left and Julie crawled out badly shaken. She scrambled into her clothes and, after a quick glance down the corridor, fled. It was only as she stumbled to the bus stop that she realized she had put on Mary's shoes and that her friend's feet were almost as large as Clementine Challans had always claimed. Walking was virtually impossible, and on arrival at Headington she was obliged to trek back to Manor House in her stocking feet.

Both knew that they would have to be a great deal more careful in future if they were to avert a scandal, not that either thought anything they did was other than perfectly natural. They did not think of themselves as lesbians because they thought what they were doing was unique, that they had invented it. If asked, they would have said they were bisexual. They often found men attractive, even if they did prefer each other.

Somehow, in the midst of all this, Mary went on trying to write, though she got no further than occasional poems. She would send them off to magazines and was overjoyed when *Queen* accepted one, but she chose to publish under the pseudonym Mary Martin, as she was unsure whether hospital rules permitted such a thing. She was paid a guinea – £1 1s od – a windfall which meant a celebration. Emboldened, she wrote to the *Oxford Times* to ask if she could review books and was taken on, probably because nobody else wanted the titles she was sent – one was a particularly hefty tome on mountain climbing – and because they did not pay. She was, however, allowed to sell the review copies of the books and, as they usually brought in half the cover price, at an average of 7s 6d it wasn't such a bad deal after all.

Of the eighteen reviews Mary preserved, most were delicately handled notices of first novels; she was not out to create a reputation for savagery. She even gave a favourable account of a book of memoirs entitled *A Banker Looks Back*. Fire was struck when the subject was one of her passions such as Shelley or Byron, or when the writer excited her admiration; Sacheverell Sitwell on Liszt evoked the comment 'how civilised' from his somewhat awed reviewer. Her most affectionate comments were reserved for a review of Colette's *The Mother of Claudine* which reveals a familiarity with all the author's work in the original French. Mary singled out Colette's delicate emphases on 'the more complex kinds of sexual emotion . . .' and her 'fineness of touch'.

*

Julie's year at Headington ended in April 1936. Mary would not complete her training at the Radcliffe until November. Neither of them wanted to continue as they were, and Julie's solution was to upgrade her training so that she could leave hospital work, obtain a post as a health visitor and find a flat to share where Mary could write full time at last. This entailed Julie moving to London, where she found a job nursing private patients at the Royal Northern Hospital in Holloway. It was a complete separation from Mary, but at least it brought in £80 a year.

Before Julie started at the Royal Northern, she and Mary took their first holiday together, as paying guests of a Mr and Mrs Summerhayes in Bourton-on-the-Hill in the Cotswolds. On the first night Julie wrote in her notebook: 'Delicious meal, roaring fire, feather bed.' The perfect holiday began perfectly; it would be an idyll forever recalled with pleasure, a world away from demanding patients and the smells of carbolic and disinfectant, from snatched encounters and the ever-present risks of exposure and discipline.

The two women had never spent so long in each other's company before. The days began with a huge breakfast, since lunch

was financially out of the question. Then there were walks down
lanes lined with hedgerows still replete with wild flowers in the
days when motor cars were still a rarity and the air smelled fresh.
Narrow bridle paths led them across country as far as Cheltenham,
reciting poetry to each other as they went. In the distance were
the hazy Malvern Hills, beside them ran a dry-stone wall covered
with clematis and honeysuckle. They would discuss Keats and
Shelley, and speculate on the latter's character. If they came to a
place large enough to have a hotel, they would sit in the parlour
and sip a liqueur (not crème-de-menthe, which was considered a
trifle 'tarty'). They could usually stretch the budget to a good tea
with cakes before returning to the Summerhayeses' and the roaring
fire and an evening meal by candle-light, the cottage having no
electricity as yet. After supper they would sit in the inglenook
and listen to their host and hostess talking about their lives.

In the front cover of her notebook Julie wrote: 'In bank £8–5s,
Mary 15s, in hand £1–14s–2½d, Total: £10–14s–2½d,' their
budget for the holiday. From the start Julie managed their finances.
In those first years she earned the most money, though it never
bothered either of them, nor would it when the situation was
reversed. As Mary had no financial sense, she was delighted to
leave it to Julie, who assiduously noted down their disbursements:
in the six weeks they smoked forty cigarettes between them, a
cigarette every day, at a total cost of two shillings. The occasional
cider cost them fourpence, while a cinema trip came to sixpence
each. Their tea might come to as much as a shilling but, if they
kept it down to tenpence, they could debate whether to treat
themselves to a luxury such as a pear or a piece of chocolate.

After such a holiday their separation was hard for both of them.
They tried to see each other at least once a month, though they
could usually manage only a day excursion – either Mary to
London or Julie to Oxford – rarely an overnight stay. On one
trip Mary suggested they see the Chinese exhibition at Burlington
House, only to discover that it was closed to the public on that
particular day. Neither minded; walking about together was happiness enough. On another occasion they joined the long queue of
mourners waiting to pay their last respects to King George v,
lying in state in Westminster Hall. It was after midnight when

they shuffled into the awesome medieval chamber and edged past the catafalque. Mary's idol was king at last, though his reign was to end miserably.

But however intense such brief moments might be, they were a poor substitute for a full relationship. Julie at twenty-three was far from mature – 'a stupid little nit', as she exaggeratedly refers to herself then. Having been sexually awakened by Mary in Oxford, she now found herself alone in London, a dangerous situation for any relationship no matter how strong.

The crisis came that Easter. Julie was asked by a colleague to help lift a patient who had just undergone surgery. The man was in his forties and of dramatic appearance: dark and Middle-Eastern looking, with receding hair which frizzed out at the sides in a flamboyantly bohemian fashion. As they lifted him from the trolley to the bed, he opened his eyes and seemed to Julie to be instantly aware, which was unusual after an anaesthetic. As his own nurse turned away, he put his hand on Julie's and told her he wanted to see her again.

That ought to have been the end of it, but over the next fortnight her duties happened to bring her repeatedly to his bedside, where she quickly realized that everything about him appealed to her. A lecturer at the London School of Economics, with the expected, though still daring, Marxist views of the time, he wrote poetry and was extremely seductive, which was what Julie was missing above all. Perhaps naively, it never crossed her mind that her growing feelings for him in any way affected the untouchable bond she was sure existed between herself and Mary. Indeed, she soon told him about Mary, but that seemed merely to increase his interest in her. When he left to convalesce, he swore he would return to see her, and he did.

Lazarus Aaronson was something new in Julie's experience. Tall and broad-chested, he wore light suits with brightly coloured shirts and ties: a bird of paradise in the grey wastes of north London. When he came to take her out, it was clear he had money, for there were always taxis and good restaurants. She told him she was a virgin, but he refused to believe her until they went to his flat and he discovered she had been telling the truth. He talked openly of sex and she enjoyed their encounters, but put them into a corner of her mind as a substitute, albeit a pleasant one, for her life with Mary. She told Mary about Laz the next time they met without considering the effect such a revelation would have on her friend. Whatever Mary felt, she kept it to herself.

*

Mary's friendships were all to do with broadening her experience outside the confines of the hospital. At some point she met the actor Leslie French, a star of the 1930s famous for Shakespearean roles and just the sort of figure Mary longed to know. Her first meeting with him was everything she could have hoped for. He epitomized the world of the theatre: Ellen Terry had given him his first make-up box, in Victorian scrap work, in 1916, when he was only twelve but already playing children's parts. Like Mary, Leslie was now in his early thirties, but was still boyishly good-looking, still playing Ariel in open-air productions in Regent's Park. But his looks and his wit masked a serious director with original views on the classics and an actor who could cope with roles as varied as Oberon and Othello.

The two met up backstage whenever Mary could get to one of his productions. He was the first of a long line of actor friends who were charmed by this rather serious woman with a keen appreciation of the performance she had just witnessed and an original view of the play itself. Homosexual men found her unthreatening, and the fact that she so openly yearned to be an actor herself completed her appeal.

Julie's affair with Laz continued through the summer and into the autumn. Anyone less naive might have sensed that this was stretching Mary's tolerance to breaking point. One day in October, when Mary had come up to London to go out for the evening with Julie, the conversation seemed to revolve entirely around Laz: what Julie and he had been doing, what interesting things he had said. That Mary was growing heartily sick of the subject did not dawn on her friend until they got back to the boarding house where Mary was to stay. It was past midnight and there was by then a tense atmosphere. Both would have liked to put things straight with a kind word, but Mary said something that irritated Julie and before she could reply, the door swung open and the landlady appeared, protesting at the lateness of the hour. Suddenly Mary was inside and the door was closing. Alone on the pavement, Julie realized at last that things had gone too far.

Julie had a disturbed night and was on duty early the following morning. Mary was meant to come to her room that afternoon, but, when two o'clock struck and she had not turned up, Julie began to feel really nervous. The hours passed miserably. She was due back on duty that evening. Perhaps Mary had returned to Oxford; perhaps it was all over. Julie was just fixing her uniform when the door opened and there she was – she had caught the wrong train and spent hours trying to find one that would get her to Holloway Road, all the while imagining what Julie must be thinking and wondering if her absent-mindedness would mean the end of everything. As they hugged each other, the decision was made that as long as they lived they would never let the sun go down on their anger, no more slammed doors and wretched nights. Julie would still see Laz, though less often than before, and while she would never lie to Mary, she would also learn to vary her conversation. In any case, Julie was beginning to suspect that she was not the only one to enjoy Laz's generosity with taxis and smart restaurants. As summer merged into autumn they began to see less of each other until, gradually, he was no longer part of her life.

*

In November 1936, now aged thirty-one, Mary qualified as a nurse and left the Radcliffe Infirmary. She took a room in the house of a don where, as she had predicted to Julie, she got down to writing a book.

She was still drawn to the idea of a historical novel, perhaps set in the Middle Ages again, but the limited free time she had would not have allowed her to do all the research necessary to avoid repeating her earlier failure. There was little choice but to write about things she knew at first hand. She decided to set her novel in a lightly fictionalized Radcliffe, with a story which, though heavily fictionalized, combined her own and Julie's experiences.

At the end of the year Julie came down with pneumonia, a serious illness in the days before penicillin, and even when the crisis passed she was weak and unable to work. When she was discharged from hospital in mid-January, Mary decided to take her to Barlaston, to her parents' house. The journey was dreadful: there was snow everywhere and the solitary taxi at Stoke had a broken window. They arrived wet and bedraggled, a sight which aroused a latent burst of motherliness in Mrs Challans.

With her mother trying to help and with Julie's health gradually improving, it proved to be Mary's pleasantest stay at her parents' house, but it was also clear that her life with Julie had reached a turning point. With weakened lungs, her friend was now at serious risk of tuberculosis, which would be much increased if she continued as a ward nurse. Mary, too, needed more congenial employment if she was to make progress with her novel, and her solution was that they should apply for posts as school nurses. While they were unlikely to be together, the holidays would be better and the duties less onerous.

By February Julie had a place at Stowe School in Buckinghamshire, and Mary went to Marlborough College in Wiltshire for one term only. Because Mary's school believed in being tough on its boys, few were ever allowed near the sick bay, leaving her ample time for writing. Margaret Lane's ancient typewriter had long since been abandoned and she was now working in longhand. She had most of the story in draft within a fortnight of her arrival, but so far had no ending, relying on one emerging as she wrote. She was planning to use some of the conventions of the popular women's fiction of the day, the type of book her mother read, but intended to subvert them to her own purposes. By setting her love story in a hospital, she would be introducing readers accustomed to the clink of teacups to the more disturbing rattle of bedpans:

> Over some of the cots that lined the walls lamps were burning, muffled in red. Under one of them, the child who presently would wear the shroud was lying with pinched, waxy face, breathing jerkily through a half-open mouth. An apparatus of glass and rubber tubing was running salt and water into her veins to eke out the exhausted blood. It was all that could now be done. Sister, going through her stock that afternoon, had

noticed that all her shrouds were too short, and had put out the necessary materials in the sewing-basket. The little nurse stitched doggedly away, thinking of a film she had seen that afternoon, of the boy who had taken her, and of what she would wear when she met him again. She had made plenty of shrouds; the first few had made her feel creepy, but they were just like the rest of the mending and darning now.

At the simplest level, *Purposes of Love* is the story of Vivian, a nurse, and Mic, a newly arrived pathologist, who meet, fall in love, have the usual jealousies and reconciliations, and work it all out in the end. Mary, however, adds a great deal of spice to this staple fare. Mic is first attracted to Vivian because she resembles his friend, her brother Jan. Mic is illegitimate and isolated; Vivian is his first adult love – his earlier passions were a crush on a fellow schoolboy and his unrequited longing for Jan. Vivian, too, has a more complex sexuality than was usual in 1930s fiction; she is not repulsed by the advances of Colonna, an openly lesbian colleague. What passes between them is tantalizingly ambiguous, but clearly a re-creation of Mary's first encounter with Julie:

> Vivian's hand touched her hair that was silky and smelt sweet like a child's. She stroked it, recalling, with infinite remoteness, the Sunday evening counsels of a careful house-mistress. Her emotions, it was true, were unstirred; but she was flattered as one is by the caresses of a fine and fastidious cat, say a Siamese. It seemed boorish to offer no saucer of milk. Vivian grieved at her own unprovidedness, burying her fingers deeper in the curls behind Colonna's ears.

Mary gets no farther than suggesting the possibility of a lesbian romance. Colonna's affair with Valentine, another nurse, breaks up near the end of the book, and she is left ruefully facing a lonely future.

Mary's intention with *Purposes* was not to celebrate lesbianism, but to propose the idea of a broad spectrum of sexuality along which people move, settling for a time at points which are not as fixed as some people would like to imagine. Indeed, the book makes it clear that it is not Vivian and Mic's 'internal' problems which hamper their affair, but the 'external' stumbling blocks thrown up by the hospital itself, its rigid disciplines and capricious hours. There is something of Caesar in Mic, and much of Julie in Vivian, and there are echoes of the Laz affair in the near disastrous fling Vivian has with the surgeon Scot-Hallard, which almost wrecks her affair with Mic. Where Scot-Hallard has refined his relationships to a polished set of finely orchestrated physical satisfactions, Mic reacts to jealousy like a wounded adolescent. Brought up by strangers, taunted throughout his childhood because of his illegitimacy, he has no defence against betrayal. Where Vivian is delightful, extravagant, impulsive, he can be cold and humourless. Unless he can defeat jealousy, she will be lost, for the underlying theme of the book is not sexuality, deviant or otherwise, but power. When Scot-Hallard's ruthlessness manifests itself, he is referred to as 'something between Hitler and the Archbishop of Canterbury', and the harshness of his character is brought out by the interest he shows in a new experimental weapons factory working day and night producing poison gas.

When Vivian casually enlists the aid of the nurses' drug cabinet to cope with a delayed period, she cannot resist telling Mic what she has done. Her excuse, that she has protected him from fathering another bastard, masks the unspoken urge to exercise power by hurt which she has so roundly despised in Scot-Hallard. Here Mary is suggesting that when the desire to enjoy control proves irresistible, it leads to a deadly self-deception. When Vivian buys a new dress for an assignation with Scot-Hallard, she tells herself the garment is to please Mic and that by sleeping with the surgeon she will somehow be sprucing herself up for her real love-making with the younger man. What began as an amusing love story has progressed into a subtler discourse on the nature of honesty and trust, hence the title, drawn from the nurses' prayer they had repeated every morning in the Radcliffe chapel.

*

Mary chose Oxford for the Easter holidays to refresh her memory as she completed the first draft of the book. She and Julie took a room above the Coq d'Or teashop in the High, where Mary could work during the day and which became Mic's flat in the book. She was still without a typewriter and worked from breakfast to mid-afternoon in longhand, after which she and Julie would go out for tea, then stroll around until it was time to buy fish and chips to eat beside the river, which they did every day. When they returned to their room, Mary would read out any remotely finished passage to Julie, who always responded enthusiastically. If she had changes to recommend, she would bide her time and propose them obliquely.

They enjoyed laughing over the private jokes embedded in the text – the references to people they knew in the hospital, especially the overtly lesbian character Colonna, who shares Mary's passion for Westerns:

Cowboys of the classic kind were a fairyland which Colonna had never outgrown. In their company she dismissed life with its painful compromises, and became her private picture of herself. Flicking open the thumbed pages, and skipping the preliminaries with the ease of practice, she was the Dude in less than a couple of minutes. Clean-limbed, with sinews of steel and whipcord, she toted his silver-mounted guns, knotted his silk bandanna, canted his elegant ten-gallon hat, confounded his hairy rivals, shot up his enemies, and kissed his pale-pink, incidental girl.

After the Easter holiday Julie travelled to Sussex, and Mary left for a girls' school in Colwyn Bay on the north coast of Wales where the pupils were once more healthy enough to leave her free to work on the book. Now pages from the manuscript passed by post, with Julie returning a stream of encouraging comments and the occasional tactful doubt. At Colwyn Bay Mary finished her draft, bought a typewriter and set about revising the work as she typed it. It was at this stage that Julie offered her single most important criticism: cut it back and drop the endless following of characters on a minute-by-minute basis – in other words, use a more cinematic technique, the famous 'bound' that they had joked about before. The main reason the manuscript had gone on growing was Mary's failure to find a plausible ending which would allow her to bring the estranged lovers together again.

Fortunately she and Julie spent their next holiday in an old cottage at Horsted Keynes, where Mary divided her time between cutting her manuscript and relaxing on bicycle rides round Sussex. For fifteen shillings a week they rented a tiny rustic building surrounded by bluebell woods. The cottage was so small they could lie in bed in the single room and watch letters being pushed under the front door. For six weeks Mary typed during the day, while Julie cooked the meals. For Julie it was 'a first taste of normal life', and much of the sensuality in the novel comes from those few weeks together when, for the first time, sex was not something to be snatched during gaps on the duty roster or before dashing to catch a train. There is a sense of physical exploration not known before. They went out into the woods, stripped naked and photographed each other with a camera Julie had borrowed.

When the holiday ended, their main priority was to find the means to make such happiness permanent.

4

Mullard – Renault

Mary found it much harder to finish the novel than she had expected. Vivian and Mic had quarrelled and parted, and merely to bring them together again hardly resolved all the difficulties she had strewn in their path. Unable to think of anything more ingenious she put her best gloss on it, parcelled up the manuscript and sent it to Arthur Waugh at Chapman & Hall. It came straight back.

She was shocked and hurt. For ten years she had cherished the Oxford encounter to the point where she had convinced herself that all she need do was run off a novel, and the kindly Waugh would publish it. When she calmed down, she realized that his letter was not an outright rejection. He liked the story, though he felt it was not right for his company and suggested she send it to the literary agent Spencer Curtis Brown.

This time there was a long, anxious wait before she received a letter from Naomi Burton, an agent with the firm, offering to represent her. The manuscript was, Burton insisted, far too long, a criticism Mary could scarcely resent as it was no more than what Julie had been trying tactfully to suggest since their summer holiday. A general rewrite would also allow her to rethink the ending. She wrote to Burton thanking her and telling her to await a new version, which she expected to be ready soon.

At Colwyn Bay she settled down to some drastic pruning, sending her changes to Julie at her new school in Horsham for comments and encouragement.

By the end of 1937 Mary felt happier with the flow of the book. Her solution to the problem of the ending seems, at first reading, a trifle melodramatic. In order to talk Mic round, Jan, the brother, takes him for a drive in his old open-topped sports car. When he crashes it, Mic is only slightly hurt, but Jan is trapped and seriously injured. Mary redeems this rather unoriginal misadventure by having Jan taken to hospital where he learns there is no hope, the least movement will kill him. When he decides to put an end to his own life, he takes on the sacrificial status assumed by the ancient Greek kings who accepted death at times of crisis in order to appease divine anger.

This sense of Jan as a scapegoat, a consenting sacrifice, and the fact that, once reunited, Vivian and Mic discover their love approaches the Platonic ideal of deep friendship untrammelled by desire, must have intrigued readers who sensed there was something between the lines which was not being made clear. It takes a second reading to realize that Plato has been a shadowy presence throughout the novel; his works are quoted by the lovers with an easy familiarity hardly credible in a young nurse and a pathologist. One suspects that Mary's readers must have looked on this as a mild affectation or at best a rather heavy-handed attempt to give her characters depth. It was only when Mary turned to writing directly about the Socratic circle that it was possible to see in these early references the signs of a more abiding interest. Even then it is difficult to dissentangle her sources and her intentions, and it was not until 1972 that a book entitled *The Hellenism of Mary Renault* provided the key. The author, Bernard F. Dick, an associate professor of English at Fairleigh Dickinson University in New Jersey, was also a considerable classical scholar and the only student of her work to persuade Mary that he had sufficient background knowledge to understand what she had tried to do. Dick was the sole researcher with whom she co-operated, and his conclusions about *Purposes of Love* were the first to break through to its hidden core:

> More important than the sexual ambiguity of *Promise of Love* [the US title] is the tenuous network of Greek allusions and ideals that is loosely worked throughout the novel. In all her early fiction, with the possible exception of *Kind Are Her Answers*, Mary Renault is demanding that the reader view her characters with a double vision and consider them as Hellenic souls imprisoned in modern bodies. An identification with

Greek prototypes and ideals may seem hopelessly naïve and even impractical today; since *Ulysses*, all mythic fiction seems anachronistic. But the reviewers who hailed Mary Renault's early novels as works of considerable depth never found the allusive undercurrents that ran beneath the narrative line like a secret spring for the educated.

In her replies to Dick's letters, Mary revealed the extent to which her interest in the literature of classical Greece had continued throughout her years as a nurse. She had even attempted to master ancient Greek again, but told Dick that she used primarily the Loeb Classical Library, in which the Latin and Greek texts were interleaved with English translations. This reading provided the sub-text to *Purposes of Love*, which in turn demonstrates the remarkable consistency of Mary's preoccupation with the classical world that had begun when she was a schoolgirl, had grown at Oxford and continued until she was ready to write directly about it in her historical novels.

*

Even with the novel completed and despatched to Curtis Brown, Plato's views on the control of desire were still on Mary's mind. Julie had embarked on another affair, this time with a teacher at her school. Julie had been chosen as one of two nurses to attend the annual Diamond Ball, where she would be partnered by Roland, a senior teacher whose wife was expecting their second baby. It was a pleasant summer's night, ending with a drive in the country and an early breakfast at Chanctonbury Ring. As they watched dawn break, Roland told her how difficult things were with his wife, how sympathetic Julie was, and how if he had met her first . . .

Wisely perhaps, Julie said nothing, though she had to admit to the other nurse when they met up in the early hours that she had enjoyed herself. Still, there could be nothing in it, for whatever he might say he was still married. In any case, they were sealed off from each other by a sudden outbreak of German measles in the school, which meant that Julie was isolated and frantically busy. It was during this time that Roland's wife produced twins, but infection set in and she died of septicaemia. Everyone felt deeply sympathetic towards the grieving widower, but, as Julie might have guessed, he was soon gravitating towards her, reminding her of their night on the downs and making it clear that he wanted to take up where they had left off.

Julie longed to tell Mary all this, but an outbreak of mumps meant that it was after Christmas before they could meet up in the Challanses' new home at Woodford Green in the Essex suburbs. Both were rather taken aback by the unexpected modernity of the place: it even had a room with a bar in jade and black tiles, quite gaudy after the subfusc conservatism of former residences.

Julie soon revealed the pressure she was under. Roland had put a lot of emphasis on the children's need for a mother; it seemed impossible that she should not step in. It was a measure of Mary's kindness that she thought less about herself than about her friend's problem. However, she was very precise about what Julie must do: she was to accept Roland's offer of a holiday at Easter and during it must make up her mind clearly and firmly what she wanted to do so as not to leave him or Mary dangling.

Julie's absence on a long car tour – through Wales, back to Stratford-upon-Avon and then down to the Three Choirs Festival in Chichester – was painful for Mary. Like the affair between Vivian and the surgeon Scot-Hallard which so tortured Mic in the novel, it was a question of letting everyone work things through. Jealousy might be inevitable, but had to be fought.

Years later Mary wrote to a close friend who had just lost a lover describing what she had felt at the time:

> . . . it might have ended in marriage, so I said she *must* go off for a bit with him and see. I'd never have forgiven myself if I'd done a Sister George on her (what a clichéd old plot, under all the gimmicks, that play has!) We hadn't a chance to acquire possessions, we were both nurses living in, but it was a curious feeling of sudden vacuum. She pitched up again at the end of a week, having found that though the bed part had gone all right, she just didn't *like* the man. But that was quite enough to give me at least a faint notion of what such a thing is like. That dream of yours about wandering through strange towns and

railway stations is utterly expressive. Those impersonal man-
made utilities are the modern symbol of loneliness. Even in a
film, an empty warehouse, a deserted car park, have this desolat-
ing effect.

Mary had said that she would be going back to Moreton-in-
Marsh for her holiday. Julie sent a telegram to say she was coming.

After a week in Moreton they travelled to London so that Mary
could meet Naomi Burton at the Curtis Brown offices in Covent
Garden. Mary was nervous and Naomi seemed slightly pompous
at first, though it was only because she was young, in her mid-
twenties, and had just been promoted from secretary to agent.
Mary was her first 'find' and she was as nervous of her as Mary
was at being interviewed by someone whom Julie later described
as 'a very sexy lady'. Whether or not Mary ever realized it, the
arrival of Naomi in their lives put Julie on her mettle, which,
coming hard on the heels of the Roland affair, was no bad thing.
Naomi was, according to Julie, 'always smiling and staring into
the middle distance, as though she had a secret'. This frankly
irritated her, the more so because Mary, who liked a touch of
theatricality in those around her, manifestly enjoyed her company.
Naomi marked a subtle change in their lives, which obliged Julie
to make some radical readjustments in her behaviour. Mary was
about to become a 'real' author with sophisticated friends in the
metropolitan world; they learned that Naomi was having a love
affair with a married man who went home at weekends – a warning
if one were needed. What Julie had to accept was that, if she went
on being the naive 'little nit' of her own description, she might
well lose Mary, rather than the other way round.

*

Both Mary and Naomi were conscious that *Purposes of Love*
contained several passages which might prove difficult in a cautious age. The 1920s and 1930s had seen the publication of a
number of works of fiction and non-fiction which touched upon
deviant sexuality. Lesbianism can even be said to have enjoyed
something of a vogue between the two world wars. Virginia
Woolf's *Mrs Dalloway* and Elizabeth Bowen's *The Hotel* had

both dealt sympathetically with emotional attachments between women, and had been criticized for it, the latter novel quite savagely. They had been published, however, which under the prevailing legal framework was never a certainty. Radclyffe Hall's *The Well of Loneliness* had been withdrawn under threat of prosecution in 1928, admittedly amid furious protest from the literary world. Mary had not thus far seen a copy, though she was understandably intrigued to learn what all the fuss was about. The only book dealing openly with lesbians which had evaded the censor was Compton Mackenzie's *Extraordinary Women*, a light, comic tale set among a cosmopolitan lesbian clique on the island of Capri in the years after World War I. It was published before the Radclyffe Hall novel was banned, but had avoided prosecution by being issued privately to subscribers. How Mary obtained a copy is not known, but she remained faithful to the book all her life, referring to it in a later review as 'a masterpiece of gentle satire, wit and pervading unbitchiness'.

Mackenzie had side-stepped the law by being funny, always an acceptable way to mask an interest in deviant sexuality. What the authorities appeared to be saying was that as long as no one took these things seriously, or as long as they were shrouded in artistic mist, the subject might be ignored. What no one had dared to do was to offer the general reader an accessible book which dealt openly and unsensationally with the variety of sexual responses familiar to most people but still censored in books. It was this that Mary had achieved.

In the end Naomi sent *Purposes* to Robert Longman, who, after having it read, enthusiastically accepted it. One of Mary's most touching and enduring memories was of the summons to London to meet her publisher for the first time. 'I remember when,' she wrote in one of her later letters, 'a shy and awkward girl terribly upset at having to wear a mackintosh because I couldn't afford a taxi, and – overthrowing all my sartorial plans – it was a wet day, I was shown through a warren of passages lined with stacks of books into Robert Longman's office in Paternoster Row. He held out his hand saying, "So this is the 200,000 word author!" '

Longman had hit the right note, at once jovial and sympathetic, yet with a clear emphasis on the fact that there was still work to be done. He found her a sympathetic editor, Eric Gillet, who suggested major cuts to give the story the pace it still lacked. Gillet then invited her to London and took her to the Ivy, the smartest restaurant in the West End, a haunt of Noël Coward and Gertrude Lawrence, and a perfect way to please someone like Mary. To complete this sophisticated whirl, Mary took Naomi to the ballet at Covent Garden – a first for both of them.

Despite the changes still to be made, a contract was in the offing, with the promise of a £50 advance. This was almost a year's salary for a nurse, and Mary suggested that she and Julie take a holiday in France. As this was such an adventure in itself, they decided to go no farther than the small seaside village of Equihen on the cliffs just south of Boulogne. It was their first foreign trip and, despite the nearness of England, which could be seen across the Channel on a clear day, everything was gloriously strange – the excitement of the crossing, the unusual shops as they passed through Boulogne. The rate of exchange was so favourable that the Hôtel des Falaises cost a mere 12s 6d a week for both of them, including real coffee in the mornings and superb meals in the restaurant, where the local children came to stare through the windows at the strange foreign ladies.

After years of nursing, this was utter luxury. Women in black with starched white aprons worked all day sanding the floors, making the beds. A tiny path led past the graves of drowned fishermen to a line of upturned boats which housed an artists' colony and which continued down to the rolling dunes of the Côte Opale. There were bicycle rides and swimming, and a shopping trip to Boulogne, where Mary bought Julie a pair of red slippers in the softest kid which she wore till they fell apart. Most amusing of all was the forbidden thrill of being able to read *The Well of Loneliness*, which was on sale to English tourists. As they did not dare risk taking it back through customs, they tore out each page as they read it, crumpled it up and threw it away – the first and last time Mary ever destroyed a book. Happily for her peace of mind, they both found it pretty silly and inadvertently hilarious in places. Both of them had fits of giggles over the men's underwear which the heroine puts on; what could this have been, Mary wondered – Wolsey combinations perhaps? Retribution for

Julie came in the form of a mild dose of bronchitis brought on by an unexpected downturn in the weather and by smoking French cigarettes. Nemesis took the form of a doctor dressed in sepulchral black who prescribed suppositories, always something to chasten the English.

Naomi came over on a day trip with her lover, which made Mary feel terrifically important and *mondaine*. The only jarring note was the news from the BBC, broadcasting the story of the Munich agreement. They were not deluded; it might sound as if everything were settled, but Mary knew that it was time to go home.

Back in London, she and Julie spent a week in a house in Cleveland Square much used by visiting nurses. The landlady was a wonderful, blowsy old thing universally known as 'the Red-haired Tart', who had a fondness for cheap sherry and a live-in lover as old as herself who wore a straw boater inside and out, all year round. Happily the Red-haired Tart took an instant shine to them, much reinforced by their turning up one day with some bottles of Australian sherry. The way the place was organized suited them perfectly. Breakfast was available throughout the morning, with the young women coming down just before their various duty times, so there was lots of familiar hospital talk over the tea-making. The place became their London home from then on. But, despite another encouraging meeting with Naomi, the atmosphere in the capital was depressing, with volunteers digging trenches in the parks and a general feeling of gloom hanging over everything.

*

Mary signed her contract with Longmans that September and moved to Cheltenham, where she had a new job as House Matron at the Ladies' College, which would be more convenient for visits to London. The British publishing contract was swiftly followed by one from Morrow in America, which would bring in $250. Later there would be £30 from Sweden and Denmark. It was breathtaking. Morrow decided to change the title to *Promise of Love*, but nothing else was altered despite the worries, shared by both publishers, that the book might be prosecuted.

More agonizing for Mary was her indecision over how she should sign herself. She was sure *Mary* would have to stay, she had struggled enough to achieve it in the first place, but what could she use so that her colleagues need never know she was the author of so risqué a book? She toyed with the idea of Mary Radcliffe after the hospital, but, when Julie pointed out how close it was to Radclyffe Hall, they both started laughing. In the end the most appealing name was Renault, that of the character in Otway's *Venice Preserv'd* who had also been the hero of her earlier, abandoned novel. She always pronounced it 'Ren-olt', though almost everyone would come to speak of her as if she were a French car.

Purposes was published in Britain in February 1939, followed shortly afterwards by *Promise of Love* in America. Over the week-end after publication the British reviews were sharply divided. The London *Observer* carried an appreciation by Frank Swinnerton, who compared *Purposes* favourably with two other books published at the same time: Robert Liddell's *Kind Relations* and *A Family and a Fortune* by no less a figure than Ivy Compton-Burnett. He commended Mary's ability to present 'very physical love-making' in an unsensational manner and praised the novel's 'very high calibre'. Ralph Strauss in the *Sunday Times*, however, went for the jugular: 'Although we are accustomed to find much in the books of today which would have shocked even the Edwardians out of their skins, there are those who still like to think that studies of the sexually abnormal, however "slight" that abnormality may be, should best be confined to the consulting room.' Such criticism was not confined to serious literary journals. Almost immediately, the 1930s equivalent of the tabloids were on to the story. The *Sunday Referee* led the pack with a banner headline:

MATRON DENIES SEX LIBELS ON NURSES
Charges of immorality among hospital nurses and of clandestine affairs between them and the doctors are made in a new novel, 'Purposes of Love', published this week by Longmans Green.

The matron of one of London's biggest voluntary hospitals told a Sunday Referee reporter:

'This book will obviously sell, and the majority of readers will think it is true. But in my experience it is **not**.

'I have been matron at this hospital for twenty-five years, and during that period I have only once come across a case of sexual abnormality between nurses.

'People seem to think that a nurse's natural instincts are bound to be repressed, because of the monastic life she is forced to lead.

'Nurses are far less repressed than the inmates of many of our big schools and universities.

CAN MEET MEN-FRIENDS

'They have ample opportunities for seeing their men-friends.

'Once a week they are allowed to leave the hospital at six o'clock in the evening, and they are free until midnight of the following day.

'Apart from this, they have two hours off duty every day, four hours on Sundays, and late passes twice a week if they want to go to a theatre or a cinema.

'How could anyone be repressed in conditions like these?

'As for clandestine affairs with doctors – well, mostly they're not clandestine and not "affairs."

'Heaps of nurses go about openly with doctors, and generally end up by marrying them.

'That's the way I lose good nurses. It makes me furious!'

Unaware that it was one of her own ex-nurses who had caused the furore, the matron of the Radcliffe Infirmary had chocks screwed to the windows of the nurses' home so that they would open only enough to let in a little air. They are there to this day.

However, the controversy did no harm to sales and by March the *Sunday Pictorial* announced that 'one of the frankest, most intimate love stories of recent years' was selling all over the country. Longmans rushed to reprint and began to take out advertisements with the title of the novel in a black banner headline beneath which was the announcement: 'It's a snowball! The publishers regret that there is no type large enough to typify the latest sales figures of Mary Renault's startling hospital novel.'

Not surprisingly, Mary said nothing of all this to her family.

She never sent her books to either her father or her mother. Even when they must have pieced together the fact that their daughter was Mary Renault, neither of them said anything. It is likely that Mrs Challans looked on the whole matter as confirmation of her worst fears; that Mary was unmarried and wasting her time on sensational novels was no more than she had predicted. But Dr Challans's attitude is harder to explain. After all, he was an avid reader and might at least have been intrigued to see what his child had done. Given the press attention for the first novel, he cannot have been unaware of the book, and even if he managed to dismiss it as 'women's fiction', the sort of thing his wife borrowed from Mudie's Postal Library, it is difficult to believe he could have resisted at least a look at what his daughter had written. But resist he did. And while Mary was initially relieved to be spared confrontation with her parents over her work, their lifelong indifference to it was to become a festering hurt.

By May the novel was banned in Eire, though this was hardly unusual since so was anything remotely concerned with human intimacy. Despite another outright attack in the *Spectator*, there were no calls for the book to be banned in Britain. Indeed, there was sufficient demand for John O'London's column A Bookman's Diary to report that the 'printers have been working night and day to get out extra editions'. (The entry also noted that the same thing applied to the recent publication of Adolf Hitler's *Mein Kampf*, which had taken four days to typeset and three to print.)

The result of all this attention was that *Purposes of Love* became a best-seller and thus the first novel dealing with bisexuality to reach a large and appreciative public. A letter from a Miss Parry of Colwyn Bay is typical: '. . . I think I want to tell you how much I have loved your book *Purposes of Love* . . . The way Vivian manages her "two lives" is so true, too. We have all had to do much the same thing, but with varying success.'

By May the *Bookseller* showed it at number eleven in its list of top sellers from forty-nine selected bookshops, by which time the American reviews were also appearing and were uniformly excellent. Edith H. Walton in *The New York Times* spread her praise over two columns, and any fears Morrow might have had that criticism of the book's sexual explicitness would cross the

Atlantic were proved groundless. A month after publication Morrow felt confident enough to indulge in some old-fashioned hucksterism:

> **Sample** PROMISE OF LOVE before you buy the copy that you will want to own always . . . **discover it for yourself.** This unique proposition will obligate you in no way whatever. Write the publishers TODAY for your **Free** copy of 'Prelude to PROMISE OF LOVE,' a sampler of the drama, excitement, romance, humor, perception that this unusual story has to offer.

The press cuttings tumbled in from Canada and Australia and India, from almost everywhere that English was read. Yellowing now, they are preserved on squares of coloured card cut out and pasted down during Mary's rare moments of quiet in the 'sicker' at Cheltenham.

*

Mary ought to have been in London enjoying her success instead of being in Cheltenham, bored and lonely. There was another nurse's post available at the school and she wrote to Julie begging her to apply. With the Roland affair behind her, Julie was happy where she was, but felt obliged to go along with her friend's request. When she got the job, the result was unsatisfactory. She and Mary could see each other only on an occasional afternoon off and, as neither cared for the place, there were now two disgruntled people.

This was too much for Mary, who went into town, drew her American advance out of the bank and bought a bright red MG sports car, the sort of glossy convertible with 'tyres like satin' more often seen in films than parked outside a boys' boarding school. There was one major drawback to this impetuous fantasy: neither Mary nor Julie could drive, and Mary had used up so much money there was barely enough left for driving lessons.

Their driving tests were hopeless. Julie was delayed at work and turned up too late; Mary was simply no good at driving and failed outright. That should have been the end of the affair, but the beautiful bright red car was too tempting and on their first afternoon off together they decided to risk a drive in the Cotswolds.

Mary took the wheel, a mistake Julie realized as soon as they drove into traffic. There was an impatient streak in Mary which rarely surfaced but, when aroused, was hard to control. She was driving with an abandon unwise for someone so obviously inexperienced, but it was a lovely day, the hood was down, the breeze was exhilarating, and Julie could not bear to spoil it. Then, without warning, Mary drove on to a patch of gravel and instinctively braked, sending the car into a helpless skid, rolling it over on to its left side. Mary was thrown out, but Julie remained trapped underneath. Bruised and badly shaken, Mary managed to raise the car just enough to pull her free. Her face was a mess, but the shock had deadened any pain, and Mary was able to sit her on the bank at the side of the road. Slightly delirious, Julie insisted they should right the car and drive away before they got into trouble, but Mary could see that the beautiful red racer was a complete write-off. More to the point, Julie needed urgent treatment. A passing car took them to a nearby cottage hospital. Mary was merely bruised, but Julie had deep flesh wounds, and her eyelids were so swollen she was blind for three days. Septicaemia set in, necessitating constant and careful re-dressing of her cuts.

Back in Cheltenham, Mary could only wait anxiously for news, reflecting ruefully on the bizarre way life had imitated art. It was another turning point: the terms of their contracts meant that Julie had to forgo her salary to pay for a replacement while she was in hospital. As neither of them liked the school, it seemed like the ideal time to resign. Both had a term's salary saved and Mary had the remains of her various publishers' advances. If they arranged things carefully, they might find a place in the country where Mary could concentrate on her writing and Julie could convalesce.

While Julie had treatment on her face, Mary scoured the advertisements to find a home for them. Trying to be practical, she settled on a cottage near Crantock in Cornwall which was said to sleep six or seven, as this would allow them to have friends to stay, sharing costs.

At first sight, the place was delightful if damp, but the other rooms turned out to be no more than an unconverted outhouse. Nevertheless, it was now summer, the weather was beautiful, the beach was close by and there was not a single chimney visible above the surrounding trees. Such splendid isolation was what they had always wanted. Civilization was a three-mile walk away in Newquay, near enough for supplies or the occasional newspaper, far enough for them to be undisturbed. Mary was thirty-three, Julie twenty-six, and at last they were living together.

*

Mary had plotted her second novel before leaving Cheltenham. It was to be called *Kind Are Her Answers* and was a simple love triangle, complicated by the new woman, whose uninhibitedly sensual approach to life and love gave the book its title. The marriage of Kit Anderson, a doctor in general practice, and Janet, a bored society woman, has foundered. A miscarriage and her subsequent hysterectomy have left little between them, except his pity for her condition and her need to manipulate this for her own pleasure. When Kit encounters Christie, the niece of one of his elderly patients, he cannot resist her vivacity compared to the arid, calculating Janet. Christie is wild and emotional; Kit is jealous. The novel sets out to show how they resolve this.

One suspects that, given time for reflection, Mary would have radically revised this outline or even rejected it for something more substantial. Although it was not set in a hospital, its medical background made it a sequel to *Purposes*, while lacking the wealth of detail Mary had poured into the first book. It was that richness which appealed to many reviewers, who praised a realism obviously lived by its author. If Mary wanted to continue writing in this naturalistic vein, she would need new experiences to draw on, yet she was now isolated in the country, shut off from the background she had chosen for her book.

Her difficulty was that contracts had been signed and, following the success of *Purposes*, there was now considerable pressure from both her British and American publishers that she should adhere to a close delivery date. Unable to withstand such demands, Mary found herself hopelessly locked into a story so slight that it offered scant prospect for development. After three months in Cornwall, she had finished a first draft and, while she was agonizing over whether to go on, a letter arrived from Morrow in America, urging her to finish as quickly as possible since the outbreak of hostilities

79

was expected at any moment and might be followed by a break-down in communications. A more established and confident author would have quietly ignored such a demand. What Mary needed above all was the chance to settle into her new life with Julie and have room to reflect on what she was doing, and how her ideas were developing. Instead, Morrow's letter galvanized her into a frenzy of work.

The most obvious effect of this rush to finish is the way her characters remain stubbornly two-dimensional. Janet is no more than a rather sour Clementine, fussy about her bedroom decor and coquettish towards susceptible young men with whom she has no intention of doing anything other than tease them for their doglike devotion. Janet has lost all chance of having children, yet Mary allows for little sympathy towards a woman she clearly dislikes. In terms of the novel, it is a wasted opportunity. Had Janet been treated more even-handedly, Kit's relationship with Christie might have had a sharper edge.

The most successful character is Christie, an exaggerated Julie – there are echoes of the Roland episode in her weakness for men with hard-luck stories. She wants to be an actress, and the book is at its best when it goes backstage at the local theatre (at one point the company performs Gilbert Murray's *Agamemnon* and Justin Huntly McCarthy's *If I Were King*), where the world of masks and role playing is used as a metaphor for the drama the lovers are enacting. When Kit auditions for a role, he recites part of the last act of *Othello*, the ultimate example of the effects of destructive jealousy. Christie's entanglements are explained by her 'theatrical' nature; she always falls for a well-acted line. When one of the actors spins her a tale about his sister dying of tuberculosis, she consoles him and, when she tells Kit, she acts out the man's tale, making her confession as much a performance as an excuse.

This awareness of self-deception shows Mary at her most observant, though the clipped, nasal, Noël Coward-like stage talk tends to undermine the realism needed to make it work:

Voices sounded along the passage; Christie said, 'Look out,' and slid from his arms.

'Dear Kit.' She settled his chain and his long sleeves. 'Don't let's be unhappy. Some time everything will be all right.'

'I'd better be getting down.'

'I'll be watching you from the back of the hall.'

'Aren't you going to make me up?' He opened the door.

'Bad luck, darling; Rollo's doing the men. Do be marvellous. I'll be loving you all the time.'

Once again, Mary's greatest difficulty was how to end what she had begun. As with Jan's car accident, she was forced to precipitate a crisis by having an embittered servant write poison-pen letters to expose the lovers, only to have them intercepted in the nick of time. Janet is conveniently removed by a hasty cruise to South Africa, where she decides to stay, leaving the lovers to their own salvation.

'Darling Kit. I'm here to look after you now.' Warmly, securely, her voice enclosed him, like the walls of a fire-lit room. 'Everything's going to be all right now. You're never going to be unhappy any more.'

Unfortunately, after so much play-acting and so many kind answers, there is no longer any reason for the reader to believe what Christie says.

Oblivious to doubts, Mary beavered away, determined to fulfil Morrow's demand. In the days before photocopying, rushed work like this was a nightmare. Everything had to be typed with carbons, and any alterations meant that whole pages had to be completely retyped. Mary sat for hours tapping at an old manual machine, while Julie brewed gallons of coffee between proof-reading and numbering pages. Then, one day in September, as they were taking a break, strolling across the nearby fields, they overheard a distant radio announcing that war had at last been declared. A few days later came another letter from Morrow, this time proposing an earlier date for the delivery of the manuscript. There was something puzzling about the date – they looked again and saw to their despair that it had already passed. Worse still, the radio began to announce that all professional personnel were needed for war work; trained nurses were urgently required and were to make their whereabouts known to the authorities. They both wrote off, listing their credentials, and waited for the summons that would propel them heaven knew where. In the meantime they reapplied themselves to the novel with something approaching panic, Mary attempting to tidy up weaker passages, Julie trying to keep her supplied with materials. First the paper would run out, then the carbons, all necessitating a long hike to Newquay and back.

The one certain factor in this shifting world was her British publisher, Robert Longman, whose letters were always received with delight for the kindly, avuncular care they offered. Longman was one of the few who knew how to offer criticism without hurt, always gently urging her not to put in too much, always tempering criticism with praise. As Julie recalls: 'She would glow after reading one of his letters.'

Naomi Burton was another ally in the alien world of London publishing, so it was a blow when she wrote to say that she had decided to accept a post in Curtis Brown's New York office. The London branch would try to find Mary a new agent as quickly as possible; but in the meantime she would be looked after by the head of the firm, Spencer Curtis Brown. As it turned out, this state of affairs could not be changed until after the war, leaving Mary in the hands of a man better known for driving women to tears than for offering them gentle support. Gruff to the point of insensitivity, Spencer Curtis Brown proved of small use in her struggle to satisfy the importunate demands of her American publishers, leaving Mary feeling increasingly isolated.

Even finishing the novel produced only temporary relief rather than creative satisfaction. Parcels were made for each publisher, and a further trip to Newquay saw them despatched. However, when Mary went from the post office to the bank, she found to her dismay that her money was blocked, the London banks having stopped transferring funds until the situation became clearer. What cash she had was nearly gone. As neither she nor Julie was inclined to indulge in what Mary called 'belly-aching and fuss', there was nothing to do but put a brave face on things, though it must have been hard for Mary to see them slipping back into the style of life she had endured after she went down from St Hugh's and was living in the flat in Bristol, trying to survive on beef cubes. At least this time their diet could be augmented with free luxuries – mushrooms from the surrounding woods, or gifts of clotted cream from one of the neighbouring farmers no longer able to despatch his produce to the cities.

*

Hopes of an early call-up were dashed when the private nursing homes were closed and there was a sudden glut of nurses. Both Mary and Julie applied to Queen Alexandra's Royal Army Nursing Corps, but were turned down because neither had taken the midwifery exams. Unable to practise obstetrics on the British Expeditionary Force setting out for France, they were obliged to look closer to home for useful employment. The newspapers were full of stories of children being evacuated from major cities as a precaution against air raids, and this seemed to offer a role for both of them which would enable them to stay at the cottage. They quickly fixed up the outhouse as a sort of hostel with home-made wooden bed frames and wrote off, volunteering to take in any children who still needed a place.

What they had not realized was the sheer chaos following the declaration of war. Orders were given and instantly countermanded. Letters went astray or lay about unanswered. No one ever responded to their offer, and the only refugees who turned up were Mary's mother and Joyce. Dr Challans had been called up for war work in Cambridge and, unwilling to face the predicted bombardment of the capital, Clementine had rented a cottage near Crantock.

Her mother's arrival in their quiet refuge was hardly what Mary would have wished. While nothing had ever been said about her relationship with Julie, her mother and father must have surmised that they were something more than mere colleagues and flat-mates. Julie had effectively distanced herself from her mother and family, but Mary's position was less clear cut. Despite the little they had in common, and her parents' lack of interest in her writing, she still wrote to them often and visited when possible. But it was quite another matter to have Clementine living nearby with her favourite daughter in attendance. Joyce was twenty-eight, but looked far younger, as if life had stopped still. She had not gone to university nor had she been encouraged to take up a career; she had also thus far failed to acquire a 'nice' husband. Although Mary knew it was irrational, she could not help believing that she had been able to escape her mother's clutches only because her sister had remained behind. That Joyce showed no desire to break free made it worse, and whenever they were alone Mary did her utmost to convince her that she should do something more with her life than act as unpaid companion to their mother.

Mary had no sooner adjusted to the new situation than she was thrown into confusion by the unannounced arrival at the cottage of her father. A good lunch from Julie helped ease the tension. The war gave them something solid to discuss, and for the first time in her life Mary found herself talking to her father on equal terms. It was what she had always wanted, and the visit might have ended well had he not enquired what her plans were, now that a general call-up had been announced. She told him about the army's rejection, and he offered to sort it out – he would use his medical contacts to get her a decent post at a good hospital. He had not approved of her having a career, but he would overlook this since she needed his help – she might even become a matron.

Mary was appalled at this development and mumbled something about her writing. He waved this away, insisting she do as she was told. Angry now, she told him she had her own life to lead and did not wish to be a hospital matron.

'Oh, God,' he cried. 'I have this daughter and all she ever says is no . . .' And with that he grabbed his coat and stormed off.

It was useless for the two friends to pretend they could continue as before. The talk about nursing had struck at their weakest point: Mary was following her chosen career, but Julie had abandoned hers. When she had gathered her thoughts, Mary suggested Julie apply for a post. Bristol might be best; there was a maternity unit there and Julie could obtain qualifications in obstetrics at last.

When the letter arrived accepting her, it ended their first attempt to make a home together. There would be ten years of considerable hardship before they were able to try again.

5

War

For Mary it was a film played backwards. They moved to Bristol and found a flat in Clifton near the bridge. The air raids had begun; they hung black-out curtains, were issued with ration cards and gas masks, and dutifully followed government instructions about laying in stocks of food, even down to the slightly dotty business of putting eggs into a bucket of isinglass, which would preserve them for months provided it was not moved. They were stoical, believing that the less they complained, the sooner it would all be over.

One evening in April, Julie turned up for night duty to find her shift had been changed without warning. She shrugged and set off for home. As she climbed the stairs, she saw a young man waiting on the landing. Even in the black-out she could tell he was handsome, with an appealing smile, blond hair and blue eyes. He introduced himself as Robbie Wilson – *Dr* Robbie Wilson. He had been on his way up to see Mary when he heard the door open and had decided to wait. He had, he explained, read *Purposes of Love* and had travelled from London to meet the author. Something about his manner convinced Julie that 'he had come with his toothbrush' and she wondered how he would react when he discovered that Mary did not live alone.

They went up together, and Julie discovered that Robbie was not a complete stranger to Mary. He had sent her a copy of the review of *Purposes* he had written for the *Hospital Gazette* at St Mary's, Paddington, where he was a house surgeon. He had come to Bristol on the spur of the moment.

What first attracted both women to him was that he was not in the least put out to find Mary living with Julie. On the contrary, he appeared to be fascinated by the situation, and within seconds it was clear that all three were going to be close friends. Robbie was to become one of the seminal people in Mary's life, a character ahead of his time, rather like a member of the hippy generation thirty years later. He was married with a daughter and was about to be appointed assistant pathologist at St Mary's, but there the conventional Robbie ended. He was seeking a divorce, which was still unusual for a doctor then, and was interested in alternative medicine, with ideas about healing through love. He explained that with diseases like cancer, still largely inoperable, it might be possible to project love to the patient as a form of therapy. It was faith healing under another name, and it was soon clear to Julie that he had come to Bristol in the hope of trying out these theories on the author he so admired.

Robbie spent the night and, when he left the next morning, they knew he would be back. In a rapidly disintegrating world, he seemed to offer a promise of a different life, younger and more hopeful and full of enthusiasm for all manner of untried possibilities, a rare thing in those grey days.

Between April and May 1940 the news swung between elation and despair. The fall of Denmark was followed by the British landings in Norway, and with Churchill's appointment as prime minister the waiting seemed to be over at last. By mid-May Holland had fallen to the Germans and the Belgian army was in retreat as the Nazis took Brussels. By 25 May British and French troops were being forced back to the Channel, and the first British wounded were being shipped home to England. One night BBC radio broadcast an appeal for all trained nurses to volunteer for war work. The need for an obstetric qualification was no longer mentioned, the 'phoney war' was over. The announcement made it clear that, while this was not conscription, all nurses were honour bound to attend public meetings to be held in all major towns.

To get to the Bristol meeting, Mary and Julie passed through a maze of sandbags to a hall where a large, masculine woman in uniform told them that this was 'woman's hour' and they were being 'called to the colours'. There was to be a new organization for them, the Emergency Medical Service, and they were all to sign up the following night.

86

When they returned, they were sent to the Bristol Royal Infirmary at once and put into an emergency operating unit. When Mary pointed out that she had never worked in an operating theatre, she was told there was a war on and every woman had to do her duty. They were ordered to return home and wait with a bag packed. They were not to go out, but should be in constant readiness for the taxi which would be sent to collect them. They should not wash their hair lest they be unprepared for what might befall. They went home and waited.

For weeks nothing happened. No taxi came. Their hair grew dirty. They ate tinned salmon and eggs. Yet, oddly enough, life was in some ways better: they received a regular state salary and Mary had all the time in the world to write, even though the sense of waiting for something to happen was unnerving – especially as nothing did. The packed suitcases stood by the door and, as they could never go out, friends came to them and helped finish up the tins and the eggs. When they felt rebellious, they hurriedly washed their hair and prayed that the taxi would not choose this moment to arrive.

They knew from Robbie's letters how bad things were in London. He had been putting in twenty-hour days at St Mary's, struggling to keep up with the flow of people injured in the nightly air raids. He was due a weekend leave around 4 June and came to visit. As they sat chatting, one of them switched on the radio, and they heard the voice of Churchill: 'We shall go on to the end . . . We shall fight on the beaches, we shall fight on the landing grounds, we shall fight in the fields and in the streets, we shall fight in the hills; we shall never surrender . . .' And they knew without needing to say anything that a turning point had been reached, that the war could no longer be viewed as a temporary break in normal life – it *was* normal life and was going to be so for a very long time. Everything that they had thought of as 'the future' was now in abeyance: Mary's writing, her desire to make a life with Julie, everything was subject to this one overriding imperative.

'Let's get drunk,' Robbie said.

They went to a nearby pub and drank there for a while, then took some beer home and sat on the floor, eating supper, drinking, occasionally talking. There was really not much to say; they might never be together again, yet there was a closeness which was possible only because they were living in the present. Robbie returned to London the following day without any idea of when he might be able to make such a trip again.

Kind Are Her Answers was published on 20 May, the day the Germans reached the English Channel at Noyelles. Amidst the general panic, Mary's book was barely noticed.

.*.

By 27 May the evacuation of Dunkirk had begun and all the hospitals throughout the south and west were put on standby to receive the wounded. Summoned to the Bristol Royal, Mary and Julie found their first task was to help clear the wards of any patients who could be moved. They were appalled. Sick people with drips dangling from them were being handed over to the care of anxious relatives; it went against everything they had been trained to do. As if that were not enough, a bomb fell on the hospital, damaging the isolation wards and hastening the evacuation of anyone who had anywhere to go, leaving only fifty patients who were either too sick to be moved or had no one to take them in.

In a way it was just as well that Mary was caught up in all this. The first reviews of her book were appearing, and those she saw were not encouraging. Anthony West in the *New Statesman & Nation* harped, somewhat unreasonably, on the fact that the novel had nothing to say about the momentous events now going on all around them:

The Ivory Tower is a nice idea, and one has a pretty picture of the artist inside, polishing, perfecting, and concentrating on lovely things, but one forgets the result of having nothing but Ivory to work on. It is rather filthy material, with a dingy colour and a soapy surface, which artists have left to the carvers of napkin rings and chessmen for the best of reasons. A book as completely divorced from the everyday world as *Kind Are Her Answers* warns one of the consequences of using that soft and deadly material.

But it was another woman and fellow practitioner, Rosamond Lehmann, writing in the *Spectator*, who touched most exactly on the book's faults:

> Her subject in *Kind Are Her Answers* is love; her treatment of it is voluptuous, with an un-English physical directness. Her manner of writing has a tremendous feminine vitality – that sort of creative gusto which has proved first the strength and subsequently – controlled by no shaping intellectual maturity – the undoing of many a contemporary woman novelist. (As with an infant on the wrong kind of patent food, the body and limbs swell out with rosy dimpling fat; the turn of the scales brings, at first, pride and delight to parents and beholders; but no bone is made; the end is rickets.)

Lehmann ended with a warning:

> Miss Renault is, I feel, at a dangerous cross-roads in her career. Popular she will be. It is to be hoped that nothing and no one will persuade her to pour herself out in an unstemmed flow of fiction during the next few years.

It would be four years before Mary published another book, though this was more to do with the war than from any desire to heed Lehmann's advice, wise though it was. Mary the author needed time to catch up with Mary the person. *Kind Are Her Answers'* most irritating fault is that it fails to reflect the way Mary and Julie's relationship had evolved. The courageous manner in which she had tackled the ambiguous sexuality of the main characters in *Purposes* made the conventionally 'straight' characters in *Kind Are Her Answers* doubly disappointing. The odious Janet turns out to be a lesbian, but only as a convenient ploy to get rid of her near the end of the book, by having her fall in love with another woman during her visit to South Africa.

At the time, the book's reception hardly mattered. It disappeared amidst the increasing chaos following the shock of the collapse of France. The Bristol Royal Infirmary had been emptied for no good reason. The wounded from Dunkirk were sent to army bases on the east coast. Those in need of surgery were treated in field stations, then sent on to hospitals in the south. Very few were obliged to travel as far as the West Country, and the evacuated hospital lay empty, its operating theatres on full alert with nothing to do except repair broken ankles sustained by people who had tripped and fallen as they entered the new Anderson air-raid shelters during the unfamiliar black-out. It was with considerable relief that Mary learned that the promised emergency medical services would come into operation. The idea was to keep as many patients as possible away from the city centre hospitals where there was an increasing risk of bomb damage. The Royal Infirmary would continue to receive emergencies, but less urgent cases were to be transferred to one of the new units at Winford on the outskirts of the city.

Mary and Julie arrived with twelve others to find scarcely more than an empty camp made up of a small, evacuated children's hospital, around which half a dozen lines of temporary Nissen huts had been built. When they looked through the windows, they could see that these sheds were stacked with unmade beds. It was a dispiriting start and, when they trooped into a bare office, they found the new matron, who looked terrified at being landed with a situation so evidently out of her experience. She was joined by a surgeon who announced that he would be 'in charge', though Julie sensed that he was just as terrified as the matron. Precisely who was to be in charge of *what* was unclear and both leaders attempted rather feeble pep talks before handing out duties. It was soon painfully obvious that the surgeon did not understand the situation and was going to treat them as if they were in the army. He began by allotting posts on the basis of seniority rather than nursing qualifications or experience, which left Julie as no more than a staff nurse.

'Where is the nurses' home?' someone demanded. But no one seemed to have thought of this. There were groans all round. Julie looked at Mary; it was another wartime bungle and here they were relegated to junior posts and forced to sleep in a hut like a troop of girl guides.

As they took the bus back to Clifton, Julie was apparently more incensed by the situation than Mary. Her solution was simple:

they would volunteer for the task no one ever wanted to do
– night duty. That way they would probably be able to work
unsupervised and might find it easier to get accommodation in the
village. The next day they went to see what was available and
encountered a young woman, married only a year, whose husband
had been called up; she was more than happy to supplement her
income by letting them have her bedroom during the day. They
went upstairs to look. The house was a tiny 1930s villa, but the
room was daintily fitted out with pink frills on everything, all
lovingly made. It would do.

The one good thing to emerge from the national call-up was
the news from Mrs Challans that Joyce was going to get a job.
Dr Challans was still in Cambridge, and Clementine had decided
that the ancient university town was as safe from German raids
as Cornwall; she therefore arranged for Joyce to train as a nurse
at Addenbrooke's Hospital.

Mary was far too busy to do much more than scribble a page
or so in moments snatched between long periods of duty. The
wounded from Dunkirk were moved to the huts, and it was clear
they would be there for some time. Mary and Julie resigned
themselves to a new life, clearing out the flat in Clifton. In due
course, once the nurses' hut was converted, they reluctantly left
the pink-frilled bedroom for partitioned cubicles in the general
dormitory. At least they were together at night with only the two
bombardiers who guarded the hospital for company, along with
the occasional wounded soldier who found it difficult to sleep and
would be invited to join them for a chat over a cup of tea. It could
have been worse: all over the country couples were separated,
often without knowing where the other was. But some at the
hospital found it impossible to submit to this sort of spartan
regime, and after a few weeks the maids who did the basic cleaning
and the laundry suddenly walked out *en masse* in protest against
their conditions. This left one of the huts empty, and a short
time later a party of conscientious objectors arrived to work as
replacement orderlies.

They were of various ages and most were Quakers; they wore
khaki jerkins without badges and were allocated the maids' hut.
Inevitably, they were insulted by some of the conscripts, one of

whom refused to be touched by a 'conchie', but most accepted
that their beliefs were honestly held and left them alone. Mary
was fascinated, listening to their stories and trying to understand
their motives. It was a touching confrontation, watching young
wounded soldiers being helped by boys of their own age who had
refused to fight. Two very different forms of courage met as one
of the orderlies offered an arm to a soldier taking his first hesitant
steps. If insults were offered, they took them quietly, never
responding, always patient. But to Mary the most fascinating thing
was that some of the conchies were homosexual. This was not the
temporary, schoolboy crush variety Mary had written about
in *Purposes*. These were young men interested only in each
other. At the time to be a conscientious objector during a world
war and avowedly homosexual as well required a special form of
courage.

Their arrival was the last excitement to enliven the slow passage
of time at Winford.

Mary and Julie never had a night off together and were soon
thoroughly bored with the claustrophobic atmosphere in the
camp. Whenever possible, Julie liked to visit Oxford to look up
old friends, and on one occasion she called in at the Radcliffe,
where she happened to meet the new matron, who was 'quite a
lady, educated and well dressed'. They certainly took to each other
and it was discreetly suggested that Julie might care to come
back. She had not thought such a thing possible under wartime
conditions; surely they were 'posted' to Bristol and unable to have
any say in the matter? To her surprise, the matron said that they
were doing new work at the Radcliffe, top priority stuff, essential
to the war effort; she would certainly be able to fix things if Julie
wanted to join them, and Mary could come too.

*

Julie was keen to accept because the work would be so much more
interesting; for Mary it was the lure of Oxford which appealed
the most. As soon as they had accepted the offer, Mary set about
ensuring that she would not be dragged down by hospital life as
she had been before. She would rent a flat where she could write

in her spare time, and where she and Julie could be together if their free time coincided.

Julie was proved right about the work – it was fascinating. They were posted to a recently created neuro-surgical department set up to cope with the influx of head wounds; it was led by the legendary Hugh Cairns and his equally famous assistant, the American surgeon Joe Pennybacker. These two men would virtually create modern neuro-surgery. As a young man, Cairns had been called to treat T. E. Lawrence after the motorbike accident of May 1935, and as a result he became the original advocate of crash helmets for motorcyclists and safety helmets for construction workers. His greatest achievement had been to set up the most important neuro-surgical unit in the country and, indeed, at the time, in the world. He had been given the wartime rank of brigadier so that he could lead the army medical team that treated wounded soldiers at St Hugh's College which had been commandeered as a military hospital because of its proximity to the Radcliffe.

For Mary, the best thing about the Nuffield Ward was the atmosphere – it was assumed that nursing staff did what was needed without waiting to be told. In the absence of the normal strict hierarchy, everyone put in even longer hours than usual without thinking about it. It was the kind of freedom and responsibility Mary and Julie needed, and one junior house surgeon, Jim MacGregor, remembers them as exceptionally friendly compared to the other sisters, who were 'starched battle-axes, if you can starch a battle-axe'. He recalled that there was always tea available on their ward and gossip about the amorous adventures currently under way in the unit – and this at a time when most sisters tended to keep aloof from mere housemen. If the surgeons were writing up their notes – a laborious business, especially under Cairns who was a very demanding chief – Mary or Julie could be relied upon to arrive with sandwiches. MacGregor lost touch with them when he went out to India and Burma, but they met up again long after the war where they least expected it.

Mary's greatest worry was the trickle of disquieting news about her father. He had been ill for some time. What had begun as a soreness in the throat was presently thought to be more serious, and he was undergoing ever more worrying tests. Work and the difficulty of travelling between Oxford and Cambridge meant that Mary could do nothing but wait for her mother's letters, which, as ever, were full of complaints about her own difficulties and the sheer unfairness of it all.

The one bright spot should have been the flat. A friend who had intended moving to Oxford had managed to find rooms at the top of a substantial Edwardian house in Leckford Road owned by a parson and his wife. When the friend's plans changed, Mary and Julie took over the flat. The owners were perfect landlords, fully absorbed in their new baby and no problem to the two women, who had a living room, bedroom and a proper kitchen with running water and a small stove. They shared the bathroom with the family, but seldom saw them. They brought their furniture from Bristol and smartened the place up. Mary planned to write there on her evenings off, but the hard work on Nuffield 1, the general atmosphere of wartime dreariness, and the bad news from Cambridge all conspired to make writing difficult. The paper would go into the typewriter, a few sentences would appear, then out it came to be crumpled into the wastepaper basket. There was never sufficient time. Mary had no sooner cleared her head of hospital matters than the interlude was over with nothing to show for it.

Just after Christmas she received word from Cambridge that tests had revealed a cancer of the pharynx. Dr Challans had had radiation treatment on his throat, but it had not been successful. He was now at home again and bedridden. Her mother wanted her to come and nurse him.

For once, Julie kept her irritation to herself. In her view Clementine Challans could have bestirred herself to do something for her husband, though there was no way she could express such sentiments given Mary's distress and her determination to go. For all her childhood attempts to isolate herself, Mary had been deeply marked by her parents' endless bickering and their indifference over her future. She still wanted her father's understanding. She wanted to talk to him about books, about life, about anything really, and now, at sixty-six, he was dying.

After four weeks Mary wrote to Julie to say that it was all over.

She returned to Oxford immediately after the funeral and, while no one else noticed, it was clear to Julie that a subtle but profound change had taken place. Mary was never 'quite the same'. She had always been forward-looking, expecting life to improve, with an exuberant streak often to the point of flamboyance, which even the first rigours of war had failed to depress. Now there was something weighing on her.

Mary told Julie what it had been like – the slow lingering death, the terrible pain exacerbated by Dr Challans's refusal to accept morphine until the very end. He suffered dreadfully, but she had gone on hoping that this last closeness to him might help erase the years of estrangement and bring them together, if only for a short time. And just when they might have talked in the way she had often dreamed, fate played its cruellest trick: the cancer had spread; he was operated on and could no longer speak. He lay, staring up at his daughter as she ministered to him, unable to give her the absolution for which she longed. Ever after the very thought of a slow death appalled her. He had been unable to swallow at the end and had virtually starved to death before her eyes. A night nurse was hired, but it was Mary who was there whenever he needed comfort.

On the morning of the funeral, Clementine, Joyce and Mary were driven to the church in a hire car. As soon as they reached the door, Clementine took Joyce's arm and walked up the aisle behind the coffin, leaving Mary to follow alone.

6

Hard Winters

Mary tried to exorcise her anger by writing.

Elsie had left school a year ago, after failing in the School Certificate Examination. The mistresses, one after another, had told her that her homework was thoughtless and showed no signs of concentration at all, and had pointed out what a disappointment this must be to her parents; a prophecy regularly fulfilled when her reports came through. All this accumulated guilt formed a steady reserve, ready to add itself to the guilt of any given moment. Where would she be, indeed? Hypnotized, she pictured herself trudging through the rain into the gates of a large, dark factory, wearing a man's cloth cap, or maybe a shawl. The factory was drawn from imagination; her travels had been few.

'Well, Elsie?' said her father.

When things of this sort happened, if there was time to see them coming beforehand, Elsie was accustomed to pray, 'Please, God, don't let them ask me to say anything.' Her tongue seemed to be swelling inside her mouth. Perhaps, even now, if she waited a moment . . .

'Arthur,' cried her mother, 'how can you browbeat the poor child like this? It isn't my fault she can't bear to be in the same room with you. Never mind, darling; tomorrow morning when your father goes out we'll do something nice all by ourselves.'

Her mother's voice trembled. Elsie edged to the door knob, and clutched it again. If only she had said something in time. She could not think what, but there must have been something. She had made her father angry, and now she had made her mother cry.

'This attitude,' said her father, 'is just what I expected. This kind of pernicious malice I see going on every day. Don't be surprised when it bears fruit. We already have one daughter outside the pale of decent society. If a second finds her way into the demi-monde, believe me, it won't astonish me.'

'Arthur!' Her mother's voice shrank to a kind of whispering scream. 'How can you be so wicked? Saying such a thing in front of a young girl.' She rose, clutching her knitting; several stitches dropped off the needle and began to run, which, to Elsie, seemed somehow to make everything more terrifying. She began to sob. 'If only one of my children had been a boy. He wouldn't have stood by to see his mother insulted in her own home.'

'If I'd had a son,' shouted her father, 'I shouldn't be subjected day by day to this petty conspiracy of women.'

Hard as it was to write, it was at least a beginning, a way of forcing herself to concentrate despite the sheer physical exhaustion of a day on Nuffield 1. When they were alone, Julie noticed how Mary had begun to look down as if bowed and, though she would quickly perk up if someone else entered the room, her former vivacity was gone. She often referred to that one day in Cornwall with her father, though now the memory was suffused with regret, but the fact that Mary wanted to be with her more than ever before did much to dampen Julie's worst fears. At least it was good to see her writing again.

Julie had been promoted to charge nurse, just one rank below sister, and was enjoying the new responsibilities. However, early in 1942 the situation altered radically with the arrival of a new matron, Miss Preddy. She liked Mary but took against Julie. Mary would be promoted to Home Sister with responsibility for the junior nurses, but, when Julie went away for a short break, she returned to find an announcement on the noticeboard that *Staff Nurse Mullard* had been assigned to the convalescent ward. Not only had she lost her charge nurse status, she was no longer in neuro-surgery. When she forcefully pointed out that she had returned to the Radcliffe specifically for that type of work, Preddy's response was classic: 'Nurse, you work where I put you!'

97

Fortunately for Julie, the doctors in the unit wanted her and made their views known, the only pressure that could possibly have affected the decision. Up went another notice announcing that *Charge* Nurse Mullard was back, but it could only be a stand-off; as Julie knew, it was impossible to achieve final victory over an antagonized matron. Shortly afterwards Preddy sneaked into Nuffield 1 and 'caught' Julie having a tea break in the kitchen. As an acting sister, she should have had her tea from a tray in the sisters' room, but such niceties had long been abandoned as work piled up. With barely a pause, Preddy ordered Julie to come to her room, an unheard-of thing on a Sunday. Her opening remark said it all: 'After your behaviour this morning, I think there's no place for you at the Radcliffe.'

Having resisted a second attempt by the doctors and surgeons to intervene on her behalf, Julie applied for a post at St Mary's, Paddington, Robbie's hospital, where she would be just down the railway line from Oxford and could maintain contact with Mary.

*

Once again, they had taken a backward step: Mary in Oxford, Julie in London. As a junior, Mary had accepted the hospital's belief in its superior wisdom, governing the sick like helpless children, controlling their treatment, releasing them when the system decided. Now she was beginning to have doubts about this misplaced 'scientific' approach, especially when dressed up as 'doctor knows best'. It touched on her relationship with Robbie when he came to stay with her in Oxford. He was still full of enthusiasm and convinced that brotherly love in the form of Communism was the only solution to the world's ills. What she found harder to take was his increasing certainty that he had found in healing through love a way of curing people which set him apart from the rest of the medical profession. When he had first set out these ideas, they had seemed amusing foibles, a refreshing change from most doctors. Now she was no longer sure they were harmless. Far from liberating the patient, such psychological 'tricks' could only increase the doctor's control. It was beginning to look like dominance masquerading as love and freedom.

Just as she had transformed Joyce into Elsie, Robbie became

Peter, a young doctor with an overweening belief in his own abilities, with herself as Leo, a young woman with humour enough to see through his pretensions:

'Have you ever,' she asked, 'found psychological treatment really decisive in curing a patient?'

Peter could have asked nothing better than this. He was off. In skilfully linked succession he recounted three instances of cases (they were, by some coincidence, all female cases) where he personally had restored the will to live at what had seemed, to less imaginative colleagues, the eleventh hour.

Leo listened, gratifyingly. There was information to be had; and, besides, she found the narrative style rather charming. At the end of the third history, however, she interrupted the flow; cutting, somewhat unfairly, into a pause whose intention had been purely dramatic.

'But,' she asked, 'what happened afterwards, when they found out?'

Peter looked at her gravely. Her trick of gaucherie, he reflected, was effective up to a point; it was a pity she overdid it.

'They went out, I think,' he said, 'happier and less lonely people than they came in. It isn't much one can do. The rest one just has to hope for.'

He means this, said Leo to herself; he really means it. This is fascinating; I'm glad I came.

'I'm sorry,' she said aloud, 'but I still don't quite get this. In the end, what did they make of it? I mean they must either have thought you were really taken with them, which would lead to a certain amount of disappointment when you didn't follow it up; or else they'd gather at some stage that you'd just been doing them good, in which case one would rather expect them to hand you a clip on the ear. Still,' she concluded reasonably, 'I suppose the great thing at the time was to save their lives. Like jabbing a boathook into someone who's drowning.'

Much of the new novel was autobiographical. Leo has left home, unable to stand her parents' bickering, leaving her younger sister Elsie to bear the brunt of their failed marriage. Leo lives on a houseboat, which she shares with Helen; together they are *The Friendly Young Ladies* of the book's title. Leo writes popular Westerns, helped by her American neighbour Joe Flint, with whom she shares an all-boys-together relationship: mountaineering and much messing about in boats. Like Mic in *Purposes of Love*, Leo's loveless childhood has acted as a block to a full adult love affair. She is forever being described as 'boylike' and even feels a 'kind of sickness at the consciousness of being a woman', though her exact relationship with the rather shadowy Helen is never fully explained.

When Elsie suddenly arrives, having run away in her turn, the Friendly Young Ladies find themselves confronted with much that they have carefully suppressed. Elsie brings Peter into their lives. He has been a temporary doctor in her home village and she is hopelessly in love with him. It is clear to Leo and Helen that Peter is more interested in them than in the lovesick Elsie. At first they tolerate him for her sake, though his arrogant belief that he can offer his patients 'guidance' through a deep understanding of their inner selves, is rather too much for both of them.

But, while Leo may be able to see through Peter's pretensions, she is ill-equipped to handle his attempts to win her over. Her usual approach to men is a form of clumsy coquettishness, leading them on before she abruptly rejects them. When she tries this with Peter, she is consumed by guilt, convinced that she has somehow betrayed Elsie. Her solution is a shock cure. She spends the night with Joe, her American neighbour, surrendering her virginity as if it were a barrier which, once broken, will allow in the love she feels she has been fighting off all her life. Predictably, the cure fails; the act is no sooner done than she knows she must leave him too. Thus the book ends with everyone back where they started. Elsie crawls home to a life of lonely subjugation. Peter remains obtusely convinced that he has somehow 'guided' all these women towards a better understanding of their emotional selves, while the Friendly Young Ladies are simply left dangling in the wind.

Forty years on, when Mary was asked to provide an afterword for a reissue of the book, she admitted that what struck her most was 'the silliness of the ending'. She did not, however, vouchsafe precisely what that 'silliness' was, though it is not hard to conclude that it was her failure to acknowledge the true nature of the relationship between Leo and Helen. There is a moment in the book which gives a tempting suggestion of what might have been. Peter brings to the houseboat a young nurse, Norah, whom he has been 'educating', presumably to demonstrate to Leo and Helen the success of his method. Leo decides she must shield Elsie from this intrusion and takes Norah out for a canoe trip which becomes, in effect, a light, witty, but perfectly open lesbian seduction:

The canoe coasted in towards the bank, kissing it neatly under Leo's practised hand. They were humming, as they landed, a verse of 'Home on the Range', which they had been harmonizing further up the river.

'Where the graceful white swan goes gliding along
Like a maid in a heavenly dream . . . '

Elsie thought the soft voices, in the gathering dusk, romantically sweet and sad.

'We must meet again,' said Leo, in the voice that means, You cannot step twice into the same river; better not try.

'Yes,' said Norah, assenting both to the spoken courtesy and the unspoken truth. She was trying, half-heartedly, to imagine what she would think about all this tomorrow morning. It had been so light, so gracefully unreal, like an indiscretion at a masked ball. She gazed at Leo curiously, over the tie-rope of the canoe. One had thought, as far as one had previously thought at all, of thick women in starched evening shirts, and intense, shy-making confidences . . . Norah found that, as after a moderate indulgence in champagne, little remained behind except a general impression that one had been unusually witty and charming, together with a feeling of light-hearted sophistication and no harm done. And indeed, anything that happens in a light canoe, even when moored, must needs be moderate enough.

Leo caught her eye and gave her a broad, outrageous, comprehensive wink.

'Come on in,' she said, 'and eat your supper like a good girl.'

*

Even with the novel to occupy her, Mary could not bear to be separated from Julie, and a month after her friend's departure she, too, resigned from the Radcliffe.

They rented rooms at 47 Cleveland Square in West London, and Mary took a job nursing private patients at the London Clinic. There were nightly air raids, and their duty periods seldom coincided. Mary worked most days, Julie nights. Even the nearness of friends like Robbie proved illusory with everyone so totally wrapped up in work. Worst of all was the sheer squalor of Paddington. Their attic rooms had several broken windows; one night a bomb hit a neighbouring house, which went up in flames, the blast shattering their few remaining panes. It was a terrible night. The curtains caught fire, but at least their building was not hit, which turned out to be pure luck when the morning revealed several gaps in the street opposite, where half a dozen incendiaries had landed. A week later they were woken at five in the morning by shouting and looked out to see an enormous barrage balloon being raised in the square below. They opened the window to wave to the ATS girls anchoring the vast billowing object and, to their surprise, saw that another building had disappeared. They went down to talk to the girls, who told them that a land mine had gone off in the night, and they realized they had grown so accustomed to such explosions that they had simply slept through it.

Neither of them could bear the air-raid shelters in the underground railway stations. Mary went down once, but the sight of the silent crowds upset her deeply. The platforms were packed with people crouched in the dark, waiting for God knew what to hit them. Both agreed it was better to take their chances above ground. Then, one night, as Julie was going on an errand to another part of the hospital, she was stopped by an air-raid warden who was in tears – a not uncommon sight at the time. The man begged her to follow him and took her to one of the windows at the front, overlooking Praed Street, where she saw to her horror that a bomb had lodged on one of the little ornamental balconies. The man urged her to look more closely and, when she did, she saw that the metal casing had split open; instead of containing a bomb, it had been stuffed with Czechoslovakian newspapers –

someone in a munitions factory, some unsung hero, had sabotaged it. Had he not done so, much of the hospital would have gone up, with unthinkable loss of life.

It was at this point that Julie decided to put things right, engineering a transfer to the Redhill Maternity Hospital in Edgware, some way from the worst of the bombing, though just as petty over regulations as anywhere else. She and Mary had always worked in 'black stocking' hospitals; the Redhill was a 'fawn stocking' hospital. New stockings would use up precious clothing coupons and, when Julie was told off for not wearing the right colour, she promptly arrived next day without any stockings at all; this provoked another blazing row, with the medical superintendent being brought in to calm things down.

It was all so pointless, and it was dragging Mary deeper and deeper into a grey depression as she began to believe that her writing was withering away, killed off by exhaustion and the trivial aggravations of hospital life. Julie insisted she apply for leave – she had had none since the start of the war, so no one could possibly object. To Mary's surprise she was given a full two weeks and was able to visit her mother and Joyce for the first time since the funeral. She arrived in Cambridge to be confronted by an instance of administrative idiocy that was extraordinary even by the standards of wartime confusion to which everyone was by then accustomed. Her mother handed her a letter – why it had not been sent to London was never made clear – which inexplicably released her from the call-up. She would have to continue nursing, but she could work where she chose as long as she continued to do 'eight hours a day, six days a week'.

At the same time, Julie, on a visit to Oxford, found that Matron Preddy had had a change of heart and wanted her back. As soon as Mary heard this, she applied for a job at the Ackland Nursing Home, directly opposite the Radcliffe. It was the final step backwards: they would be in Oxford and, just as before, they would not be able to live together. On the other hand they would at least be very close.

Mary rented a room near the Ackland, but no sooner has she started on *The Friendly Young Ladies* than Robbie turned up.

He had had a suspected bout of tuberculosis and wanted to be near her while he convalesced. She could not put him up, but he stayed in a nearby pub and was constantly on her doorstep. His Marxist diatribes and global solutions wearied her, especially since he refused to stop arguing until she agreed with him; and even when she gave in and managed to persuade him to go to bed, he might suddenly return, ring her door bell and ask her to come outside to admire the stars. This sort of fey behaviour did not appeal to Mary and her distaste increased when the owners of the house made it clear that they approved of her having a young man, whom they considered less suspicious than Julie.

Mary was therefore much relieved when Robbie returned to London early in 1944 and resumed his healing-through-love at St Mary's. His most notable success was with a young woman terribly injured in an explosion who later wrote a book explaining his methods and praising his help. Mary, however, was beyond caring what he did. They saw each other from time to time, though the periods between visits grew longer until, almost unnoticed, he ceased to be part of her life. However, he had given her a character and, with the original out of the way, she made herself finish the book.

Longmans had kept a precious cache of rationed paper against the day of delivery, but no one could have foreseen the hopelessness of bringing out a book in the summer of 1944. When the Normandy landings began that June and *The Friendly Young Ladies* was published a month later, it was Dunkirk and *Kind Are Her Answers* all over again. Predictably, the reviewers were as much imbued with war-weariness as everyone else. Lionel Hale in the *Observer* got no farther than the dust jacket and appeared to think that the novel was the story of a man on a boat. Henry Reed in the *New Statesman & Nation* simply dismissed the whole thing as too complicated. Even her American publishers Morrow were far from enthusiastic. Worried by the increasingly explicit sexual relationships in her books, they waited a further five months before publishing it and then only under the anodyne title *The*

Middle Mist, taken from a sonnet by Rupert Brooke which was the book's epigraph.

Mary was shattered. It had been so hard trying to write in such impossible conditions and then to see it all tossed aside. The book might have its faults, but it was more adventurous than most, with a rich array of characters, finely drawn, and with much humour. Ten years later Jeanette Foster's classic study *Sex Variant Women in Literature* described Leo as a 'portrait as piquant as any since Mlle de Maupin', while the incident with Norah in the canoe gleamed 'like an unmatched gem'. Mary needed just such encouragement in 1944. Dragged down by the war and her separation from Julie, she was in no state to cope with careless criticism offered by reviewers whose minds were on other things.

In the past, she had always had another novel in progress by the time the previous one was published. Writing was something to be done every day, even if it was no more than a page or two to keep her hand in. Now the habit was broken. For the first time since she had scrambled into the loft of the stable at Dacre Lodge to work on her cowboy book, an exhausted and disillusioned Mary threw in the towel and stopped writing.

*

Mary was by this time thirty-nine. With three published novels under her belt, she should have been enjoying a literary life – a flat in London, the friendship of like-minded people, the theatre and ballet she so loved. Yet here she was, still walking the wards, changing beds, bathing old bodies, wiping and sluicing, with nothing but another freezing winter to look forward to.

Just occasionally there was a flicker of interest. At one point she had the artist Paul Nash as a patient. He was a great friend of Gilbert Murray, which must have added to his appeal, and Mary later revealed that they had been quite friendly.

For most people the war was finished. The Germans were being pushed back. It was only a matter of time, but Mary remained unimpressed. Hitler might be dead and the Russians in Berlin, but she was still not satisfied. It had lasted five weary years, and she wanted the absolute, the official end. It came on 8 May 1945, VE Day. In Oxford, as in all towns and villages throughout the nation,

there was dancing in the streets with milling crowds singing patri-
otic songs. Mary was not among them. In her attic room she put
a sheet of paper into her typewriter and started work again. There
had been nine months of silence.

Return to Night was the book she should have written earlier,
would have written if so many things had not conspired to prevent
her. It was set in a hospital in 1939 as if the last five years had
never been, as if she were determined to exorcize the faults of the
past, the novels flawed by the pressure of war work, scribbled
down in exhausted moments snatched between long hours of duty.
This time there would be a very tough female character at the
centre of the book, a doctor called Hilary Mansell, who is in love
with one of her patients, a man eleven years younger, Julian
Fleming. All the usual Renault elements are there: the ambiguous
first names, the medical background, the problem mother. Elaine
Fleming is a World War 1 widow whose difficult, possessive
relationship with her son provides the book's psychological tension. As with all Renault's male 'leads', Julian is breathtakingly
good-looking:

Hilary stared, forgetting her trespass and the apologies she
might need to improvise. She felt a little detached from reality.
The light, the setting, the hour, seemed a theatrical extravagance,
exaggerating, needlessly, what was already excessive, the most
spectacularly beautiful human creature she had ever seen.
Because her habit of mind had made her hostile to excess,
she thought irritably, it's ridiculous. It's like an illustration to
something.

At thirty-four, Hilary is at an acutely difficult moment in her
life and career, and Julian's arrival on the scene throws everything
into chaos. Having liberated herself by entering the medical profession against her parents' wishes – like the Challanses, they had
hoped for marriage and family – she has had a drifting love affair
with a fellow hospital doctor, but since the end of that has settled
into a fairly mediocre post in a country hospital with outdated
methods and equipment, a place clearly beneath her talents.

Tired after a night of coping with an emergency premature

delivery, Hilary goes for a walk in the countryside and falls asleep on a grassy bank, only to be awakened, like the sleeping princess, by her dashing knight riding by on his magnificent charger. The roles are then swiftly reversed. When Hilary next sees Julian, he is unconscious, having been thrown from his horse, and only her prompt action in getting him emergency brain surgery saves him from being reduced to a vegetable – a section of the book which vividly recreates the work Mary and Julie had done at the Radcliffe:

The porter slid a rubber sheet under the quiet head as the nurse lifted it. Whistling faintly between his teeth he picked up a pair of clippers from the tray and nibbled them in a broad arc. A deep soft swathe of black hair slid down on to the mackintosh; the balance and composition of the face were instantly changed. Sanderson looked again, said thoughtfully, 'I think we can keep the flap clear of the forehead,' and went on into the theatre. The porter, clipping away, remarked, 'S'right. Shame to spoil 'im for the girls,' and winked at the nurse, who, conscious of Hilary's presence, ignored him. Hilary picked up the stethoscope and took the blood-pressure.

Sanderson had the reputation of being able to turn an osteoplastic flap quicker than anyone in two continents. This time, having nothing else to do, Hilary watched the clock. The lid of bone was lifted in just seventeen and a half minutes. As far as she knew it was a record. As she stood under the great frosted window, out of the track of those who had work to do, she fell back into the old impersonality. There was, indeed, nothing personal to see. The shape on the table was only a coffin-like oblong, a stand placed across the chest supporting a long green drape so that not even a human outline was recognisable below. All the varied activity in the room was focused on a six-inch oval; already even the bone-flap, with its fringe of artery-forceps, had been swathed with sterile gauze. There was only one reminder of the incidental presence under the green cloth; the anaesthetist on his low stool, the stethoscope in his ears connected to something unseen, making at intervals a tiny point on the chart beside him. This vigil over the hidden life was his only function. Nature had done his work for him; he could have added nothing, except death.

After several months, despite considerable resistance on Hilary's part, the now recovered Julian discovers his saviour and begins to court her. He has secret hopes of becoming an actor, but, while brilliant on stage, he chooses character parts where his physical beauty is heavily disguised.

There are several clues suggesting that his possessive mother is responsible for his continuing failure to assert himself. He cannot make love to Hilary until Elaine Fleming goes away, and then only after a strange and violent rite of passage, a bloody fist fight with a drunken lout encountered on their walk to his mother's empty house. A brutish struggle ensues which ravages his face until he looks as if he has been made up for Caliban. Only then can he make love to her in his mother's home.

By mid-novel we have learned that it is Elaine Fleming's constant warnings of the dangers inherent in his good looks, her public and humiliating criticism, which have destroyed his confidence. Realizing that, under the influence of Hilary, he may at last break free, she reveals that as a nurse during World War I she had been entranced by a flamboyant actor, a Canadian, André O'Connell, but discovered, after their wedding, that he was already married. She had reported him to his commanding officer, precipitating their divorce and his court martial. Elaine is 'saved' by a Major Richard Fleming, who marries her despite everything. As Fleming is killed shortly afterwards, the reader is left with the near certainty that Julian is O'Connell's son. Hence Elaine Fleming's horror at the boy's 'dangerous' good looks and her repugnance at any hint that he may one day become an actor.

Having heard out his mother, Julian leaves the house and goes to Mott's Cave, an eerie subterranean cavern with a dark watercourse which he has visited earlier with Hilary. All their previous encounters have been by night in dark places and now, at the novel's climax, Hilary guesses what he is planning to do and makes a wild night journey to save him. She arrives just as he is about to plunge into the dark pool; by throwing on the artificial lights rigged up by a local farmer, she startles him into drawing back from the abyss. At Hilary's hands darkness has become light; she has saved him, but knows that she can never possess him totally:

> She was only the Madonna of the Cave, Demeter who fashions living things and sends them out into the light. All she had done, and had still to do, must work to accomplish her own loss; to separate and free him, to make him less a part of her, and more his own. Already the new claimants were waiting to receive him from her; the dangers of the coming years; death, perhaps, not this that he would have chosen but alien and lonely; if he lived, the work which would be his most demanding love; the men who would be his friends; the women who would be beautiful when the last of her youth was gone.

*

As in *Purposes of Love*, the ending of this novel leaves the reader with a nagging feeling that there is another story lying just beneath the surface. *Kind Are Her Answers* and *The Friendly Young Ladies* both have their share of Greek references with quotations from Plato dropped into otherwise ordinary conversations, but in this fourth novel there is a suspicion of something more consistent at work. There is a clue to Mary's intentions in her original title, *The Sacred River*, which was rejected by Longmans on the grounds that the public might think the book was about the Ganges. She settled on *Return to Night*, a quotation from a poem by Robert Binyon, but also a sign that the novel was based on the Greek birth and rebirth myth. As Bernard F. Dick pointed out in *The Hellenism of Mary Renault*, Hilary is Demeter, the earth mother, and Julian is the symbolic grain, 'which must be allowed to grow unimpeded'. With the benefit of hindsight – he was writing in the early 1970s – Dick felt that this mingling of antique and modern had not been entirely successful, that Mary's characters were 'historically misplaced' until she allowed them to slough off the contemporary costumes in which she had clothed them. According to Dick, it was only when she began writing historical novels that the conflict was finally resolved.

It would be wrong to assume that Mary was unaware of the problem. There are many indications that she longed to abandon contemporary life in her fiction, but was restrained by the memory of her first failure. It was one thing to toy with quotations from the *Dialogues*, quite another to contemplate the research necessary if she were to recreate accurately the time and place which had produced them.

She did, however, attempt a compromise, weighing up the possibility of writing a historical novel set in a period close to the present whose habits of thought and action would require little effort to reproduce. But even this foundered, as she explained to the artist Rowland Hilder, whom she had chosen to illustrate the cover of *Return to Night*. She had hated most of her early covers with their underhand pretence that her books were conventional love stories. In an attempt to pacify her, Longmans agreed to her choosing the most famous illustrator of the day, and it was when they met at his studio that she revealed to Hilder that she had just abandoned a novel about Byron. It had, she explained, been a hard decision. She had spent the six months since the completion of *Return to Night* researching the project and had been ready to begin drafting the story when a newspaper reported the discovery of the previously unpublished correspondence between Byron and his last love, Teresa Guiccioli. Without access to this cache, Mary felt her book would be seriously flawed and, when she read later that Iris Origo was planning a book based on the Guiccioli letters, she realized there was no point in continuing.

Byron remains one of the more intriguing might-have-beens of Mary's career, and the question of why, having gone that far, she did not proceed to another historical subject remains unanswered. Her chief worry, that her work left her insufficient time for research, was laid to rest six months after VE Day when obligatory service ended. Officially classified as an author, Mary was allowed to return to her profession. Her royalties were enough to survive on and, when she rented a tiny flat at the top of a professor's house in the Banbury Road, she had all the elements necessary to embark on such a task; the Oxford libraries would have been available to her. Instead, she wavered, unsure what to do.

There were distractions – old friends began to resurface: Leslie French, full of outrageous stories about how he had been bombed out of every theatre in England, and her old schoolfriend Beryl, who came to lunch with her daughter, a meeting so friendly and relaxed it seemed hardly possible that they had not seen each other for eight years.

The most bizarre of these post-war resurrections occurred when Mary and Julie took their first holiday for a decade. They went to Ireland in the summer of 1947, a brief idyll with 'Lovely days in a leaky boat on a loch'. It was while they were passing through Dublin on the way home that a strange encounter took place. They were walking by the Liffey when Mary said, 'You know, if you asked me, I'd say there was a man walking along, just over there, who is exactly the way you used to describe Laz.' Julie looked, and it was Laz. Mary told her to go and speak to him, but as Julie ran across the road he slipped into a restaurant and, when she followed, he was nowhere to be found.

*

1947 opened with a bitterly cold January and a shortage of heating fuel. Mary was still having difficulty finding a subject. *Return to Night* had been a summing up, an ending. The war was too near and too disturbing to write about, and her mind drifted back to a brief holiday she and Julie had spent at a pub called the Blue Anchor in Devon some time in 1937. During their meals they fantasized about the other guests: over there was a divorcé wooing the young girl he had just met; at the next table were two spinsters, one lively, the other cold – what could they be talking about? It seemed a promising situation, such different people briefly thrown into close contact, forced to adapt their true thoughts to the social niceties of this temporary community.

In Mary's novel there is an unmarried female don, Miss Searle, and an unmarried nurse, Miss Fisher: the first an intellectual, divorced from the physical side of life; the second none too brainy, but sensible, open-minded and full of humane sentiments. At one point they both reach for a fallen ball of wool:

For a moment their hands met on the ball: the hand of the scholar, meticulous, with fineness but no strength in the bone, taut veins blue under the thin skin at the back, the nails ribbed, brittle and flecked here and there with white; the other broad-

111

palmed and short-fingered, with aggressive smooth cleanliness that comes of much scrubbing with antiseptic followed by much compensating cream, the nails filed short and round, their holiday varnish spruce.

Miss Fisher is outgoing, longing for contact, whereas Miss Searle is sharp and cutting, using her superior knowledge to highlight the other's educational shortcomings.

This was a fair beginning, and for almost a third of the book it is possible to believe that there will be a keen dissection of the intellectual versus the physical in human affairs. However, this is abruptly abandoned in favour of a conventional love story between two other guests: Neil Langton, a schoolmaster in bitter retreat from a failed marriage, and Ellen Shorland, much younger, a secretary still obsessed with a childhood crush. This rapidly becomes a re-run of the journey into self-knowledge theme which was effectively dealt with in earlier books. The one original element, which gives the book its title, *North Face*, is Neil's decision to climb a mountain without adequate preparation or the appropriate equipment as a personal test of will. This nearly kills him, but in the end convinces him of the certainty of his love.

Love, or rather the absence of it, is the link between the seemingly unconnected halves of the book. Great literature has taught the scholarly Miss Searle nothing of human affection; Miss Fisher, in her blunt, good-natured, working-class way, is far more concerned with real people. A close reading of Miss Searle's opinions might lead to the conclusion that in this, the last of Mary Renault's novels to concern itself primarily with heterosexual love, we are being given some form of manifesto about the dangers of a literary life:

The only modern novels that found permanent room on her shelves were about women of exquisitely refined sensibility, to whom a dozen unkind or tasteless words, a moment's falling away from perfect tact by a loved one, were lethal, the end of the world. They reinforced her faith that she was herself adjusted only to relationships like this. Her own loneliness had become for her simply the proof of a discrimination to which nothing was tolerable but the best.

If Mary's intention was to use *North Face* as an affirmation of the life force and a plea for the physical, she did not succeed. It is the only one of her books fully to justify her later rejection of the novels she wrote in England. Much of it consists of internal monologues as the characters attempt to rephrase their private thoughts for public consumption. Its main concerns are old themes which had been brilliantly handled in *Return to Night* and on which Mary had little fresh to say.

*

While she was finishing *North Face*, *Return to Night* was published in England on 28 July and by Morrow in America one month later; the latter event changed everything. A few weeks after the New York launch Julie was called to the telephone at the Radcliffe to speak to Mary – a worrying event in itself, as casual calls between them were unheard of. Mary's agitated voice excited the worst possible fears until Julie pieced together the facts that her friend had won some sort of prize and that it was to do with MGM, the film people. Julie delightedly imagined it might be £1,000 or thereabouts and was dumbstruck when she realized that Mary had said $150,000, over £37,000 at the time. Her publishers and agents would get part of it, but that still left a sum quite beyond belief.

The MGM Award had been inaugurated three years earlier, when someone in Hollywood decided that successful films were often based on novels and the easiest way to find one would be to offer a prize. The flaw in this plan was that the award was made for literary merit rather than suitability for cinema adaptation. The result was that none of the winning books was filmed, and the scheme was abandoned shortly after Mary won. With so much interior monologue and so little action, Mary's novel was virtually impossible to dramatize effectively, but nothing could alter the fact that the prize had been awarded, thus transporting her, as if by some act of Hollywood magic, from genteel poverty to wealth beyond her wildest dreams. To put it in context, at the time a decent middle-class home in Oxford might cost £400, a war widow's pension was a mere thirty shillings or £1 10s 0d per week. She had, in effect, won a schoolteacher's lifetime earnings.

Little wonder that in the first heady days following the announcement she believed all her troubles were over. There was a tremendous amount of press coverage, which brought Mary to the attention of the non-reading public, briefly making her a minor celebrity. More important was the possibility the money offered of rebuilding the life she and Julie had surrendered when they left the Cornish cottage at the outbreak of the war. Mary could at last buy a houseboat, her one fantasy to have survived the passage of time, which had found its fullest expression in *The Friendly Young Ladies*. An advertisement led them to a firm at Brixham, near Dartmouth, in the West Country, which had boats suitable as homes for sale. When they travelled down to see what was on offer, however, they found only a collection of war surplus vessels, none of which had been converted into living quarters. They ought to have left, but the lure of that long-established dream was too strong; oblivious to the problems, Mary settled on a large grey gunboat – it even had a gun turret, though the gun had been removed. They were rowed to its moorings and shown round while its dimensions, none of which meant much to either of them, were rattled off. It hardly seemed to matter, so unreal was the whole experience. The owner wanted £500, hardly a great deal if one wanted to found a navy, but far too much for a home. Nevertheless, with the MGM prize to spend and the vendor promising to move it round the south coast and up the Thames to whatever canal or river-bank they chose, Mary paid.

As 1947 drew to a close, the boat occupied every free moment they could spare. They chased up and down the Thames, measuring lock gates and discussing with the Thames water conservancy engineers the extraordinary difficulties of moving a gunboat.

Still flushed with the thought of her great windfall, Mary persuaded Julie to give up her job at the Radcliffe and, while the boat set off on its lengthy sea journey towards the Thames estuary, they began to plan their new life together. It was only by gradual degrees that doubt began to creep in. Such wealth seemed almost surreal for two people accustomed to the barest necessities of life.

Something had to be wrong somewhere. At last a friend pointed out that, with wartime income tax still at 19s 6d to the twenty-shilling pound, they had probably already spent more than they would receive from the prize. All their high spirits evaporated. That she might end up in debt had not crossed Mary's mind, and it terrified her. When she consulted an accountant, he suggested she should not touch the money until the exact tax liability could be assessed. At a stroke her massive good fortune had been transformed into a threat. They tried none the less to resume their former lives. Julie moved in with Mary, to her landlord's open disapproval. In the end, they were forced to accept that the gunboat could not be moved and Mary's dream had to be abandoned. It remained in Brixham, a mournful grey hulk, like some abandoned piece of wartime booty, strange and useless.

*

The winter of 1947–8 was the worst for many years and dragged on interminably. It seemed so unfair to have endured all the hardship and work during the war, and suddenly to become rich, only to have the riches snatched away again. Even their lodgings were precarious, with Julie unable to use the bathroom and forced to creep up and down stairs, hoping she would not be thrown out. Mary was forty-three, and a morbid feeling that life was slipping away increased with every cold day that passed. There was no running water in the kitchen, and the landlord's wife began to record Julie's arrivals and departures in a book, though why she did this was never made clear.

The weather turned even colder, and Mary took to wearing the lining of an air-force flying jacket, a sort of padded, zipped up body suit, in a desperate attempt to keep warm. She delivered *North Face* on 8 January 1948, but it no longer seemed central to her life. Longman was not especially enthusiastic and took more than eighteen months to publish it.

Mary often fantasized about going away – to Italy or Greece, anywhere warm – but there were strict limitations on taking money to countries outside the sterling area. Even if she could evade the tax man and draw out some of her prize money, she would be allowed to travel only to countries within the British

Empire – Canada, Australia, India or Africa. Europe, which she most wished to visit, was closed to her; America was out of the question.

One day in late March, they were both sitting, swathed in sweaters and dressing-gowns, close to the cooker whose single gas ring was their only source of heat. Mary was reading *The Times*.

'Julie,' she said, 'what do you think of South Africa?'

Julie tried to think of South Africans she knew; there had been one or two; they had all seemed very healthy, good legs and teeth, good-looking generally. She mentioned the name of one of them.

'She was very nice,' Mary said. 'They all have big cars and farms. It says here in *The Times* that there's a boat going out there – shall we go?'

'Yes,' said Julie, and that was that – no proper discussion, no doubts, no enquiries. Mary went to London and made the bookings: they would sail from Marseilles in a matter of weeks, just time enough to make their farewells and pack all their patched and darned wartime clothes.

Before leaving, Mary wrote to her cousin Alan, son of Aunt Cathy, third of the Baxter sisters, who had gone out to Rhodesia as a junior in the colonial service. He invited them to stay. They would leave the ship at Beira and travel inland to Sinoia, where he was posted.

On 15 April they left London by train for France and dashed across Paris to catch the train for the long overnight journey down the length of the country. In France there were post-war restrictions, too, and typed instructions advised them to bring food for their evening meal. The train was old and dirty, and when they finally chugged into Marseilles, they hurried to a hotel in order to bathe before rushing to the shipping office, where their papers were processed. They were put into a waiting area, which was like a cage, through the bars of which they could see the ss *Cairo*. It was small and dirty.

*

The *Cairo* turned out to have been an inter-island steamer from the Hebrides originally called the *Prince Charlie*; long since super-annuated, it had been bought and renamed by its present Italian owners, who had registered it in Panama. It was obliged to terminate in Beira, as no British or South African port would take it in. The captain, a Greek, grieved a lot, wringing his hands as tears streamed down his face. The mate was an Italian who liked women. Any who happened to be passing were invited into the chart room and offered a sweet vermouth, while he traced a finger over the charts to show where the captain, during his spell of duty, had allowed the ship to stray off course and explained how he, the mate, was retrieving the situation. He would finish by pointing out that he alone – 'not the captain, no, no' had 'the certificate of navigation'. The radio officer was a White Russian. With the Mediterranean still full of mines, he was supposed to operate some kind of detector device, but he was always in the bar singing melancholy Russian dirges. When one of the more concerned passengers climbed into the lifeboats and reported that they were full of holes, the mate shrugged his shoulders and said, with a charming smile, 'But of what use? If she sink, she sink in three minutes.' Which was unarguable, as the bulk-head doors had been removed to cram in more passengers, and the crew were sleeping on the dining-room tables, because their cabins had been commandeered.

For Mary none of this detracted from the simple, wonderful fact that she was standing on deck looking out at the waters of the Mediterranean. Of course, with the first sun, all the Englishmen changed into baggy shorts, exposing chalk-white knees which had not seen daylight for a decade, but Mary and Julie found themselves teaming up with two men in their twenties who seemed rather more sophisticated and who had done some travelling before. The younger, Peter Albrecht, who was twenty six, had been born in South Africa and spent some time in India. He was making this journey with his lover, Jack Corke, for much the same reasons as Mary and Julie, and probably quite a few others on the boat had they but known it – to escape the misery of austerity Britain, in the hope of finding a new life in the sun. The best thing about the two men was that they had been acting on the London stage, always a passport to Mary's approval, as was Jack's appearance – tall and handsome – though Peter hardly came up to the high standard of male beauty Mary preferred in her men friends.

From photographs he appears to have been rather puffy and frog-like, though Jack seemed more devoted to him than he to Jack.

Later Peter Albrecht would return to acting in England, and would adopt the stage name Peter Arne, achieving some success as a bit-part player in films and, later, television. But at the same time they were full of wild schemes for making money in Durban. As Mary and Julie had no plans of their own, it was impossible not to be drawn into these dreams, especially since everything was expressed in that rapid-fire camp wit Mary found so amusing.

Port Said was a shock, their first experience of poverty and squalor. When the ship docked and haggling traders came aboard, all four friends bought deck-chairs the better to enjoy the slow passage through the Suez Canal. That accomplished, there was a day in Aden which provided a moment of high excitement. The quartet went ashore along with most of the crew, but, when they returned, they found chaos. The *Cairo* was surrounded by little boats full of screaming Arabs trying to clamber aboard. The captain had tried to make a quick profit by offering passage to 100 pilgrims heading for Mecca, a move that risked capsizing the already overloaded tub. Reinforced with their first taste of plentiful cheap booze, the English passengers, Jack and Peter among them, stormed to the anchor and refused to let the captain raise it if the Arabs boarded. He wept and wrung his hands. In the end the harbour master negotiated a compromise, allowing on board only those Indians who held British passports, while the Arabs were forced to row back to shore screaming abuse and waving cutlasses, looking to Mary like the pirates in *Peter Pan*.

It had been frightening and funny at the same time, but it served to confirm Mary's growing conviction that they could do worse than put their trust in the two men, who had proved so resourceful in a crisis. Lounging in their new deck-chairs, watching the sunset over the low African coastline, it was only natural that they should tell Peter and Jack about Mary's prize money, and inevitable that they should all dream up ways of turning it to good use once they arrived in South Africa. A restaurant in Durban was a recurring idea, but there were several others. Peter, it transpired, was very good at interior decoration, though it was left rather vague as to who would do the cooking.

Having sailed down the Somali coast, they crossed the line on 9 May 1948, with the two women undergoing the usual ceremony. A hand-drawn certificate, lovingly preserved, shows the boat with a jovial King Neptune and announces that 'Our trusty and well-beloved Mary Challans has this day entered our domain and been rightly and duly initiated with all form and ceremony as Our subject, signed – Neptune Maris Rex.'

Their arrival at Mombasa harbour in Kenya was, in Mary's words, 'too wonderful', with a slow glide past palm-fringed beaches before their first real sight of Africa: women in brightly coloured *kangas*, the Indian *dukas* selling everything from paraffin to tins of condensed milk, the thudding heat and the dusty roads, the neat colonial bungalows. They had met a district commissioner on board, and he invited them to lunch at the Manor Hotel, where, in an elegant dining room with revolving fans, bowing white-jacketed waiters offered a full menu and the prospect of eating whatever they wished for the first time in nearly nine years. They had what Julie remembers was 'a fabulous luncheon'. That evening they went to the cinema and sat entranced among Indian women in beautiful saris. For ever after the memory of Kenya would bring a glow to Mary's face. 'Very gay and partyish', was how she described it, and the pleasure that brief stay gave her was certainly a major reason why she took to Africa with hardly a backward glance. Kenya was a revelation. She had expected many things including adventure, strangeness and shock but had hardly been prepared for luxury and fun.

Back on board, they set sail for Beira where the four would split up, Jack and Peter going on to Durban, while the two women went by train to Salisbury and then on to Sinoia, where Mary's cousin Alan Beale was stationed. There was no doubt that the four of them would meet up later and that some project or other would be launched. In fact, it seemed as if Jack and Peter were going on ahead only to get things ready for their arrival. They would keep in touch by telegram.

It was an overnight journey on a little chugging train to Salisbury. Before the rapid sunset obscured the view they could glimpse African villages clustered near the narrow-gauge track. They were awakened early for breakfast in a station hotel and were amazed to see Rhodesian settlers eating enormous quantities of steak, eggs and hash, a sight which, more than the sounds and smells of Africa, convinced Mary that she had truly left ration-bound Britain behind. Every hotel in Salisbury was full, but she was determined to enjoy this unexpected abundance and decided to have dinner at the most luxurious restaurant she could find. It was only when they were settled at their table, wearing their usual darned and patched utility clothes, that she realized the settlers' wives at neighbouring tables were all in full evening dress and some were even wearing tiaras. It was a grotesque parody of forgotten pre-war England, of the days when she and Julie had had to wear long gowns to eat at Fuller's after the theatre. The situation might have been funny had Julie and Mary not been confronted by a wall of disapproving looks.

Relieved to be outside again, they hunted for a taxi willing to drive eighty miles to Sinoia. The driver they found turned out to be a garrulous old fellow who passed the journey trying to scare them with stories about man-eating lions. It was so dark they were aware of being there only when dogs began to bark and oil-lamps sputtered into life as people hurried to see who could be arriving so late in such a remote place. They were directed to Alan's house and, at the sound of their car, his wife Wyn appeared on the veranda wearing what Mary described as 'a sort of frothy negligée', part of her wedding trousseau.

They were by this time thoroughly exhausted and were shown straight to their rooms. When Mary awoke the next morning and looked out of the window, she saw all their faded and darned clothes hanging out to dry. She was even more amazed when she learned that the laundry had been done by prisoners 'rented' from the local jail.

The 'house' was made up of round hutlike dwellings called rondavels, roofed with corrugated iron. Because Alan (known as Jo, a nickname he had picked up in the army) had been born in Australia and raised in New Zealand, he had few connections with Britain and had met his wife Wyn, an Anglo-Indian, while serving in the sub-continent. He had chosen to join the Rhodesian service because the territory was a quasi-independent, self-governing colony. He visited Britain rarely and was already a settled African hand with strong opinions about the 'native' population, which surprised his visitors. Until then everything about Africa had been rather light-hearted; Alan's views were an intimation of another, less easy-going attitude.

They flew to Johannesburg on 26 May 1948. The plane was an old Dakota. After take-off, the air hostess disappeared into the cockpit for a time; when she re-emerged, she began to pass along the lines of passengers, most of whom looked like businessmen, bending down to whisper something to each in turn. Mary and Julie could not hear what was being said, but could see that it had an immediate effect on each listener, some of whom looked very distressed. The young woman eventually came to them, bent close and said with stagy emphasis, 'It's the Nationalists.' As this meant nothing to them, Mary asked her neighbour to explain; she was told that there had been a general election which the Nationalist Party had won. Why this should have so bothered everyone was a mystery to Mary, but she realized it was far more serious than she could yet comprehend.

The plane refuelled in Kimberley, then flew to Johannesburg. Driving into the city, they noticed how the Africans standing at the roadside were wearing dull grey blankets, hardly a match for the brilliant cloths of Kenya. The hotel was like something out of a frontier movie, which ought to have appealed to Mary's love of Westerns, but did not. There were polished brass spittoons on the landings, and in the foyer a fat man sprawled on a sofa with a tart on his knee. Johannesburg was not for them. They were only too glad, the next morning, to board a train for Durban. They had telegraphed Jack and Peter, who met them at the station, full of a marvellous, infallible plan to get rich quick. There was, they explained, a huge influx of people like themselves coming out from England to escape the rigours of austerity. What did these people need most? Houses, of course – they would use Mary's prize money to build houses to sell to immigrants. It was a sure way to cash in on the new world that was opening up.

Having no other plans, Mary could only agree. The little of Durban she could see from the car looked more than satisfactory. There was an imposing town hall and the elegant sweep of the tree-lined esplanade with ocean liners riding at anchor. The quaint

Victorian shops with their wrought-iron verandas were no less exotic than the domes of the Grey Street mosque serving the largest Indian population of any city outside India. Best of all were the Zulus, proudly striding down the broad avenues in their traditional dress, the women bare-breasted with only a small leather apron to cover their loins. It was deliciously, tropically hot. Harsh English winters and the predatory tax man simply melted into the past. Durban was fine. A new life was possible.

Part Two

========

South Africa 1948–1983

7

Very Gay and Partyish

Mary and Julie were driven to the Metropole Hotel, where, for the first time in their lives, they had the luxury of their own bathroom. It was a promising sign, like seeing shop windows piled with goods, and passers-by wearing new clothes. Jack and Peter were staying with friends, but the Metropole was fine with a jolly, footloose crowd of youngish people, mostly recent refugees from austerity Britain, plus a sprinkling of actors hoping for work, a surprising number of whom seemed to be 'queer', as they self-mockingly referred to themselves.

When Jack and Peter returned, they took the two women to Durban North. The city was spreading out along its northern coastline and white-painted English homes with tidy gardens were edging along the flat sandy scrubland, turning the hot tropical shore into a replica of the Home Counties on the Indian Ocean. Here, the men explained, was the place to buy land and build houses. And with all the recent arrivals, their plan seemed foolproof.

They began at once. The accountant in England reached an agreement with the tax authorities, after which Mary was able to transfer £5,000 to South Africa. With this she purchased three empty plots near the beach, on which they would build desirable homes.

They began by forming a company: CAM Construction – C for Challans and Corke, A for Albrecht, M for Mullard. With the first plot ready, white tradesmen and black labourers were hired, and a nearby house was bought where the four of them could live and run the operation. They engaged a house-boy called Peter, who willingly agreed to become Paul to avoid confusion. He was from neighbouring Lesotho, the son, he explained, of a witch doctor, who had passed on his powers just before his death. However, the only sign of any deep knowledge of plants and herbs they could see was his penchant for brewing illegal beer from pineapple stems. He arrived with a wife and two children, and soon acquired a second wife. His importance to Mary went beyond his duties about the house: he was the first African with whom she had any close contact and thus his reactions were studiously observed and his opinions carefully dissected.

To Mary, at forty-three, there was pleasure enough in having acquired her first house at last. She wanted all the things which had been forbidden to her when she lived in nurses' homes or rented accommodation, and promptly bought two dogs: Horace, a Scottie, and Simba, a Rhodesian Ridgeback, which romped about as she strode along the nearby beach on her morning and evening walks. Of course there were disadvantages in being a pioneer on the outskirts of the urban area. It proved difficult to obtain a telephone, so a car, a Studebaker, was needed to cope with frequent trips into town for orders, as well as a truck to collect building materials. As work progressed, a second, smaller car became essential. Not surprisingly Mary's £5,000 was soon exhausted and she was obliged to mortgage the land to keep going.

Much of her time was spent in planning meetings, the four of them sitting on the living-room floor, working out the next stages in the building, which Julie would draw on graph paper and take to a trained draughtsman in the city, who would prepare scale drawings for approval at the Town Hall. Mary was chairman, Peter managing director, Jack treasurer, and Julie secretary. It was time-consuming, and Mary resigned herself to being unable to write; in any case what was she to write about? Better, she thought, to wait.

An advertisement in the *Natal Daily News* brought an immediate response from a recently widowed woman looking for a new home. They now had a real reason to press on, making the days ever longer and more tiring, and on Friday nights, when the labourers packed up, they were ready to relax. In the early days they piled into the Studebaker and drove off to see something of their new country. Mary thoroughly enjoyed visiting the game reserves and sleeping rough in the game camps. She loved the animals. If they did not go away for the weekend, they were often invited to the houses of Peter and Jack's friends for tennis or swimming. After years of freezing winters in cold flats, it was heaven.

Mary, however, still looked upon Durban as an adventure which would one day end. Many English-speaking South Africans felt the same, retaining their British citizenship and clinging to a somewhat idealized image of pre-Nationalist life. Indeed, in those early days, it looked to Mary as if the thrust of Nationalist legislation was aimed not at Africans, but at replacing those of English origin with Afrikaners. Judges, town clerks and every conceivable public official came under scrutiny as the descendants of the Boers attempted to redress what they saw as the occupation of *their* country. The English could only fume and mutter among themselves, failing for the most part to appreciate the enormity of the changes affecting the African community until the more pernicious *apartheid* acts were already in place. Nearly all of Mary's friends were English; the Indians kept to themselves, the Africans were Zulus to be admired at a distance, and the Afrikaners were as alien as Martians.

Meanwhile, six months had gone by; the first house was still unfinished and two more barely started. Mary's money was running seriously low, yet Jack and Peter were taking the Studebaker and driving off for long weekends in the countryside. Mary did not complain. The two men could be very entertaining, but their war stories were becoming a bit repetitive, and she was pleased to have time to herself with Julie. There was also something disturbing about Jack and drink – one glass seemed to make him drunk and boorish.

It was difficult to know what to do. So much of their lives depended on the two men. They had met most of their new friends because of Jack and Peter – which meant that nearly all of them were homosexual. It was not the least of South Africa's anomalies that, while its politicians were obsessed with racial divisions, sexual ones flourished. Most big towns had a thriving homosexual community, technically contravening the country's laws, but largely ignored. Durban had a mainly English-speaking group, which led a life parallel to that of the straight community. Thanks initially to

Jack and Peter, the two women were swiftly admitted as honorary members and were soon sharing the passions and miseries of the shifting relationships within the group.

The main unifying events in the community were impromptu parties. Couples would drop by for tea on Sunday, others would arrive, and a party would evolve. Occasionally this was a more organized affair. When Mary, Julie, Jack and Peter had settled in, they held a *braai* – a South African barbecue – on one of their building sites, a novelty which gave them considerable notoriety within the group. Mary's much depleted funds still ran to lashings of drink, and as it was usual to bring a bottle of brandy, the party went with a swing long into the night. There was dancing to an Afrikaans accordion band, with some revellers falling into the foundations which had already been dug.

A lot of the guests were acting connections of Peter's. He was still trying to keep his old career going and had contacted the South African Broadcasting Corporation [SABC], which at the time was the only consistent employer of professional actors in Durban. He had been auditioned by the young Cedric Messina, who had started up an SABC drama unit in Durban after returning from war service in Italy. Messina was obliged to turn out a play a week, rehearsing and recording in the evenings, after which there might be a get-together of some sort, to which Mary and Julie were often invited. Peter had been quick to spread the word that Mary was a highly successful, prize-winning author and had even persuaded her to start work with him on a radio play he wanted Cedric to produce. If he was trying to keep her happy, this was certainly a clever move, given Mary's love of acting and actors.

Cedric Messina was the descendant of Italian immigrants who had settled in southern Africa in the 1820s. His father had worked in the Rhodesian copper mines, though Cedric had been brought up in Johannesburg and had joined the SABC as an announcer, just before the war. He had served in the Western Desert and in Italy until an army resettlement grant enabled him to go to England to work for a short time with the BBC. On his return, the SABC posted him to Durban to set up the drama unit, but he had the promise of a post in London at some future point which he was determined to take up when he could.

Almost everyone in the group had had some form of military experience, and the contrast between the rather flamboyant parties and the memories of war and death reminded Mary of the wounded soldiers and the 'conchies' at Wingford. There was much talk of wartime experiences, and Mary was always a good listener who seemed to enter into the stories as if she had been there. She once confessed to a friend that she had battle dreams in which she, as a man, led the fighting. In one especially vibrant encounter, she was a crusader crossing a battlefield after the conflict, when she saw a mortally wounded man whom she despatched with a single swing of her sword.

Mary rapidly realized that these young men longed for stable, enduring relationships, yet often found it impossible to create one. She became accustomed to temper tantrums and jealous spats, to broken hearts and threats of suicide. To her, there was an explanation for all this in Plato, in the *Phaedrus*, where he distinguishes the soul as having

> three parts, two of them resembling horses, the third a charioteer. One of these horses we said was good, the other vicious. The better of the two is an upright noble animal, a lover of honour, sensible to shame, and obeying the word of the driver without the lash. The other is crooked, headlong, fiery . . . Now, when the driver is inflamed by love and desire for some beautiful human being, the tractable horse holds himself back, and restrains himself all he can from attempting any sensual enjoyment of the beloved object, but the other, setting whip and rein at defiance, struggles on . . . to unchaste intercourse.

This was a fair description of the building-site party. Two guests turned up in a covered wagon dressed as *Voortreckers*, and the amount of food and drink available gave the four hosts a reputation for being what one guest called 'dizzy rich'.

Among the guests was a young English actor, Dennis Folbigge. He had answered an advertisement for a photolithographer in the British *News Chronicle* and had arrived in Durban two years before Mary and Julie. Having managed to join Messina's radio drama team, he had transformed himself into an actor. Unusually, he had an Afrikaner friend, Gerry Strydom, a budding sculptor and potter, though, as Dennis put it, he was 'more English than the English'. The two lived in the Connaught Hotel on Seaview Street, an old Victorian pile with a wide cast-iron veranda which Dennis described as looking 'as though you should gallop up and tether your horse to the rails'. Many of the SABC drama crowd, including Cedric, were permanent residents at the Connaught, where everyone repaired after the late-night recording sessions.

Dennis, more than anyone, was puzzled by Jack and Peter. Why, he wondered, did they always have the big car, while Mary and Julie, who were clearly paying for everything, always had the small one? It seemed everyone except Mary and Julie knew the gossip about Peter and Jack – that they lived very high indeed, always eating at the best restaurants, always with money to throw around.

The first crisis came just before Christmas 1948. Mary and Julie were in bed asleep when their door crashed open and Jack staggered in. He was hopelessly drunk and flung himself to the floor, bawling that Peter had left him. They calmed him down long enough to find out that Peter was at the house of a friend close by. Julie went to find him and he quickly told her the full story – Jack was an alcoholic. Drink fuelled his crazed jealousy. He had tried to disguise his drinking, which was why he seemed to get instantly drunk on what appeared to be his first drink.

They returned to the house, and Peter took Jack to their room. Alone again, Mary and Julie tried to work out what this meant. They had suspected for some time that the two men were not pulling their weight – there was always more planning than action where they were concerned. Jack, as company treasurer, never seemed to pay any bills until their credit ran out, yet the money still disappeared faster than Mary could borrow it. This drunken incident had exposed the awkward situation they had got themselves into, though for the moment they could think of no way to put it right.

*

The house for the widow was almost finished, but the other two were worryingly behind schedule. In their ignorance about local conditions, they had not taken account of the rainy season. The monsoon-like gales made all outside labour impossible, and they were forced to lay off the workmen. When the weather eased and they could start again, there was a new crisis over funds, but this time there was no hope of borrowing more money. The four of them were sitting discussing the dilemma when Mary suddenly said, 'Do you know what yesterday was? It was the first anniversary of CAM Construction'. A year had gone by with nothing solid accomplished. The sense of adventure had dissipated, Mary had not written a word, and nothing but debt and failure were in prospect. Everything was tied up in the unfinished houses and, when she began to question Jack and Peter about what could be done, they were disturbingly offhand, almost uninterested.

To outsiders, however, they still looked like a team. The local artistic community had begun to discover Mary, and the *Natal Daily News* of Thursday, 12 May 1949 carried a profile of her in Peter Quain's 'Talk' column:

> Living shyly in Durban is a young woman novelist who two years ago won £25,000 as the Metro-Goldwyn-Mayer award for the best novel of the year – and had £20,000 of it taken from her in supertax by the British Government.
>
> Her pen name is Mary Renault. She flatly refuses to disclose her real name for publication, and when she talked for Talk, she gave the very first Press interview of her life – an astonishing thing in a novelist who has picked one of the richest plums the world has ever offered writers.
>
> It was only after lengthy persuasion that Mary allowed the taking of a photograph.
>
> And she has been living in Durban almost a year, known to few people as an authoress.
>
> **She is philosophic**
> Mary is tall, blue eyed and charming, and has little to say about her prize-winning book, *Return to Night*, which was selected from several hundred submitted by writers in all parts of the world.
>
> MGM have temporarily shelved the story – because they con-

sider it 'a bit complicated for the screen'. This spring Longmans, Green will publish her latest work, *North Face*. She finished this shortly before she left England, and has already had it published in America.

Since her arrival in the Union she has been collaborating with a friend, Peter Albrecht, a South African with London stage experience, in writing a play, provisionally titled *Dark Freedom*. He wrote the plot – the effect on a family of the return after 15 years of the father, a criminal lunatic – and she wrote the dialogue. It is hoped to produce this play at the Journey's End Shellhole some time in August.

The accompanying photograph showed Mary rather awkwardly posed with her typewriter on her knees. Bending over her is the solicitous figure of Peter, one hand behind her, the other resting on the head of Simba, the Rhodesian Ridgeback. Only Julie knew that this scene of domestic tranquillity hid an altogether more disturbing reality. She had begun to go through the pile of company records and stacks of unpaid bills, and had been forced to face up to the evidence that Peter and Jack were undermining the business. Cedric Messina later confessed that he had never trusted Peter, who had seemed plausible but a bad lot. However, as no one said anything at the time, there was nothing the two women could do except stagger on, hoping that the whole sorry mess would resolve itself.

Mary's patience finally snapped when two friends from Johannesburg came to stay. The six of them were supposed to be having lunch, but Jack had not appeared. Half way through the meal they heard a noise and Peter hurried out to intercept Jack before he could launch into another drunken scene. When Peter returned, his expression made it clear that this was something far worse. Jack had swallowed a bottle of aspirins, washing them down with a bottle of brandy. The local doctor was summoned, and they hauled him to the bathroom, where they attempted to get a tube down him to flush out his stomach.

The next day Mary went to her lawyer and told him the whole story. How, she asked, could she extricate herself from such a mess? The lawyer was surprised; he had met the two men and had thought them 'decent types'. He gave the impression that she was being difficult. When Mary insisted something be done, he suggested she go away for a while and leave him to sort out the problem.

She was reluctant to accept the advice: the house was hers and surrendering it to Jack and Peter only weakened her position. But with no one else to turn to, she laid off the workmen, packed a few belongings and drove with Julie and the dogs to a hotel on the outskirts of town, where she waited, in some disquiet, for what might happen next.

Six weeks went by. She walked the dogs and made worried telephone calls to the lawyer, who she felt should have been doing more. She decided to confront him. As Julie was about to drive her into town for the meeting, the hotel manager asked them to take his wife along to the shops. The meeting with the lawyer turned out to be pointless: they were treated like two hysterical females who needed to be pacified. In low spirits they collected their passenger again and headed out of town, Mary in the back, the manager's wife in front beside Julie. It was a two-lane highway; traffic was slow. Suddenly a lorry pulled out in the on-coming lane, heading straight towards them. The driver had totally mis-judged the distance, and they met head on. The manager's wife crashed through the windscreen, while Mary hurtled across the seats into the bakelite dashboard, which shattered under the impact.

The steering wheel saved Julie, though the blow knocked her out. When she came to, there was a terrible pain in her chest, her passenger was covered by a snowstorm of shattered glass, and Mary was head down against the dashboard, not moving, with blood everywhere. Julie felt for a pulse, but could not find one. An ambulance arrived and, as they lifted her, Julie could see that Mary's forehead had split open. They were rushed to the nearest hospital, where Mary was taken immediately to an operating thea-tre. The hotel manager's wife was badly injured, with a fractured jaw and pelvis. Julie was led away to be x-rayed, and found to have broken ribs. When she was strapped up, they let her return to the ward to wait for Mary. She expected the worst, but, as the trolley was being pulled back, she could hear Mary, still high on the anaesthetic, singing 'Lord of our Fathers known of old . . .'.

133

She had a broken collar bone, and her face looked dreadful, swollen and stitched, but at least she was alive.

After three weeks in hospital, Mary still needed a cosmetic operation to remove the scar, but she felt fit enough and discharged herself, with a distinct mark above her left eye.

She and Julie moved into a double room in Cedric's hotel, where life improved enormously, largely because of all the friends who were in and out of each other's rooms in a continuous jolly party. The hotel's two owners had once been singers; they called everyone 'darling' and generally created the type of camp atmosphere which always cheered Mary up. A week after settling in she was due to return to the hospital so that the surgeon could assess her injuries for insurance compensation, but just as Julie was about to fetch the car, she was handed a telegram from their Johannesburg friends who were returning to Durban and wanted to be picked up at the air-strip. Mary said she would take a taxi, and Julie drove to what in those days was scarcely more than an isolated field where small aircraft could land. The place looked deserted, but suddenly one of the CAM Construction lorries drove up behind her. It was Jack and Peter, who must have sent the telegram. Before she could start the car, Peter was in it, pushing Julie aside and taking the wheel. He drove off furiously towards the town. 'Where is Mary?' he demanded. 'Why isn't she with you?' Jack, grim-faced, was driving the lorry behind. Julie refused to speak. They were approaching the hotel and a policeman was slowing down the traffic when Julie threw open the door, jumped out and ran into the lobby. Glancing back she was relieved to see the Studebaker driving away. She had never been so terrified in her life.

In the hotel, she at once telephoned their lawyer who was shocked when he heard the news. He said he would phone the police and report the car as stolen – the Studebaker was one of the few things registered in Mary's name – and he arranged a meeting for that evening. The meeting produced everything that Mary and Julie hoped for. The lawyer had seen the two men and had their written resignations from CAM Construction. They would hand over the firm's books the next day and were to be out of the house within a week. Within days Jack and Peter were gone.

Jack disappeared from their lives for good, though an occasional word about Peter Albrecht living in London, using the stage-name Peter Arne, filtered back to South Africa. In 1983 a friend sent Mary a bunch of newspaper cuttings. One bore the headline SCREEN 'VILLAIN' MURDERED and told how sixty-two-year-old character actor Peter Arne had been bludgeoned to death by a homosexual prostitute in his apartment behind Harrods. A Filipina maid had found a blood-stained piece of wood in the corridor. The article listed Arne's film credits as *The Return of the Pink Panther, Straw Dogs* and *Moonraker*. Arne's agent, Roger Carey, said, 'Everybody loved him and he had friends all over the place.' Thirty-five years earlier Mary had simply been delighted to see the back of him and his drunken friend, and relieved that she would never have to have anything to do with either of them again.

*

Now that the money had run out, it was time to return to their original way of life – Mary must write, Julie must work. First they repossessed their house and threw the inevitable party for all their friends. Then Julie got down to sorting through the mass of papers and bills to see what could be salvaged. The situation could hardly have been worse. The post-war boom was over; South Africa entered the 1950s with its economy in the doldrums and a depressed housing market. CAM Construction now had three completed houses, so Julie decided they should live in one and let the others. But she also knew that they would need an income if they were to pay off the loans, and this proved more difficult than she had imagined. As in England, major hospitals in South Africa preferred to train their own staff, and a working knowledge of Afrikaans was often required. Even though Julie was willing to work below her level, no one would consider her, until a friend of a friend introduced her to the Matron of the King George V Hospital on the far side of town. As it was doing interesting work with tuberculosis, a field in which Julie had considerable

experience, there was a chance. The hospital staff was still integrated, with no racial divisions between the nurses. The wards,
however, were split along racial lines and Julie would work as a
sister on a ward for Indian men – a distinction maintained more
because of social and dietary differences than from any political
imperative.

Money aside, Julie's work was to prove invaluable to Mary as
it opened a window on the world beyond Durban North. While
the English-language press was remarkably liberal and outspoken
in the face of increasing harassment, it too was imbued with the
prevailing belief that the 'Nats' were a temporary aberration. In
1949 it was still possible to be white in South Africa and to imagine
that all would be well, decency would prevail. Even when there
was a riot in Durban in 1949 and 142 people were killed in Zulu
attacks on Indian shopkeepers, it was hard for Mary not to view
it as something unreal or fictional, which was how she described
it to the *Spectator* journalist Richard West:

It all started with a rumour, which flew around among the
Africans with astonishing speed, that an Indian stall-holder had
killed an African boy whom he caught stealing from his stall.
(Years later this boy, now a youth, turned up in the juvenile
courts charged with theft, but sound in wind and limb. What
the Indian seems actually to have done is give him a clout on
the ear.) I was then about a year out of England, living in
Durban North, a respectable suburb which you probably know.
The stall incident had happened in the Grey Street Indian
Market. But wherever you looked, Zulus were emerging from
the *kias* where they 'lived-in', or the shops where they had been
working, carrying pangas or choppers or just sticks, waiting at
the bus stops to go into town.

It seems extremely odd to look back on now; but I and
another equally recent immigrant got into a car and drove down
to see what was going on. It was not so reckless as it seems,
because the climate was quite different from that of any riot
today; one sensed that the Africans were totally uninterested in
white people. We had a curious sense of being invisible. As we

drove through one of the main streets, Smith Street I think, we met an *impi* coming down the middle of the road. They were marching along, or rather dancing, in step, chanting, and waving their weapons. They looked quite happy, not a scowl on any face, they could have been going to a beer-drink. I suppose they were just looking forward to killing Indians. They passed our car, dividing either side of it, then closing up again. We went home after that. I forget now how many people they killed when they got to the Indian suburb. Not many by more recent standards, but it seemed a lot at the time. Two Jewish friends of ours got stopped. He had a rather swarthy Levantine colouring; they wanted to pull him out of the car and kill him. His wife, who is fair, flung her arms round him and assured them he was white and her husband; they believed her, on account of her being willing to embrace him, and let him go.

On the way back we passed an Indian tailor's shop with the window smashed. The bolts of cloth were still there, he must have left in a hurry. A Zulu girl was passing; they used still to come into town then in tribal dress, topless, with a striped towel round the hips and the red mud head-dress modelled on Queen Nefertiti. She hauled a big bolt out of the window, rushed up to the car in front of ours, which contained two ladies in prim hats, and with a beaming smile tried to present it to them through the window of the car. They waved it away with apprehensive gestures, and we hurried on before she could offer it to us. She was obviously enjoying herself and wanted to spread the festive spirit. (A couple of days later, when the loot began to appear, we saw another of these tribal girls decorated, among her beads, with a black lace bra.) I suppose what we should really have done was accept the cloth and give it to the Indian later, if he was still alive.

Our house-boy was a Basuto and thought the Zulus frivolous. 'They don't care for nothing, missus, only singing and dancing.' He used to say they would never combine against the Government because on the day arranged half of them wouldn't remember to turn up. But he all too clearly thought that on this occasion they had done rather well. 'I'm sorry for those Indians. But they don't worship God, missus, only snakes and monkeys.'

137

Such detached levity of tone was possible only from someone who was still essentially a visitor. Apart from the occasional outing in Natal and trips to the eastern Transvaal with its stunning mix of mountain and ocean, Mary's only real journey across South Africa had been to the Cape, the most European part of the country. She had loved it on sight and would have moved had she not been tied to the unsold houses.

By 1950 this sort of isolation was no longer tenable. Friends who worked in education told Mary how the night schools, which had done so much to help the Africans, were being forced to close. Julie introduced her to Consiva, one of the African nurses at the hospital who was married to an Indian, and Mary learned something of the appalling difficulties experienced by those who dared cross racial lines.

Such matters confronted her with a basic dilemma. Could she continue to be a visitor, enjoying the natural beauty and the material benefits of the country for as long as it suited her, or did she mean to stay and accept some responsibility for South Africa's future? One side of the argument was easy to resolve. She had no wish to return to Britain, which she associated with the hardships of hospital life – the petty restrictions, the meaningless discipline – overlaid with grim memories of those last freezing austerity winters. For all her worries about where things were heading in South Africa and despite the mess her finances were in, she had found a home at last, and so had Julie. In 1950 they both became citizens; they were allowed dual nationality, but they never again used their British passports. They had made their decision, and they stuck to it.

*

As if to finish with the past, Mary decided to write a novel about her final years in Britain; it would also be her last work of contemporary fiction.

To many, *The Charioteer* is the best British novel to come out of World War II. To others its significance lies in its position as one of a tiny group of important books which take homosexual love as their subject. In that regard, the novel was also a reflection of her new life in Durban.

The members of Mary's Durban circle were confronted by the same ethical choices as existed on the broader political stage, which she had first observed at the EMS Hospital at Winford, where the wounded soldiers from Dunkirk had been tended by the despised 'conchies'. Like pacifists in wartime, homosexuals were outcasts in 'straight' society, struggling to adjust to a sexuality which could not offer the support of a traditional ethic – the struggle symbolized by the chariot in the *Phaedrus*: one horse heaven bent, the other plunging earthwards. To Mary the moral choices needed to live decently as a homosexual seemed no different from those one needed to make in a complex political situation like South Africa's – except that the former was something she felt able to write about.

The Charioteer follows its central character, Laurie Odell, from childhood through his schooldays to young manhood in a way so sympathetically and roundly portrayed that the book becomes not only a moral exemplar for homosexuals, but also a counterblast to the wave of homophobic prejudice which characterized the early 1950s in Britain and America.

Mary had left Britain when homosexuals were still enjoying the relatively free atmosphere engendered by the wartime easing of many social taboos. As an avid reader of the British press, she knew of the recent revival of prosecutions for homosexuality and she had read about the Cold War hysteria in America which identified 'perverts' as subversives trying to undermine capitalist society. Set against such happenings, the comparatively lax situation in Durban could give the illusion of liberation. But it was an illusion. White South Africa tolerated homosexuals as long as they played by unwritten rules.

While Mary enjoyed the camaraderie to be found within this close-knit secret society, she was also aware of the dangers that arise when people are forced to lead double lives. Camp humour was fun, but there was also back-biting and bitchiness. To someone like Mary, motivated by the highest ideals of Platonic friendship, the way that society's rejection induced furtive sex and selfishness in love was something to be resisted. *The Charioteer* would show the way.

Purposes of Love, with its lesbian undertones, would seem mild in comparison with what she was now planning to write. Since the Oscar Wilde trial, homosexuals in British fiction had appeared as either sick or funny, or both. The E. M. Forster stories which touched on the subject were distinctly low key. Because Forster suppressed *Maurice* until after his own death it appeared too late to affect anyone, except Christopher Isherwood, who read it in manuscript and became the one British author to give deviant sexuality a central role in his work. His 1930s Berlin novels treat the subject openly, though with a tendency to relate homosexual 'soul-sickness' to the greater malaise of a decaying society. But no British author since Isherwood had tackled the subject.

In America, in 1948, Gore Vidal's *The City and the Pillar* became the first major work of fiction to show a homosexual sub-culture free of moralizing conclusions. Vidal's stated aim in writing the book was to show that, while legal and social pressures against homosexuals can make them neurotic, a man who enjoys sexual relations with his own sex is not by definition so. Not only did Vidal draw the obvious conclusion, that a removal of repression would end the worst aspects of the sub-culture – the freakish behaviour, the constant search for sexual gratification without affection, the impermanence of most relationships – he also made the then extraordinary point that being 'gay' was not merely acceptable but could be a positive good.

The City and the Pillar was the obvious precursor to the book Mary was planning to write, but, immured in Durban North, it had passed her by. Later she and Vidal became distant admirers of each other's work, but for the moment neither knew of the other.

The Charioteer offers a wholly believable world, without the quirky theatrical language or overindulgence in literary quotation that tended to mar Mary's earlier books. From the very opening there is a sense of amazed discovery, which the book never loses; as here, where the hero, Laurie Odell, five years old, lies in bed, unable to sleep:

It was the first time he had ever heard the clock strike ten at night. If he had been asleep and waked to hear the strokes, it would have been different, a small manageable fragment broken off the unknown hugeness of night, from somewhere in the middle. He would have been a little uneasy, perhaps, in his waking solitude, and, if he heard anyone stirring, would have found something legitimate to call out for, such as a drink of water. Only babies called out about nothing. The ten months which had passed of his fifth year felt like at least half his remembered life, and he was used to his responsibilities.

Tonight was unique. Tonight he had not been to sleep at all, and it was ten.

Seven o'clock was familiar and domesticated. With luck and good management, at seven his mother might still be sitting on the edge of his bed with an unfinished story. Eight was unusual, associated with trouble: having been punished, or being sick. Nine was the wild outpost of an unknown continent. Ten was the mountains of the moon, the burial-place of the elephants: white on the map. He lay staring with round birdlike eyes at the dim lapping of light on the ceiling incredulous of the journey he had made alone.

Outside a man passed the house, whistling. The noise had an absolute foreignness, like the note of a jungle bird. It had no link with humanity; it was simply a mysterious feature on the face of night. Somewhere, so far off that in the daytime one never heard it, a line of railway trucks was shunted together. The metallic clangs, melancholy with distance, not quite harsh and not quite musical, made a loose chain of sound, then stopped inconclusively, leaving the ear suspended and waiting.

If one sat up as long as an hour past bedtime, except on Christmas and birthdays, one would be ill. Laurie, who had had this explained to him many times and accepted it as incontrovertible fact, inferred from it that after three hours, one would probably die.

Sensing the tension in the house, Laurie gets out of bed and finds his father packing; his parents' marriage is ending. When he bursts into tears, his mother takes him back to bed, where he is comforted by the certainty that she loves him best. He never sees his father again.

The story flashes forward to his schooldays in a taut episode in which he discovers that his idol, the head prefect, Ralph Lanyon, his idealized father-figure, is to be expelled for sexual misconduct with a junior boy. To prevent Laurie from organizing a wildcat protest, Ralph admits that the charges are true and, as a final gift, presents him with his copy of the *Phaedrus*, the book whose message will order the pattern of his life, with Ralph remaining in Laurie's memory as the very epitome of courage and honour.

With another leap in time, we find Laurie in hospital, wounded in the leg during the flight from Dunkirk. In scenes closely drawn from Mary's own experiences, the maids walk out and are replaced by conscientious objectors, with the inevitable polarization of feeling among the wounded soldiers. We learn that, before being propelled into the army, Laurie had had a year at Oxford, where he was introduced to the homosexual sub-culture. But schooled in the *Phaedrus*, with his image of Ralph intact, Laurie is looking for a more uplifting love than the forced gaiety which 'queer' life has so far offered. Taking a walk to escape the claustrophobic atmosphere of the ward, Laurie comes across one of the youngest 'conchies', Andrew Raynes, and without hesitation falls unreservedly in love with him.

Even at a distance of some forty years and at a time when variant sexuality is a commonplace in novels, the matter-of-fact treatment of this event is still startling. There is no question of an attempted seduction. The subsequent encounters between the two young men convince Laurie that Andrew's innocence must not be violated. Laurie's will be a one-sided love, Platonic, with the dark horse of wilful passion subdued. They meet in a neighbouring garden, which they dub 'Eden'. When Andrew explains his Quaker beliefs, he defends his pacifism in a manner that bristles with Mary's approval of individuals who stubbornly oppose any attempt to regiment their actions. When the owner of the garden, angry at a 'conchie' defiling her property, expels them from Eden, they meet in a nearby field, which they appropriately call 'Limbo', the eternal consolation prize the early church offered to good pagans such as Plato.

Andrew has had to struggle against his family's military traditions and the war-fever gripping the nation; Laurie must fight

Sandy

the furtive herd instinct of many homosexuals. He meets Alec, a medical student, in town during an air raid and is persuaded to go to a 'queer' party when he is told that the long lost Ralph will be there. This party, a full chapter long, offers the inverse of Limbo, a hell of camp screamers sporting names like Bunny and Bim who spout a bitchiness that fails to mask an inner loneliness.

Inevitably, Ralph's appearance, resplendent in his naval officer's blue and gold, is like a vision, obscuring the fact that he, too, belongs in this shadow world, having had a brief affair with Alec and being now at the end of another with Bunny. All Laurie sees is his hero, wounded like himself, a shattered left hand masked with a padded glove.

Thus Laurie, the charioteer, is yoked to the light and dark horse: his friendship with Andrew, Platonic, innocent, asexual, and his affair with Ralph, a sensual minefield of complex choices. Ralph also aspires to the Platonic ideal; as he puts it, 'It's not what one is, it's what one does with it.' But Laurie quickly realizes that he sees their relationship as one between older and younger, the type of role-playing Mary had observed among her Durban friends: active/passive, dominant/submissive, teacher/pupil, all ways of aping the sex roles of a 'straight' marriage. Ralph falls short of the Platonic ideal by wishing to manage his lover and thus block his progress to full maturity. Even when he learns about Andrew, he tries to manipulate the situation.

> Laurie realized now that, from the moment when Ralph had learned that this was a love without physical bond, he had thought of it as something not quite real . . . Laurie remembered how he always said 'this boy', on a certain inflection, faintly indulgent; it would have been patronage in someone a little less kind. As far as he was concerned, Andrew was someone by whom Laurie had been refused.

Laurie, then, is presented with a clear moral choice: life with his schoolboy hero, with whom he will remain a managed youth, never growing to full adulthood, or his love for Andrew, unspoken and therefore pure.

In the end the choice evaporates. His mother announces her

intention to remarry, and Laurie weakens. Ralph turns up at the wedding and, as in *Return to Night*, when the mother has gone, he and Laurie have sex in her home, a scene redolent with 1930s Freudianism. With this act, the dark horse bolts, the charioteer plunges earthwards, and it is the innocent Andrew who suffers. Driven by jealousy, Ralph's ex-lover Bunny goes to see the boy, hoping to unearth a little scandal with which to tarnish Laurie and thus punish Ralph. Andrew, however, assumes that Bunny must be Ralph, a misconception quickly realized by Bunny, who uses it to reveal, in the worst possible light, the true nature of his 'friendship' with Laurie. Shocked, Andrew violates his deepest principles by punching him on the jaw and running away.

Laurie's world has collapsed. When he tracks Andrew down, he leaves without seeing him, knowing that if he tells him the truth, any friendship they have would be altered by Andrew's knowledge of his sexuality. Back at the hospital, he learns of Ralph's innocence, but can forgive him only to forestall his attempted suicide. Laurie must accept that theirs can never be anything but an imperfect love, and that he must do what he can to make it work. After all, none of the lovers in Mary's earlier novels had been allowed the delusion of a perfect marriage. An enduring relationship is not a woolly dream, she seems to say, and applies this even-handedly to the 'marriage' of Laurie and Ralph – though by ending the book with a final quote from the *Phaedrus*, she indicates that such a compromise can still aspire to a certain goodness:

Quietly, as night shuts down the uncertain prospect of the road ahead, the wheels sink to stillness in the dust of the halting place, and the reins drop from the driver's loosened hands. Staying each his hunger on what pasture the place affords them, neither the white horse nor the black reproaches his fellow for drawing their master out of the way. They are far, both of them, from home, and lonely, and lengthened by their strife the way has been hard. Now their heads droop side by side till their long manes mingle; and when the voice of the charioteer falls silent they are reconciled for a night in sleep.

*

Despite the obvious sensitivity and maturity with which she handled her subject, there was consternation at Longmans when they received the manuscript in the late autumn of 1952. Mary's much-loved Robert Longman had by this time retired, and the company's fiction list was being handled by his nephew Mark. While he could hardly have expected another of Mary's English nursing novels, he was in no way prepared for the awkward fact that he was expected to handle the first openly homosexual novel by a serious writer to be published in Britain since the war. Gore Vidal's *The City and the Pillar* was little known in the United Kingdom, and set no precedent for Mary's novel. Indeed, there would be only three major works of fiction dealing with homosexuality – *The City and the Pillar* (1948), *The Charioteer* (1953), and James Baldwin's *Giovanni's Room* (1956), between the end of World War II and the 1962 publication of Christopher Isherwood's *Down There on a Visit*, which marked the opening of the present era of liberation and the end of most literary taboos about homosexual love. None of this was any comfort to Longmans in 1952.

The difficulty was compounded by the author's ambiguous position. She had been well known, famous even, for her earlier books; but it was now five years since she had published anything, and those fans who might still remember her and rush out to buy *The Charioteer* would be in for a shock. It was one thing to be entranced by a love story with a slight suggestion of unrequited lesbianism, quite another to come face to face with the story of a young man's homosexual awakening, let alone his love for a very young conscientious objector. Longmans' worries were doubled when Morrow, still Mary's publishers in New York, flatly refused to bring out the book on the ground that it would lay them open to prosecution. Mary never doubted that their decision sprang from McCarthyism, which had placed 'sexual perverts' on a level with Communists. Eisenhower's Executive Order of 1953 would bar homosexuals from federal posts, and the Burgess and Maclean scandal in the British Foreign Office would reinforce the connection between homosexuality and treason. The idea of a homosexual love story involving soldiers and pacifists must have seemed to the editors at Morrow like a scenario for their worst Cold War nightmare.

As Longmans was primarily a publisher of school text books, a market traditionally sensitive to any kind of impropriety, the news from America added weight to those voices in the company that worried lest their educational division be tarnished by association with a book some might consider pornographic, and it is to Longmans' great credit that, despite these misgivings, they decided to proceed. It was to be another six years before an American publisher found the courage to follow suit.

Fortunately for Mary, her book was given to John Guest, who would be her editor from then on, and who gradually replaced Robert Longman as her trusted ally in the distant world of London publishing. John Guest had been brought from the publishing house of William Collins to expand the fiction list at Longmans and, although he knew of Mary's former success, he was as surprised as anyone by the book he was given to edit. Not, as he admits, that there was ever much editing to do. Mary was fastidious about her manuscripts and utterly resistant to any tinkering with her style. Her views on punctuation were unbending (she had, he recalls, an especial fondness for the semi-colon), and Guest soon learned to leave well enough alone, confining himself to the rare suggestion that something he 'had not fully understood' might perhaps be clarified 'a little'.

The Charioteer was published on 5 October 1953. A few weeks later Sir John Gielgud was arrested and charged with 'importuning male persons for immoral purposes'. After a humiliating trial, he was fined a tawdry £10. For Mary, who remembered his brilliant Hamlet and his haunting Cassius, the coincidence was especially upsetting. One of the saddest aspects of her book is the way Laurie, despite being a wounded war hero and a person of undoubted moral worth, grows increasingly furtive about his true nature. He sinks farther and farther into a mire of half-truth and innuendo so that one of his Dunkirk comrades will not know that he is homosexual; and, when he tries to stop a young boy from falling out of the next bed in the ward, he is instantly consumed with fear lest the nurse think he is doing something disreputable.

TOP *Frank Challans (front row far right), Mary's father, as a medical student at the London Hospital, Whitechapel, in 1900.*

ABOVE LEFT *Dr Challans outside the Old Vicarage, Barlaston.*

ABOVE RIGHT *Clementine Challans, Mary's mother, still handsome in old age.*

ABOVE A St Hugh's College
production, If I Were King,
Michaelmas term 1927, with Mary
(centre) as François Villon and
Margaret Lane as Katherine.

RIGHT Mary on the downs near
Barlaston, Staffordshire, in the
autumn of 1932, soon after her
parents had moved there.

Nursing in Wartime

TOP LEFT *Mary in 1940.*

TOP RIGHT *Robbie Wilson, unconventional doctor and friend, in 1939.*

ABOVE *Julie Mullard (right) in 1944, wearing her 'Sister Dora' nurse's cap.*

LEFT *Julie and Mary on board the Cairo in 1948, on their way to South Africa, where they settled in Durban.*

BELOW LEFT *Julie at the King George V Hospital, Durban.*

BELOW *Mary in a Black Sash protest in 1955. She was among the first to join this women's movement against* apartheid.

ABOVE OPPOSITE *Julie and Mary (right), with Chi-chi, at Delos, the house they moved to in Camps Bay near Capetown.*

BELOW OPPOSITE *Delos with a view over the beach at Camps Bay.*

ABOVE Mary (centre) with
friends outside a taverna in
Samos, on her first trip to Greece
in 1954.

RIGHT Mary and Michael
Atkinson installing her cast of the
Roman statue of the Apollo
Belvedere in the garden of Delos,
Camps Bay, in the late 1970s.

ABOVE OPPOSITE Lunch with
David Poole and the author
during the filming of the BBC
documentary in 1982. The
microphone is hidden in the
cherub centrepiece.

BELOW OPPOSITE Working in her
'Swiss bank' study with Mandy
and Coco, the dogs.

ABOVE *Mary and Julie walking the dogs on the beach at Camps Bay, 1982.*

LEFT *Portrait of Mary Renault in 1982.*

To counter this slow descent into shame and secrecy, the book clearly sets out the case for reform:

When Laurie got back, they were all discussing a recent black-mail case. Sandy and Alec had met someone who knew the victim, and had all the details, which were sordid enough. Remembering long discussions at Oxford, Laurie remarked that the present state of the law seemed to encourage that sort of thing; it was unenforceable, and merely created racketeers.

'I agree,' said Alec. 'You could add that it gives the relatively balanced type, who makes some effort to become an integrated personality, a quite false sense of solidarity with advanced psychopaths whom, if they weren't all driven underground together, he wouldn't even meet.' He caught Sandy's eye fixed on him reverently, and, as if he were giving way to a suppressed irritation, added, 'Not that I can feel much pity for anyone who'll submit to blackmail, myself.'

Sandy said at once, 'No, really, that's a bit sweeping, Alec. What about his job, what about dependents, what if his mother's got a weak heart and the news will kill her? It's not like you to be so rigid.'

'Oh, Sandy, we've been over this so often. It's a matter of what your self-respect's worth to you, that's all. Isn't that so, Ralph? In the first place, I didn't choose to be what I am, it was determined when I wasn't in a position to exercise any choice and without my knowing what was happening. I've sub-mitted to psychoanalysis; it cured my stutter for me, which was very useful as far as it went. All right. I might still be a social menace, like a child-killer, and have to be dealt with whether I was responsible or not. But I don't admit that I'm a social menace. I think that probably we're all parts of nature's remedy for a state of gross overpopulation, and I don't see how we're a worse remedy than modern war, which from all I hear in certain quarters has hardly begun. Anyway, here we are, heaven knows how many thousand of us, since there's never been a census. I'm not prepared to accept a standard which puts the whole of my emotional life on the plane of immorality. I've never involved a normal person or a minor or anyone who

147

wasn't in a position to exercise a free choice. I'm not prepared to let myself be classified with dope-peddlers and prostitutes. Criminals are blackmailed. I'm not a criminal. I'm ready to go to some degree of trouble, if necessary, to make that point.

For some reviewers Mary's strong, polemical line and the coincidence of the Gielgud trial linked the book to the growing movement for reform and even drew the support of the Church of England's official newspaper:

The whole theme of the book is the conflict between the better self and the lower self which is torn by the temptations of homosexuality. The fact that it has been published by such a first-class publishing house as Longmans is itself a proof that this subject is treated with complete sincerity and restraint.

This set the tone for the great majority of reviews, but it was a letter from a reader that best revealed the way the book had caught the moment:

I had been reading about the John Gielgud case and in my mind I judged him harshly.

After I read your book I felt I viewed that problem from a different angle. Now I feel great sympathy with those in that category, who try to struggle against it. I feel they ought to be helped and encouraged as far as humanely possible. I do not know when I read a book which affected me so much. I had to read it over and over. Your handling of the subject was so beautifully done that no one could take exception to it. I only wished I had had more knowledge of Ancient Greek and Roman History. Perhaps you will excuse this outpouring when I tell you I am a widow and elderly.

One letter, surprisingly from Bloemfontein in South Africa and written by a schoolmistress, offered an acute insight into the exact consequences of sexual repression:

Dear Mary Renault,

This is just to say a grateful thank you for the mental help your last book *The Charioteer* has given me, and I am sure it must have lifted the hearts of many who have come up against that problem and its effects.

Early this year I had news that a friend had thrown himself under the tube train at Marble Arch because he was shortly to be brought up in court on that sort of charge! He was a Music Examiner and had been out here a few times – we were very close mental friends and I never dreamt he was anything but a 'sensitive'. He had one of the loveliest minds I have come across and was a practising RC (I am a believing Anglican).

Once I said, 'I do not know how Jesus himself managed to suffer certain sorts of fools gladly, it's too difficult,' and his answer was, 'He did not need to, nobody would be a fool with Him.' And from that height to suicide!!!

Morrow's refusal to publish in America was not entirely successful in preventing enthusiastic readers from getting hold of copies. One of the earliest, Christopher Isherwood, gave a copy to his friend Gerald Heard, who wrote to Mary from Santa Monica, a long letter full of praise: 'The dialogues are really amazing – as Isherwood said to me, how can an author who must in many respects be "above the battle" and outside that particular circle of Purgatory understand it so well?'

Whatever else, the almost forgotten author had returned as a challenging contemporary writer with a new audience. Her Durban friends rushed to have *The Charioteer* sent out from England, though whether they realized that the book's strictures on 'queer' behaviour applied to them is doubtful; people rarely do. But, if nothing else, they now knew that Mary was far more than a minor scribbler of women's fiction. Her status among gay men was brought home when Cedric invited her to a performance of *The Tempest* in Durban and took her backstage to meet the lead, John Boulter, a young actor recently arrived from Britain. Before leaving, Boulter had visited a sympathetic bookseller in Charing Cross Road to buy something 'amusing' to read on the boat. The man suggested Gore Vidal's *The City and the Pillar*, but added that, if he liked it, he might also care to take a new book called *The Charioteer*. Boulter had been particularly impressed by the latter, though like so many he also concluded that 'she' had to be a man. Now here *she* was, in his dressing room in Durban, and he was, as he told her later, 'completely overawed'.

*

Shortly before the publication of *The Charioteer*, Cedric Messina had begun to play a leading role in Mary's life. Being so close to the SABC drama group, Mary was aware that he was having family problems which threatened to damage his career just as it was about to take off. The BBC in London was on the point of finalizing the contract he had been waiting for when he was summoned to Johannesburg, where his mother had been undergoing psychiatric treatment since the recent death of his father. The mental hospital wanted to discharge her, and Cedric felt he had no alternative but to bring her to Durban and install her in the Connaught Hotel. Within days she had shut herself in her room and was refusing food. When the locks were opened, she was found sitting on the bed, staring into space, refusing to budge.

When Mary learned of this, she offered to take in Mrs Messina while Cedric worked out a solution. The old lady was no trouble as she rarely left her room, taking her meals off the trays Julie prepared and brought to her. If they had to communicate, she always referred to them as Miss Challans and Miss Mullard, while to them she was always Mrs Messina. But a week became a month and still no alternative had been found. Cedric's contract appeared, but how could he leave without finding a solution?

'We did it for God,' is Julie's rather flippant explanation as to why they decided to keep Mrs Messina while Cedric went off to London for a year. They must have known that after such a length of time the situation would be permanent and, given their relationships with their own mothers, it seems hardly credible that they should have been willing to take on someone else's. To Dennis Folbigge, this selfless act was the most admirable thing about them, and was possible only because both women were so close to each other that even the permanent presence of a third person could not affect them. Dennis remembers arriving one day and catching a glimpse of Mrs Messina sitting in her room, immobile, silent; then seeing her, still there, in the same position, when he left three hours later. Although Dennis and his friend Gerry counted themselves among their closest friends, it was clear that the two women were in a world of their own. Dennis and Gerry always referred to them as M and J, never separately, and often marvelled at the way each counterbalanced the other. Mary was the sheet anchor, holding the more excitable Julie steady, while the latter's bubbling energy, busily coping with day-to-day life, left Mary free to withdraw into her writing.

Before leaving for London, Cedric asked Mary to write a play for his radio drama group, no doubt as a way of thanking her for her kindness to his mother. He was, however, nervous about what she might come up with and was pleasantly surprised when she proposed an eight-part serial based on the ever popular story of Captain Bligh, Fletcher Christian and the mutiny on the *Bounty*. She rejected the Charles Laughton version, which portrayed Bligh as a monster, and created a more complex man from a humble background who finds himself placed in authority over the better-born Christian. Initially the two men are close friends, but, when Christian challenges his authority, Bligh's feelings of betrayal have something of the rejected lover about them. It was a twist to the story which would be used, over thirty years later, in the Mel Gibson film version, but was, at the time Mary worked on it, an unusual view of the well-known quarrel.

Mary was thrilled to be working with actors, and they clearly adored her eccentricities. Cedric is still amused by memories of her talking about the Battle of Salamis to a somewhat puzzled Indian shopkeeper, or discussing a philosophical point with a waiter as if he were a professor. She was no anecdotalist, however, and seldom told jokes; her humour was unforced and spontaneous. Dennis recalled that they had no lesbian friends, and Julie confirmed they found women couples hard to accept and refused to use the word of themselves. As Julie put it, 'If people talked about "lesbians", we used to draw our skirts away.'

Mary's reactions were more complex and applied to women in general. She hated to find herself 'trapped in female company'. She resented any invitation that led to her being placed among the wives while the husbands enjoyed themselves elsewhere. Although this was partially an understandable refusal to be treated as second class, it also grew out of her distaste for marriage, engendered by her mother's bitter nagging. She simply did not wish to be a woman. Dennis once quizzed her about fixing the scar damage to her face, but she merely shrugged and retorted, 'What's the point? I'm no fashion plate.' Yet she did care about her appearance, worrying over her clothes, concerned about what people would think of her. For parties she would dress up in bright, sometimes flamboyant colours, as if a theatrical splash would provide her with armour against the world. She was an impressive figure. At fifty-three the thin, boyish look had given way to a squarer, more handsome face with the same fresh complexion, enlivened by her usual broad smile. There was by this time a considerable contrast between her and Julie; where Mary was solid, Julie was as thin and sharp-featured as when they first met.

Julie had become one of the four under-matrons at the hospital and, because of her good relations with the nurses, she was given the job of sifting through the thousands of applications from African girls who saw nursing as a means of liberation from the drudgery of village agriculture. It was hard to refuse such hopeful candidates, but Julie tried to be as fair as possible and, when a Government directive ordered her to select only applicants of Zulu origin, her initial reaction was favourable. The African nurses had enormous problems with travel, especially in getting home for the holidays, and this would be taken care of if all the girls were local. It was only when Julie proposed to write to the failed candidates and was ordered not to that she understood she had been deceived, that this was simply an underhand ploy to implement the resettlement acts whereby only Zulus would be allowed to work in Natal. In order to prevent any protests against this back-door segregation, the other candidates were to be simply left dangling, with no word one way or the other about their future. Furious at being gulled in this way, Julie proceeded to flout her instructions, writing to all the other applicants, apologizing for the fact that they could no longer be considered for training. It was the first skirmish in a running battle which was to bring her into open conflict with her superiors, and the first sign that politics were about to dominate all South African lives.

The elevation of Heinrich Verwoerd to the Nationalist cabinet in 1952 put an end to any hopes that its more illiberal policies might be diluted by parliamentary action. Under Verwoerd's influence, a new crop of draconian laws came into effect, including a more thorough pass law, aimed at keeping all Africans except servants out of White areas. At the same time, the infamous Section 10 of the Native Laws Amendment Act began the process of forced removals and resettlements, which culminated in the bulldozing of Black and Coloured neighbourhoods, and the consequent growth of squatter camps, with all their deprivation and misery.

Mary's sole means of protest was to write to the newspapers in the hope of prodding the weak conscience of the English-speaking community. She was under no illusion that this was going to achieve very much, but it was impossible to sit by idly while such injustices went unchallenged. The largely English-speaking liberal tradition in the country was fragile – it was, after all, the English who had first perpetrated racial division; the Afrikaners had merely given it a name, *apartheid*, and a legal framework. To put up a sign in a White neighbourhood telling everyone that the park benches were for Whites only was simply to tell them what they knew already. It was easy to believe the Government's apologists when they explained that the pass laws were just a forceful attempt to control the increasing problem of urban crime. Even Mary's servant Paul was initially in favour of such moves, which he thought would keep trouble-makers out of the area – Africans being as much the victims of crime and violence as their White employers. It was only when Mary realized Paul could be arrested for not carrying his passbook while he was outside the house cutting the grass verges that she saw how far things had gone. She had occasionally been obliged to visit the local police station to pay Paul's fines when the police caught him brewing beer. Now she was more often bailing him out when he was arrested for infringing the pass laws. She found them petty and degrading and wanted to do something about them, but felt constrained by her lack of knowledge. Unlike those authors who had been born and brought up in South Africa, Mary felt too much the outsider to write directly about the country. Its problems were too new for her to consider fictionalizing them. Nor did Cedric's suggestion, on his return from London in 1953, that she follow up the *Bounty* experience by writing a historical novel about the Zulu hero Shaka, have much chance of striking fire.

What Cedric could not know was that she had worked out her own way of resolving the dilemma. She had decided to write a historical novel at last, not because he or anyone else had suggested it, but because she believed there was a telling parallel between the crisis in South Africa and events in fifth-century Athens. She had edged towards the idea while working on *The Charioteer*, which had brought her so close to Plato again that she had been unable to free herself once the novel was finished. Her thoughts began to gell while she and Julie were making another of their favourite boat journeys up the East African coast to Kenya.

To while away her time on board Mary had taken Xenophon's *Memorabilia of Socrates* to read and was immediately struck by the difference between this view of Socrates and the one she knew from the *Dialogues*. In 1981 she described to me the image of Xenophon which emerged from the book:

> This was a man who had also known Socrates and had obviously met him on an entirely different level, I mean Xenophon was a soldier, and he was rather conventional, not very conventional or of course he couldn't have been a friend of Socrates, but he was fairly conventional, and very practical. And I thought how interesting, what must the rest of his circle have been like? I mean what was Phaedo like who was rescued out of a brothel after he had been enslaved and was originally an aristocrat? Critias, of course, turned out to be a vicious dictator when he had the chance, yet all these people were there in this circle. What must it have been like? And I thought I must write a book about it.

This sounds almost offhand until one remembers how near the surface the idea of writing a historical novel had always been. Where a contemporary story might get side-tracked as its charac-ters struggled to come to terms with complex events whose outcome they could but dimly perceive, time and distance would offer her the broad structure and the finished conclusions she wanted. She was not suggesting that events in the Athens of 420 BC were the same as those in the Pretoria of AD 1953 but rather that the moral choices offered to individual citizens were comparable.

Mary had not set herself an easy task. Although she had long been familiar with the primary sources – Plato, Herodotus, Thucydides, Plutarch – she needed a great deal more to flesh out the story if anything like historical realism were to be achieved. Memories of her first attempt, that blithely unresearched first novel of the Middle Ages, were still too painful to allow any sloppiness. She knew the broad outline of the period she wished to cover – from 415 BC, the year when the war between Athens and Sparta reached crisis point, to 402 BC, when Athenian democracy was restored after the tyranny of the Thirty – just before the trial and death of Socrates. These were the thirteen years when the pride of the Athenians caused their downfall, when their armies were betrayed by their generals, and their democracy ruined by mob rule and despotism. It was the age of Socrates, but also of Nikias the tyrant, who had been his pupil. There would be enough wrong choices in this story for it to be a lesson to even the most obtuse.

8

The View from the Acropolis

In Mary's first novel about ancient Greece there is a moment where one of her main characters hurries out of the gymnasium to greet a friend, who notices that his 'right shoulder, which one always leaves till last in cleaning off, still had dust and oil on it'.

It is the word 'always', with its total assurance of how things were, which is so utterly convincing. Even her editor, John Guest, tended to refer to her 'psychic vision of life in Ancient Greece', though that was fairly tame beside the claims for reincarnation made by some of her later fans. Actually it was more a question of skill and ingenuity than magic. Chunks of description are traceable to Thucydides, and sections of philosophic talk paraphrase Plato's *Dialogues*, though this hardly explains the rich visual texture, those details of behaviour and dress, that 'always' which makes the text live and for which there is no single traceable origin. When asked how she achieved it, her explanation was refreshingly simple: 'If you look at a collection of Greek vases, you'll find all kind of daily things you wouldn't know about. All the little implements they have hanging up on the walls, or in the gymnasium, or what the women are using, you know in the kitchen. You can even see a sculptor's workshop, and there is a huge statue of Achilles sort of half finished slung up more than life size with all these little people working around it, and you can see potters working. You can get a tremendous amount of background from the art work, and, of course, the spirit of the art work is important too. I mean the difference you find, for instance, between something of the severe classical period and then later on the much more romantic Hellenistic period.'

What Mary needed were the secondary sources, the more anecdotal accounts of the Socratic circle found in Diogenes Laertius,

Macrobius and Atenaeus. Durban's city librarians, unused to such serious research, were scant help and in the end she turned to Blackwell's bookshop in Oxford. Orders were despatched to England, and parcels of archaeological records, works of history, guide books, books on pottery and sculpture, volume upon volume, began to fill her study in Durban. It took two years, from 1952 to 1954, to complete the research. Each morning after Julie had left for the hospital, Mary would wander about the house and garden, book in hand, sitting where fancy took her, dashing off notes to herself, occasionally taking a break to chat with Paul. She was happy; it was what she had always wanted to do. At forty-eight, she was embarked on a new life and it was as if everything which had gone before had been a preparation for it. The English novels seemed no more than apprentice pieces, while all the reading in the classics she had done over the years was at last falling into place.

When she was ready to start writing, Mary confined herself to her study, surfacing for lunch, then immersing herself in the book again until Julie returned and it was time for a beer. Because the novel stuck closely to historical events, she soon had the plot drafted out. It was the painting of individual scenes with the minutiae of Attic life that took a further year, but that gave the book its commanding air of authenticity.

Mary had decided the novel would take the form of a memoir written by Alexias, a fictional Athenian gentleman whose personal story is woven into the historical events that comprise the plot.

The Last of the Wine spans the thirteen years of Alexias's young manhood: he is fifteen years old when the action begins, twenty-eight at its close. He shares his story with the older Lysis, his lover and mentor in the military campaigns which punctuate the story. Lysis is drawn from a single line in Diogenes Laertius's notes, 'By conversing with Sokrates, Lysis became an excellent person', but all else is Mary's invention. And it is this mix of fact and guesswork, based on careful research, which gives the story its plausibility. Keeping Alexias and Lysis at the forefront of the action, Mary bridged the gaps in the historical record while working her 'real' characters – Plato, Socrates, Phaedo, Xenophon – into the narrative, without the false notes which so often reduce historical fiction to low comedy. One day Lysis is admiring a young wrestler, Aristocles, whom he finds 'too square for beauty'. When he next encounters the youth he finds his fellow athletes have nicknamed him 'broad-shouldered' or 'Plato', and the name has stuck.

Mary was unusually sensitive to the mores of the age she was writing about. As she explained in an article she wrote for the *London Magazine* in 1979: 'You cannot step twice into the same river, said Herakleitos [Heraclitus]. People in the past were not just like us; to pretend so is an evasion and a betrayal, turning our back on them so as to be easy among familiar things.' The open nature of Alexias's and Lysis's relationship, the way no one doubts that the flight of a bird is a meaningful portent before a battle or that a man has an unquestioned right to decide whether or not his child shall live, are as important to the validity of the book as the details of a hoplite's armour or the design of a fighting vessel. All such matters were, as her article makes clear, part of a search for truth:

> I have never, for any reason, in any historical book of mine, falsified anything deliberately which I knew or believed to be true. Often of course I must have done through ignorance what would horrify me if I could revisit the past; at the best one is in the position of, say, an Indonesian resident who has never met an Englishman, trying to write a novel set in London from documentary evidence, pictures, and maps. But one can at least desire the truth; and it is inconceivable to me how anyone can decide deliberately to betray it; to alter some fact which was central to the life of a real human being, however long it is since he ceased to live, in order to make a smoother story, or to exploit him as propaganda for some cause.

When we met, I watched Mary correct a film script based on her life of Alexander the Great. The text was clearly a riot of errors and she was not best pleased, explaining that it had been 'written by somebody knowing very little about Greece. You have Aristotle saying to Alexander, don't believe the old stories that glorify humility. Well, no old stories glorify humility; it was the last thing they glorified. They thought humility was mean-spirited and slavish, and the magnanimous man was somebody they approved; he not only knew he was the best, he was the best. I think it is particularly wrong to impose Christianity on the ancient world, otherwise you get a whole lot of characters whose values you have got completely wrong.'

Having swept her mind of contemporary prejudice, Mary's skill lay in transforming her sources into fiction without distorting the spirit of the original. It is fascinating to see how she uses passages from Thucydides's history of the Peloponnesian Wars, drawing out the facts she needs while adding her own characters. Near the opening of *The Last of the Wine* there is a scene where the Athenian fleet sails for Sicily to put down a rebellion in Syracuse, the details for which are taken directly from Thucydides's account of the departure:

When all the equipment was loaded, and the crews were in position, a trumpet blew for silence, and the usual prayers were offered up. A single herald led them, and his words were repeated by all the crews together. Wine was poured into the mixing-bowls, and on each ship officers and crew made libations from gold and silver cups. Everyone on the shore joined in these prayers and offerings, both the actual citizens and any other sympathetic bystanders.

At the end of the ceremony a hymn was sung, and the fleet set sail. They went ahead in line for some way, then broke ranks and raced each other as far as Aigina. From there they made their way to Kerkyra, where the other allied forces were waiting.

In her novel Mary transforms this simple piece of reportage into a glittering farewell to Alkibiades, the city's golden hero, later its villain, whose exploits she will weave through her book. The interpretation is hers, but the visual detail and measured, Attic cadences cleverly echo the original:

The Generals joined their ships, the bustle grew less and ended. A trumpet blew a long call. Then one heard only a dying mutter, the slap of the sea on the jetties, the cry of gulls, and the bark of some dog grown uneasy in the hush. The small clear voice of a distant herald cried the Invocation. It was taken up in the ships and on the shore; the sound flowed and rolled like surf; on each poop gold or silver flashed, as the trierarch lifted his cup to pour the offering. Then ringing across the water came the paean, and the shouts of the pilots, bidding the ships away. The chantymen began to give the time to the rowers; up went the great sails painted with suns and stars and birds. So they put out to sea, the crews answering song for song, and the pilots calling out to each other challenges to race. I saw Nikias' white beard flutter as he prayed with raised hands; and on the poop of Alkibiades' trireme, which already was standing away, a little shining figure like a golden image, no bigger than the Adonis dolls the women had carried in the streets.

The sails filled; the oar-blades all together beat up and down, bright-feathered wings; like swans the ships flew singing towards the islands. Tears stung my eyes. I wept for the beauty of it, like many more. Happy for the Athenians, if the tears that followed afterwards had been like mine.

The tears come when news is brought to the city that their vacillating general, Nikias, has led the army to total defeat. When word of his father's death in the massacre is delivered to Alexias, he is brought abruptly to manhood, responsible for his young stepmother and her newborn daughter, and for the land and slaves that are the family's wealth and status as free citizens of the democracy.

This interlude in the war is the last sunlit day of the Athens of the great philosophers before evening descends. With his childhood friend Xenophon, Alexias becomes a follower of Sokrates, around whom the characters assemble – Phaedo, Plato and Kritias, and the semi-fictional Lysis, who courts the beautiful Alexias, becoming his lover and, as was expected of the elder, his tutor. The nature of their relationship is precisely delineated and contrasted with the 'love of the agora', the lust of the bath-houses, where the enslaved Phaedo had been forced to sell his body, before being bought out at the urging of Sokrates. In their 'good' relationship, Lysis must train his young companion for manhood,

to be honourable in the city's service and brave in battle. One day
Lysis will marry as, later, will Alexias. Love binds them, but its
effects are spiritual rather than sexual; such a friendship, Mary
suggests, is a stage, not an end.

Alexias's struggle lies in resolving his bisexual nature. His
mother died when he was born. He was a sickly child, and he
learns later that his father wanted to expose him and was prevented
from doing so only by a sudden Spartan attack on the city. Thus,
Alexias, like Laurie in *The Charioteer*, is in search of a father
figure and at the same time must reject this in order to grow to
maturity. When his father takes a new child-bride, Alexias
becomes deeply attached to her and, when his father is presumed
dead, he feels that he has become almost her husband. The high
moment in his youth is his victory in the foot race at the Isthmian
Games, but his joy is tarnished when a hulking creature nearly
kills Lysis during a wrestling bout, which Mary uses as a symbol
of decline in the Hellenic ideal: where once a sportsman trained for
physical perfection, for beauty, now they will become anything,
however gross, to win.

All this ends abruptly when Alexias's father, having been
enslaved, not killed, suddenly reappears, an embittered man, who
finds his farmland ravaged by the Spartan siege and his son con-
sorting with those he considers dangerous free-thinkers. He
quickly joins the aristocratic group who blame the mob and thus
the democratic system for everything that has gone wrong. To
escape this poisoned atmosphere, Alexias and Lysis join the
expedition to Samos, where they help the democrats defeat the
oligarchs, and return to Athens only to find that a similar group,
supported by Alexias's father, has taken power there. From this
point on the city will lurch between tyranny and mob rule. A
counter-revolution, led by the moderate Theramenes, is short-
lived when the newly restored democracy again fails to hold back
the Spartans. With weak generals the city cannot hope to resist
the new Spartan leader, Lysander. After the entire fleet is lost
at Aegospotami, Lysander seals off the city and starves it into
submission, imposing the Thirty Tyrants, who reign by terror and
corruption.

Among them is Kritias, once a pupil of Sokrates, who uses the skills in argument he learned from the philosopher to sway his audience. Mary has already linked the historical Kritias with the fictional Alexias in an early scene, where the older man spills wine on the boy's garment in order to fondle him without his father noticing. Kritias's behaviour is contrasted with that of the two lovers playing *kottabos*, tossing the lees of wine to spell out the beloved's initial in the dust. Throughout the book wine is used as an ambiguous symbol, the bringer of release and joy, but also of loss. Kritias is the villain. Not having sought the good in himself, he can bring nothing but harm upon the city when he rules it. His sexual desires are impure, therefore he cannot but be corrupt. That he listened to Sokrates without desiring to follow where he led is the grossest example of his weakness. After Kritias murders Alexias's father, Alexias leaves with Lysis to join the rebellion forming outside the city, and, when the Spartans abandon the tyrants, the democrats return. In the battle for liberation, Alexias kills Kritias in a potter's stall in the market place, amongst empty wine jars and cups. But Lysis is also slain and, when his dead body is brought to Alexias, so much blood has drained from it that his flesh looks like clear yellow marble.

The city is free, but humbled and at the mercy of Sparta. There is democracy once again, but Mary has depicted enough to show that this is not an automatic benefit – if a citizen is not motivated by the good and the beautiful, neither will his city be. The book ends on an image both hopeful and sad: a torchlight race on horseback between the youths of the city, a relay symbolizing the handing on of the sacred fire, a symbol of civilization. As the race is about to begin, the voice of one of the new democratic leaders, Anytos, is heard, railing against Sokrates, whom he is soon to accuse of corrupting youth. As the horses gallop away, there is a last prophetic image of the philosopher, silhouetted against the burning torches, a wine cup in his hand.

*

Historical novelists are often portrayed as insatiable bookworms, utterly obsessed with vacuuming up facts about their chosen period, not altogether sane. Yet in her article for the *London*

Magazine, it was not the collecting or ordering of data that Mary emphasized but the use of language:

> Greek is a highly polysyllabic language. Yet when writing dialogue for my Greeks I have found myself, by instinct, avoiding the polysyllables of the English language, and using, as far as they are still in the living language, the older and shorter words. This is not because the style parallels Greek style; it is entirely a matter of association and ambience. In Greek, polysyllables are old; in English, mostly Latinized and largely modern. They have acquired their own aura, which they will bring along with them. Their stare, like that of the basilisk, is killing. Take the following sentence, which I have just picked at random from a magazine: 'High priority is to be given to training in the skills of community organizing and conflict resolution.' It contains no concept which Plato did not know, or, indeed, did not in fact deal with. But it comes to us steeped in notions of the company report, the social survey, and so forth. When I see writing like this in a historical novel I know what the author is after. He wants us to identify with the situation of his characters as if it were our own. But it isn't, and identification thus achieved is a cheat. You cannot, as an advertising copywriter would say, enjoy a trip to fifth-century Athens, or Minoan Crete, in the comfort of your own home. You have, as far as your mind will take you, to leave home and go to them.

> Does all this really matter? Yes, I think so; and not just aesthetically. Every era of man's development, from the palaeolithic upwards, is still in living existence somewhere on earth. Indeed, the metropolitan technocrats whom self-centred intellectuals glibly call Twentieth-Century Man, are as few today in relation to all humanity, as the spores in a mould-spot on a grape where it has scarcely begun to spread. We live in blindness if we forget that history is not only vertical; it is also horizontal.

> However, one does not go to the past as a public utility. So why? One can say, 'Because it is there.' But unlike Everest, not only is it there, but we are its products. We go, perhaps, to find ourselves; perhaps to free ourselves. It is certain we shall never know ourselves, till we have broken out from the brittle capsule

of Megalopolis, and taken a long look back along the rocky road which brought us where we are.

By early 1954 the novel was at the scribbled-over typescript stage, but Mary hesitated before starting the fair copy. Most of her early books had been set in her much loved Cotswolds, in countryside lived in and walked over, but *The Last of the Wine* not only described scenes and places she had never known but also some that no longer existed and had been imaginatively reconstructed from archaeological evidence:

Our house stood in the Inner Kerameikos, not far from the Dipylon Gate. The courtyard had a little colonnade of painted columns, a fig-tree and a vine. At the back were the stables, where my father kept his two horses and a mule; it was easy to climb on the stable roof, and thence to the roof of the house.

The roof had a border of acanthus tiles, and was not very steep. If one straddled the ridge, one could see right over the City wall, past the gate-towers of the Dipylon to the Sacred Way, where it curves towards Eleusis between its gardens and its tombs. In summer-time, I could pick out the funeral stele of my uncle Alexias and his friend, by a white oleander that grew there. Then I would turn south, to where the High City stands like a great stone altar against the sky, and search between the winged roofs of the temples for the point of gold, where tall Athene of the Vanguard lifts her spear to the ships at sea.

The hours of work involved in calculating that deceptively simple 360 degree vista in seven sentences is awe-inspiring, but worrisome for the author. Mary had long since decided that, when the book was sufficiently advanced, she and Julie would make their first visit to Greece. She had been planning the journey throughout 1953 and had decided to visit Italy first. To see everything she needed would take four months. Mrs Messina was placed in a nursing home and the house let to an English couple who would take care of the dogs. They left at the end of March 1954 aboard the Italian liner ss *Africa*, which called in at many of the ports they had seen on their original voyage out six years earlier.

They ate at a table with four other women, two British and two Australian, younger than they but, as Julie recalls, great fun: 'Lots of screaming with laughter and everyone else very envious.' They called in at Zanzibar, which, in those pre-revolution days, Mary thought was 'pure Arabian Nights', though the Red Sea was even more unbearably hot than she remembered – the Italian purser dropped dead from heat stroke and made the remainder of the journey to Trieste in the fridge.

They disembarked at Venice, staying in a modest hotel behind St Mark's before travelling by train to Florence, where they spent six days in a palazzo with a painted ceiling and delicious food, and walked the banks of the Arno, staring into the jewellers' windows, hating the noise of the traffic and the crowds.

In Rome they were booked into the Hotel Inghilterra, then a cheap boarding house close to the Spanish Steps. They breakfasted every morning in the El Greco near Keats's lodgings, before marathons of walking, interspersed with long sessions sitting in the Forum.

The old train which took them to Brindisi rattled into the station at nine in the evening. There was no one to help and they lugged their own suitcases over to the Hotel Jolly. By the time they had washed and changed, it was a little late, but they were surprised to find the huge dining room completely empty, and even more surprised to be told that there was no service on Friday nights as they were 'Jolly Nights'. This appeared to mean some sort of dance, but they were tired and unwilling to walk round a strange town looking for a restaurant late in the evening so they insisted on being served. As they waited, groups of men, some rather flamboyantly dressed, began to arrive. The music struck up, and one or two took to the floor to dance together. Mary and Julie looked around; they were the only women there.

They left for Greece the next day. Although Mary had insisted that the travel agents book them a cabin from which they could watch the arrival at Piraeus, there had been a mix-up and they were told they would have to take two single first-class cabins. Nevertheless, it was what Mary had most longed to see and, after steaming through the Corinth Canal, there it was, exciting despite its ramshackle air. They were arriving in pre-tourist Greece, which was still reeling from its catastrophic civil war. Immigration control consisted of a hut on the harbour where two men stared at their unfamiliar passports. Outside, they had to pick their way through the fish sellers on the quay until they saw an ancient cab and could begin the slow process of explaining their destination. They were driven over bumpy roads, more pothole than tarmac, passing several overturned buses, until they entered the city. Their driver deposited them at a handsome three-storey house, where their host, Mr Pakis, welcomed them with almost excessive warmth, showing them a room with a balcony giving an uninterrupted view of the Acropolis. It was everything Mary had expected and more. The air was deliciously clean, bright and sharp. There were almost no cars and little rubbish in the streets since no one had anything to throw away except countless cigarette ends. The house had a large dining room, with a large, polished table, where they had breakfast and dinner with the other guests. Mr Pakis sat at the top and Mrs Pakis could be glimpsed in the kitchen as the fifteen-year-old serving girl came in and out with trays of food.

Mary was determined to see everything. They had arrived on a Saturday, and the following morning Mr Pakis invited them to join him on a trip to his family's village. They took a bus packed with peasants with enormous bundles who were shamelessly interested in them. When they arrived, they were taken to visit Mr Pakis's friend the mayor, who was sitting with his wife on kitchen chairs outside in the garden, but who immediately insisted that the foreign visitors come into the best parlour; like every room in Greece, this had a bed in it as if, in Mary's words, 'Odysseus might return at any moment'. This courteous reception seemed close to the manners of ancient Greece. In spite of the obvious poverty, they were offered the traditional spoonful of rice and raisins, and everyone made great efforts to converse despite their limited vocabulary. The bus back was again packed and just as friendly.

The following week they climbed the Attic hills. While they were standing on Mount Parnes looking down at Eleusis, a black cloud suddenly passed over the ground below, a sinister effect Mary recalled later as the moment when she knew how people could believe that the god Pan caused herds to run about in terror in a lonely place.

However, it was when she stood on the Acropolis, peering towards Piraeus, that she realized her one error. She had written of Alexias staring at the ships in the harbour when, in fact, it was hidden by the curve of the land. Extraordinary as it seems, this solitary lapse was her only 'mistake'. More often, she discovered something new to work in. While on the Acropolis she sat close to the shrine of Asklepias and began to draft the scene in which Alexias is ordered by the priest to run down to the Agora and back to see whether he should compete at Olympia. It is a key moment, one in which the young man must learn to accept the limits of ambition, for the final judgement is that, by running, he risks death from a weak heart, and there is little doubt that had Mary not been there, looking down from the high city to the Agora and the modern town below, she would not have seen so graphic a way of conveying it.

Over the following weeks it was less a matter of checking or adding to *The Last of the Wine* than of storing material for future books. At the time, the only convenient way to see the islands was an official Government tour, which rushed past Poros and Mykonos, stopped briefly in Crete, then hurried back via Santorini. The first part of the trip yielded little, and it was only on the day-trip from Mykonos to neighbouring Delos that Mary had reason to take out her notebook. The tiny island was an entire archaeological site with three temples dedicated to Apollo, whose childhood home it was said to have been.

Crete was impossibly brief. The boat docked at Heraklion for one day only, just time to hurry by taxi to Knossos, but Mary knew she was in for an extraordinary experience, one for which she had been preparing herself since her days at St Hugh's. To step into Sir Arthur Evans's dramatic reconstruction of the House of the Axe was bound to be an important moment, though she could not have foretold just how deeply moving it would turn out to be. Evans's brightly coloured restoration has many critics, but Mary Renault was not among them. While Evans may have leant towards the Art Deco taste of his day, there was nothing in her experience to match the sensation she felt as she wandered through the top-lit inner chambers, down the painted stairwells, through the Queen's Megaron, the King's Megaron, the Halls of the Double Axes, and the Colonnades to that dark chamber where Minos's scallop-backed throne waits, guarded by its gryphon frescoes.

It is clear from what she wrote later that it was here she decided that her experience must be put into words:

Picture to yourself all the king's palaces you ever saw, set side by side and piled on one another. That will be a little house, beside the House of the Axe. It was a palace within whose bounds you could have set a town. It crowned the ridge and clung to its downward slopes, terrace after terrace, tier after tier of painted columns, deep glowing red, tapering in towards the base, and ringed at head and foot with that dark brilliant blue the Cretans love. Behind them in the noonday shadow were porticoes and balconies gay with pictured walls, which glowed in the shade like beds of flowers. The tops of tall cypresses hardly showed above the roofs of the courts they grew in. Over the highest roof-edge, sharp-cut against the deep blue Cretan sky, a mighty pair of horns reared towards heaven.

The sight winded me like a blow in the belly. I had heard travellers' tales third-hand, but pictured them in the likeness of what I knew. I felt like a goat-herd who comes in from the back hills and sees his first city.

As if all that were not enough, she was about to experience one of the coincidences that made people think she had some form of supernatural link with Greece. Mary and Julie had returned to the town with scarcely sufficient time to visit the recently opened museum and, as they hurried in, they saw a group of workmen setting up a newly restored mural taken from the palace. To Mary's utter amazement, it was the original of the Bull-leaper which she had discovered all those years ago in the Ashmolean, the single most famous image from Minoan art. The frozen beauty of the slim-waisted Cretan youth, barely touching the tips of the great curved horns at the peak of his elegant somersault, brought vividly to life, as nothing else could, all that she had seen that day:

He ran smoothly up to the sullen bull. It was the leap I had seen often in the Bull Court. But that was a shadow; now, he had a living thing to dance with. He grasped the horns, and swung up between them, going with the bull; then he soared free. The beast was too stupid to back and wait for him. It trotted on, when it felt him gone. He turned in air, a curve as lovely as a bent bow's, and on the broad back his slim feet touched down together; then they sprang up again. He seemed not to leap, but to hang above the bull, like a dragon-fly over the reeds, while it ran out from under him. Then he came down to earth, feet still together, and lightly touched the catcher's hands with his, like a civility; he had no need of steadying. Then he danced away. There was a joyous screaming and cooing from the bird-trees, and shouts from the men. As for me, I stretched in secret my right hand earthwards, and whispered under all the noise, 'Father Poseidon! Make me a bull-leaper!'

If ever a book insisted on being written, it was *The King Must Die*, much of which was dreamed up as Mary wandered around Knossos and let her mind journey with Theseus to Crete and back. Theseus, the king's son, who offers himself as part of the Athenian tribute to Minos, slays the Minotaur, half-man, half-bull, dwelling in the labyrinth below the palace. In 1964 Mary would write a new introduction to Charles Kingsley's *Theseus: A Greek Legend Retold* in which she sets out her own view of the myth: 'Kingsley called it a fairy-tale. So it may be. But in our day, things have come to light that he did not know, and I would rather call it a legend, a marvellous rumour which grew up about something real.' She went on to explain how scholars now knew that the word 'labyrinth' in old Cretan meant 'the Palace of the Axe', while 'Minotaur', in Greek, was 'Bull of Minos'. Assuming that the old tales had been embellished by wandering bards, it was not hard to see how the story of the half-man, half-bull had been based on a real figure wearing an animal head, as the earliest priests had done during sacrificial rites. She had seen for herself that the labyrinth *was* the palace, as the word implied. She had experienced the uncanny *frisson* of stepping down those gloomy stairs, into the darkened throne-room where Minos would have sat, terrifying in his bull mask. It was reasonable to assume that the Athenian youths were not taken to Crete as human sacrifice but as slaves to be trained for the bull court – a religious rite and a sacrifice only if the bull-leaper fell and was gored to death by the sacred beast.

*

The boat left with Mary still lost in spirit in Minos's labyrinth. When they docked at Santorini, she refused to go ashore for fear of breaking the spell, preferring to remain aboard and gather her memories of Knossos. Julie waited with her. They could see from the deck how beautiful Santorini was with its donkeys and pretty churches, but they had no wish to diminish the power of the House of the Axe with lesser sights.

They arrived back in Athens to find Mr Pakis in a disagreeable mood. A letter for Mary *Renault* was waiting on the hall table, but, when Mary claimed it, Mr Pakis was not pleased. She had registered as Mary *Challans*, and he immediately assumed that she had been deceiving him. He had not kept their room for them as they had arranged. They tried to explain to him about writers and pen-names, but even when he eventually calmed down, he would only let them have a bed in the scullery. It hardly mattered; they were planning to set off on their travels again.

They sailed for Samos one late afternoon, pulling into Karlovassi at seven the following morning. The town looked new and uninteresting, so they hired an ancient taxi to take them over the mountain to Samos town. Their driver took the hairpin bends at terrifying speed, but delivered them safely to the only decent hotel, where the owner was so overwhelmed by the arrival of two English ladies that he offered them his own room. This was reached by a ladder to a landing with three doors and a communal tin bowl with a tap above it. A policeman had one of the other rooms, though theirs was clearly the best, with an enormous double bed and gaily painted Easter eggs still arranged on the heavy, polished dressing-table.

The first night they set off to find a taverna their driver had recommended because its food was good and its owners spoke a little English. The scenery on the way was almost as Mary described it in *The Last of the Wine*:

> After killing time in a small colonial town, it was good to see the great city of Samos glowing between hills and blue water, into which the town thrust outward like a spur, with the harbour in the curve of it. Westward on the strand was the Temple of Here, the biggest of all Hellas. Eastward, the barley-terraces fell like a broad stairway to the sea. Across the strait, quite near, stood up the lofty coast of Ionia, violet-coloured, just as it is named.

They found the taverna because the owner was standing in the street, looking out for them. His restaurant doubled as a barber's shop, but the food was as tasty as the driver had promised – freshly caught fish, lightly grilled and soaked in lemon. They ate there every evening, and the owner would invite the island's various notables to come and watch them – the chief of police, the head of the fire brigade, the doctor. There is a photograph, taken by Julie, of Mary sitting outside, surrounded by a large group of men, clearly happy to be so completely accepted, talking 'like one of the boys'. As they chatted, tidbits would appear from the kitchen and more Samian wine would be poured. When they finally left, some of the men escorted them home. The most amusing evening was when one of the men revealed that their wives were afraid the two foreign ladies might decide to go bathing; they had heard about swimsuits and did not approve. Mary was happy to reassure them that there were no plans to indulge in this worrisome practice.

Water was, however, much on their minds. After several days of splashing it out of a tin can, they felt the need of a bath. There were rumours of a four-star hotel on the other side of the island, and so they set off early one morning by bus. There had been no time for breakfast, but all their drinking friends came to say goodbye, insisting they join them in a last glass of Samian wine. It was light and delicious, but was poured in such great quantities that the two women were tipsy in a flash. As the bus pulled away, everyone was giggling and laughing, which was just as well: the island had two buses and they had caught the new one, which lurched over the narrow mountain tracks at a terrifying rate, at one point narrowly missing the old bus coming in the opposite direction.

When they finally reached the town, the luxury hotel turned out to be just another taverna with a barber's shop and a guest-house, but it did have a bath, which, as their host explained, no one had ever asked to use before. They quickly saw why – an enormous wood-burning stove had to be lit to heat up the boiler, but they refused to be cowed and insisted on seeing it done, until, amidst clouds of glorious steam, they had the only bath of their entire time in Greece.

When they had dried off, they went for a walk in the surrounding hills. The path went up and up, and gradually they began to feel that they were being followed. They turned to see a crowd of ragged, sullen urchins. They hurried on, hoping to lose them, but, when they turned again, they were shocked to find that this time there were adults in the group, too, gypsy figures with scowling faces. There was an indefinable air of menace about this silent, tightly packed group. They seemed to Mary like ancient, near-savage creatures, living half-wild on the mountainside. She could imagine the superstitious tribe that had once lived there, its wild womenfolk scurrying through the undergrowth during the earliest Dionysian rites. Without a word she and Julie turned back, pushing a way through the barely moving group, and hurried down the slope, trying not to look back.

There were three more trips: Olympia, where they sat in the ruins of the great stadium sharing Easter eggs with a local family having a picnic; Marathon, where the swoop of mountain to sea reminded them of their lingering desire to live at the Cape; and finally Corfu, where Julie came down with typhoid despite all the injections she had had. The doctor advised Mary to nurse her, even when he was shown the hotel's filthy toilet with its 'mushy' floorboards.

'Hospital is worse,' he said and prescribed chloromycetin, then the newest and best antibiotic, though, at £5 a bottle, cripplingly expensive.

The room was hot and full of flies, there was no hot water, and from the square below rose the incessant blare of an amateur brass band as a group of cadets rehearsed for Liberation Day. When this dawned, the streets were loud with the shouts for *ennosis*, the union of Cyprus with Greece.

Julie was mildly delirious for three days, with Mary bathing her to keep down her temperature, taking great care lest any movement prove too much for her heart. She could eat only packaged soups and was very weak by the time they were due to leave. The departure was a nightmare. First they took a taxi to the harbour, then they were rowed out in a small boat to the ship that would take them to Brindisi, another night in the Hotel Jolly, then finally on to the liner for Durban, with Julie giggling deliriously the while. Thankfully, they had time at sea for Julie to recover and for Mary to reflect on all she had seen. Her one regret was that she had not been able to say goodbye to Mr Pakis, who, for all his occasional bad temper, remained something of a symbol of their time in Greece, at once emotional, hospitable and passionate.

9

The Labyrinth

Having been given no warning that Mary was writing a historical novel, Longmans was thrown into confusion when the manuscript arrived. Like all publishers, they were keen to build a certain reputation for their authors and, while *The Charioteer* had been a jolt, it could still be passed off as another of her hospital novels. The new book offered no such escape clause, and from the moment it arrived, the publishers had the deepest misgivings about its suitability for a public totally unprepared for such a radical change of direction by an author they had assumed was neatly pigeon-holed.

Mark Longman's first reaction was based entirely on commercial considerations. For him the novel was simply too long. Whatever its literary qualities, and he does not appear to have been much concerned with them, at 160,000 words the book would have to be priced at a guinea (£1 1s 0d in the pre-decimal currency, and certainly a considerable price for a novel at that time). Out went the order – the manuscript was to be hacked back to 120,000 words. John Guest was given the disagreeable task of conveying this news to the author, though he attempted to mask the cuts as necessary editorial pruning, a deceit still painful to Mary when she recounted it many years later: 'I got a demand from Longmans to cut one third of the book. This really shocked me. I knew it was the best thing I had ever done (it probably still is). I knew it didn't need that amount of cutting. When I first started writing I was very wordy. But I'd learned by that time how to prune, and been all over it before I sent it in. I could tell in my bones this demand was purely economic. I refused to do more than about an eighth. Even that was too much. I have got a file to this day of the cut bits; sometimes I read them over, and I still feel bitter.

Nearly all the stuff that came out should have stayed in. There was a whole lot about the Greek navy at Samos, and Alkibiades. In the original version, Lysis and Alexias were both in the battle of Notium (Cape Rain). I cut all that and just had them hearing the news. I cut all about the fall of Euboea and Lysis losing his family estates. There was no sense in cutting any of this, it just saved bloody Longmans some bloody paper. If I had stuck it out, I think they would have put up with it, and I always wished I had.'

What restrained her was the memory of how the now-retired Robert Longman had always gently rebuked her for being prolix, and how she had never doubted that he had been right in persuading her to make radical cuts in *Purposes of Love*. With this in mind, she wavered, made the changes and lived to regret it. In 1968, having received a particularly sympathetic fan letter from M. Simister in Birmingham, England, she sent her the excised pages in the hope that one reader at least would know what she had really intended.

Mary never quite forgave Longmans – they even tried to charge her a £10 'author's corrections' fee – and her shock and anger were exacerbated by having to waste time on the changes when she could have been marshalling her ideas for the Theseus story. She had already begun with the bare outline, from Plutarch's *Life of Theseus*, which recounts the popular version of the legendary boy, raised by his mother in Troizen in the Peloponnese, who proves himself the son of Aigeus, King of Athens, by lifting a heavy stone under which his father had left his sword. After many adventures, Theseus arrives at his father's palace, where he bravely volunteers to join the tribute of Athenian youth sent to Crete at the behest of King Minos to be sacrificed to his monstrous son, the Minotaur, half-man, half-bull, who lives in the unfathomable labyrinth built by Daedalos below the palace in Knossos. Helped by Minos's daughter Ariadne, Theseus slays the Minotaur and sails for home, forgetting to raise the white sail, which is the agreed signal to his father of his safe return. Assuming that Theseus is dead, Aigeus throws himself into the sea now named after him, whereupon his son becomes king in his stead.

175

With the unwelcome corrections to *The Last of the Wine* out of the way, Mary was looking forward to fleshing out her new project, but, just as she was beginning her research, in late 1955 she received a letter from Joyce in England telling her of their mother's declining health. Clementine had arthritis and was in considerable pain.

She and Joyce were living in Newton Abbot, where Joyce was a sister at the local hospital. To Mary, this was a spectre of life as it might have been. Joyce had charge of a ward for geriatric women and the fact that she seemed to enjoy her work only made it harder for Mary to bear. Reading her sister's letters was a form of punishment. It appeared that Clementine was spending more and more time in bed, and it was all too easy for Mary to visualize what this meant for Joyce, forced to wait on her hand and foot after an exhausting day with her senile patients.

Clementine refused to be hospitalized and Joyce could not give up work to devote herself to her mother, though undoubtedly Clementine resented her failure to be there when required. Early in 1956 Mary received a sharp note from her mother, telling her formally that she would be receiving nothing in her will. Even bedridden, Clementine was capable of twisting the knife, of making it quite clear that her daughter had failed her and must be punished, even when the blow was meaningless.

Her mother had long succeeded in inspiring in Mary a revulsion towards any form of conventional female life. This was now moving towards a thorough-going aversion to femininity itself. When an American correspondent suggested that she, like him, must be attracted to the female form, he was quickly disabused:

So you really think most women are beautiful? That must be nice. I wish I did. Sometimes I look round a lot of housewives shopping, or business men's wives stuck at some awful party when the men go off talking shop and leave them to go on about knitting or servants or something (one does inadvertently get let in for some like that, though of course, if I am, I never go there again) and I have a terribly sad feeling like looking at a lot of animals that have moulted and got silly from being kept in a cage.

All Mary's books deal harshly with mothers. The later ones extend this to women in general, but the book on Theseus which she was planning would make this one of its principal themes. Her chosen sources for the novel show a marked preference for theories of prehistoric matriarchy, which many scholars nowadays believe to be suspect. Chadwick's *The Earliest Greeks* had already provoked in Mary a near-obsession with the Greek Bronze Age, but it was Frazer of *The Golden Bough* and Robert Graves's *The Greek Myths* that led her into the realm of the 'mother-goddess' and the often contentious theories of kingship and worship that divide academic debate over the roots of Mycenaean culture.

Those who follow this line take as their starting point the Hellene belief that when their ancestors swept into the Greek peninsula from the wild grasslands to the north, they brought with them the sky worship of Zeus, displacing the earth worship of the mother-goddess practised by the coastal people they conquered. By calling her book *The King Must Die*, Mary highlights the key struggle at the heart of the book: the replacement of the matriarchal system under which the reigning queen chose a new king each year, sacrificing him after his year of glory in a ritual intended to ensure the cycle of death and rebirth of the crops.

She could not have chosen a better moment to embark on such a subject. The recent discovery of the Mycenaean royal tombs had revealed a startling difference between the rougher mainland culture and the more effete society on Crete. The archaeological reports were described by Mary in the article she wrote for the *London Magazine* in 1979, which still conveys the excitement she felt when first reading of them:

Here with their skeleton hands still folded over their long gold-pommelled swords lay the tall princes whose descendants took Troy; beside their domed tombs had stood the great stone walls of their fortress-palaces, the gates with their huge lintels, lifted no one knows how, and their lion-carved capstones. The written tablets shadowed a warlike society, well organized, aristocratic and art-loving, but primitive and barbaric by the standards of Crete's millennial sophistication.

But as her visual image of Mycenaean society developed, so too did her dissatisfaction with her portrayal of Theseus himself. She had already written several chapters depicting him in the Homeric image of the larger-than-life warrior of the *tholos* tombs.

> Somehow, I couldn't tell how or why, I found the story resisting me. Something was dragging, something stuck. I went on, with an increasing instinct that I was going to fetch up against some block or other which would refuse to be side-stepped and would make me a lot of work. I was, and it did. I had already accepted fully the view now held by most scholars that the tribute of youths and maids from Athens, prey of the Minotaur (which just means 'Bull of Minos'), the doomed company which Theseus joined as a volunteer, must in fact have been conscripts for the bull game, whose astonishing athletics are so dominant a theme of Minoan art. Two discrepant images had thus been wrestling in my subconscious imagination. Among these light, slender, wiry young acrobats, who possessed the only possible physique for the bull dance, what on earth was this six-foot-three warrior doing?

It was her memories of the slim, wiry Bull-leaper which enabled Mary to liberate herself from the dilemma. The Theseus legend claims that he was the inventor of wrestling. As Mary realized, this was something only a short man would have needed to do. Theseus the giant was obviously a product of later legend. For Mary, he would be of slight build with lightning reflexes:

> Obviously, there was now no alternative but to rewrite from the beginning. But from this decision on, I started to enjoy myself. Nothing is more exciting, when one explores the past, than the sense of having, perhaps, found a new lead into truth. Someday, no doubt, new documents will be deciphered, which will restore the lost history of the Helladic age, and some or all

of my guesses will be disproved. Never mind; it is better for us all, including me, that more truth be known.

Thus Theseus, in Mary's version of the story, while bound for Athens, passes through Eleusis where he is forced to wrestle the year-King to his death and marry the Queen:

I put my knee in his backbone. Keeping him pinned, for he was not a man to give an inch to, I hooked my arm round his head, and pulled it back till I felt the neckbone straining. Then I said softly in his ear – for it did not concern the people about us, who had given nothing to the sacrifice – 'Shall it be now?' He whispered, 'Yes.' I said, 'Discharge me of it, then, to the gods below.' He said, 'Be free of it,' with some invocation after. It was in his own tongue, but I trusted him. I jerked his head back hard and fast, and heard the snap of the neckbone. When I looked, it seemed his eyes still had a spark of life; but when I turned his head sideways it was gone.

I got to my feet, and heard from the people a deep sighing, as if they had all just finished the act of love. 'So it begins,' I said to myself; 'and only a god can see the ending.'

They had brought a bier, and laid the King on it. There was a high scream from the throne. The Queen rushed down and threw herself on the corpse, rending her hair and clawing her face and bosom. She looked just like a woman who has lost her dear lord, the man who led her a maiden from her father's house; as if there were young children and no kin to help them. That was how she wept, so that I stared amazed. But now all the other women were crying and howling too, and I understood it was the custom.

They went off wailing, appeasing the new-made ghost. Left alone among staring strangers, I wanted to ask, 'What now?' But the only man I knew was dead.

Presently came an old priestess and led me towards the sanctuary-house. She told me they would mourn the King till sundown; then I should be blood-cleansed, and wed the Queen.

In Mary's version, Theseus refuses to accept his role as king in name only. At the end of his year he kills the Queen's brother and leaves for Athens, where his struggle with the sorceress Medea, who dominates his father's court, continues his purge of the old ways. When he volunteers to go with the Athenian tribute to Crete, Theseus offers himself up to the old religion by becoming a performer in the bull court, whose rites were dedicated to the mother-goddess, with Ariadne transformed by Mary into her priestess.

This second, Cretan section of the book transmits all the excitement Mary felt when she visited Knossos. The chapters set in the House of the Axe, in the bull court and in the training room where the Cranes, Theseus's bull-leaping team, practise on the mechanical bull invented by Daedalus, architect of the laby-rinth, are all rich with the detailed research she had been doing since her return home and are some of her finest descriptive writing:

I went down the steps, and heard the trap close softly. Around me every way stretched the vaults of the Labyrinth; long pillared passages lined with bins, or shelves for jars and boxes; crooked nooks full of clay-sealed vases with painted sides; tunnels with bays set back for casks and chests; a maze of dim caves, stop-pered with darkness. A great grey cat leaped past me, something fell clattering, and a rat gave its furious death-squeal.

I went round the grain-jars, of which each could have held two men standing, and found the pillar. It had a ledge with a little lamp, a twist of wick in a scoop of clay. Joined to the dressed stone was an offering-bowl, smelling of old blood. Black stains with feathers stuck in them ran down to the floor and a shallow drain. It was one of those master-pillars of the house, at which the Cretans offer sacrifice, to strengthen them when the Earth Bull shakes the ground.

The thin cord round it had been tied there lately, for it was clean of blood. When I picked up the slack from the pavement, a house-snake went whipping into its pierced clay pot, not a yard from my hand. I started back with gooseflesh on my arms; but I had the cord, and followed it.

It led winding through dark narrow store-rooms, smelling of

wine and oil, of figs and spices. Every so often, at a turn, there would hang on the black dark a little seed of light, from such a lamp as the first, beckoning the way rather than showing it. As I groped round a pillar, a strange harsh cry, low down, made my hair rise. In the moist floor an old well smelled dankly; a great frog sat on its coping, pale as a corpse. Then the way narrowed, and either side I touched rough stone walls, where creeping things scurried from my fingers. And as I paused, I heard from within the wall a muffled beating, uneven like a heart in terror; when I laid my ear upon the stone, faint and deep a voice was cursing and shouting, calling for light, and upon the gods. But only a few feet on I could hear it no more; the prison must have been a good way off.

Thus Theseus descends into the labyrinth for a secret tryst with Ariadne, priestess of the mother-goddess, at which point Mary forces the legend into her own framework. By carrying off Ariadne, after his revolt against her brother, Theseus shatters the old religion on the island. When he abandons Ariadne on the island of Naxos, Mary explains this away by having Ariadne revert to her former faith, joining the Bacchae on their night of bloodlust.

After a while I reached out, and touched her shoulder where her torn bodice bared it. She sighed, and murmured something I could not hear, and her eyelids fluttered. She stretched out her hand.

It had lain closed on her breast, like a child's who has taken her toy to bed with her. Now when she tried to spread it out, the blood on it had stuck between the fingers, and she could not part them. But she opened her palm, and then I saw what she was holding.

Leaving Ariadne on Naxos, Theseus continues to Athens, where, according to Mary, his deliberate refusal to raise the white sail causes Aigeus's death. The old King had allowed himself to be dominated by the old religion; his son must sweep away the women's mysteries and usher in the golden age of Athenian enlightenment in a male-dominated city.

*

While Mary was working on the novel, she let Cedric deflect her once more into writing another radio play. *The Day of Good Hope* is a ninety-minute piece dramatizing the voyage of the Portuguese explorer Bartolomeu Dias, the first white man to land on the southern tip of Africa. To Mary the event was especially poignant, for, when Dias encountered his first Hottentot, he killed him. But one suspects the true reason for Mary plunging into the task was the pleasure of production: the evening rehearsals, the parties back at the hotel, the gossip and the jokes. It was to be her last play for Cedric, who had been offered a permanent job with the BBC and was about to leave South Africa for good. Before his departure, he invited Mary and Julie to a party he was giving for some dancers who were visiting Durban with the Sadler's Wells Ballet, among them the young dancer David Poole, who was performing in *Blood Wedding* and *Pineapple Poll*. Poole was South African and, as a Coloured child in Cape Town, he was not destined to be a dancer. He was eighteen before he saw his first ballet, but the experience so fired him that he presented himself at the Cape Town Ballet School, where Dulcie Howes immediately cast him as Kostchei in *Russian Tale*, her version of Stravinsky's *Firebird*. After the war, Poole left for England and leading roles at Sadler's Wells, where his fellow South African, John Cranko, choreographed some of his best ballets around him. Too old to expect to be a strong classical soloist, Poole concentrated on his considerable acting skills and became an important choreographer and director. But, in 1954, it was his background as much as his undoubted talents that the two women found so moving.

They had been greatly disturbed by recent legislation aimed at disenfranchising the Coloured population. The suppression of their voting rights and the moves to separate them from White society seemed utterly preposterous, a clear misuse of Parliament. Here, at last, was a clear-cut issue, and when in May 1956 the Women's Defence of the Constitution League was formed, Mary was among the first to join. The movement became popularly known as Black Sash from the shoulder-band worn by its members as they picketed public places, or doggedly haunted cabinet ministers, standing silently outside Government buildings with their placards, or handing out leaflets. The League's first actions were intended to highlight the extreme measures being enacted by the new Strijdom Government, which was forcing through the Coloured Vote Bill by packing an enlarged Appeal Court with sympathetic judges to resist any constitutional moves that might block its wishes. There is a photograph from the *Natal Daily News* of 13 February 1956 of Mary draped in her sash, handing out leaflets on a street corner. She dutifully attended meetings and protests, though her every instinct revolted against such an all-female organization. The women gathered at one of their members' homes, where a black maid served a sumptuous tea while the members discussed their next moves. They finished about noon and returned to their homes, where their maids had already prepared lunch. Mary found all of this faintly ludicrous, but, as it was the only protest movement open to White women, she made the best of it.

✻

At last there was cheering news from America. Naomi Burton wrote to say that Pantheon, a new publishing house, was very keen to have *The Last of the Wine*. Had Mary known just how small Pantheon then was, she might have hesitated – but she would have been wrong to do so. Its distinguished co-founders, Kurt and Helen Wolff, combined experience and freshness in ways that would enable them to launch Mary with more *élan* than a more staid publishing house might have shown. With Morrow's refusal to publish *The Charioteer*, Mary had not been heard of in the United States since *North Face* in 1948, and there was no eager public awaiting her latest book. It was fortuitous, therefore, that when John Guest told Helen Wolff about *The Last of the Wine*, she reacted decisively. Her husband Kurt had been a leading figure in pre-war German publishing and numbered Kafka among his authors. Forced to flee to America, the Wolffs had founded Pantheon and were adding names like Italo Calvino, Georges Simenon and Günter Grass to a list that would become one of the most impressive in American publishing. When Helen decided she wanted Mary's book, the company was uniquely placed to promote it. They had just had their first major financial success with Anne Morrow Lindbergh's *Gift from the Sea*. As Helen Wolff

183

describes it, Pantheon was 'a shoestring enterprise' which suddenly had cash 'pouring in', so that they were able to advertise *The Last of the Wine* 'in a way out of all proportion to the advance sales, which were a meagre 3,000'.

More important than money, however, was the Wolffs' decision to emphasize the novel's serious historical and literary qualities in all their promotional material, rather than playing up the thrilling adventure aspects as Longman was doing in Britain. This was to have a profound affect on American reactions to Mary's work.

Longmans published *The Last of the Wine* on 4 June 1956, and reviews and letters show that many readers considered it a sequel to *The Charioteer* as a study in homosexual love. The novelist Simon Raven wrote of the 'moving celebration of the Attic virtues', and William Golding hoped she would allow 'a thoroughly heterosexual male to put on record that you have made him understand how fruitful and beautiful such love could be'.

Following publication, Mary's correspondence was dominated by letters from men, thanking her for explaining their own feelings to them:

Some years ago after a major illness I was sent to a children's home in South Devon. Such a place for a withdrawn and isolated lad of just fifteen could have been hell but luckily I was befriended by a fourteen-year-old boy who gently taught me how to cope. Our relationship was both intense and beautiful but for a while restricted by the feeling that we were somehow unusual. Then one day while wandering round a second hand book stall in a Plymouth market we came across a copy of *The Last of the Wine* price 3d. I bought it thinking it would be a good read of battles and glory but found instead a sensitive study of the sort of love we were beginning to experience. From it we learned that we were not the only kids in the world to feel this way and from then on accepted the emotions that we had for what they were. For eighteen months we knew a very special joy and shared the dream of being ratings together in the Royal Navy. My friend left and became a boy seaman while I became Head Boy of the home and went on at school to do 'A' Levels (the medical authorities said No Navy) but later I managed to serve at sea with the R.N.R. We became separated by circumstances and have our own family commitments – but are still very close (I'm godfather to his daughter). Thanks to you we both share something which might otherwise have passed us by – an adolescent love without chains.

As a result of the Wolffs' advertising campaign following Pantheon's publication on 15 October 1956, the critical emphasis was quite different in America. The book was given handsome, individual review space, often with a prominent photograph. The most notable success was with *The New York Times*, whose Book Review section on Sunday, 16 October had a substantial review by Edmund Fuller, along with a three-quarter-page advertisement from Pantheon containing selected quotes from the British reviews. Fuller's piece was enthusiastic, but was exceeded the following Wednesday, when the daily edition of the paper devoted its 'Book of the Times' column to *The Last of the Wine* with a review by Orville Prescott which stood alone in showing a clear understanding of what had prompted Mary to write the book in the first place. Prescott was the first to highlight the fact that Mary lived in South Africa and that her novel, while set in ancient Greece, had a great deal to say about her adopted country:

Too close to the events in which he played a part to see all their significance, Alexias was unaware of many matters that disturb a modern mind. The parallels between his age and ours are deadly – wars and the loss of liberty, political passions and the terrors of dictatorships, atrocities and retaliations. Miss Renault does not overemphasize these similarities, but they are there and they are disturbing.

By an extraordinary coincidence the *New York Times Book Review* had also carried a critique of James Baldwin's *Giovanni's Room*, which many critics now rate along with Mary's *The Charioteer* as one of the four or five key books on homosexuality published in English this century. Both Baldwin's and Mary's reviews emphasized the blend of subtlety and candour with which the still 'delicate' material was handled.

There was soon a homosexual following for *The Last of the Wine* in America, as there was in Britain, but the Wolffs' greater emphasis on Mary's scholarship also won her another audience, as her American correspondence makes clear. An associate professor at Adelphi College, New York, wrote to ask her advice on Greek costume, and an art historian in California, who had been advised to read the book by a curator at the National Gallery in Washington, wrote to say that he had left instructions in his will that he was to be buried with a copy of *The Last of the Wine* in his coffin.

In January 1958 Mary received a letter from an American author, Jay Williams, praising *The Last of the Wine* in terms that showed a much deeper understanding than usual. Williams, who was forty-four and married with two children, was a budding historical novelist, though he earned his living then as a writer of children's stories. He would eventually publish over sixty books, but, before he joined the army in 1941, he had been an actor, which was bound to appeal to Mary. Williams enclosed an article he had written for the *American Scholar*, entitled 'History and Historical Novels', which defended the genre against the charge of triviality often made by academic historians, arguing that imaginative reconstruction, if based on thorough research, can usefully flesh out areas closed to scholarship. Mary replied enthusiastically and a twenty-year correspondence was under way, Williams becoming the only person, apart from Julie, to whom Mary spoke freely about the craft of writing. They never met, but, as they passed from Miss Challans and Mr Williams to Mary and Jay, they settled down to an exchange of books and a quiet intimacy which bolstered the confidence of each when writing became difficult or critics irritating. She liked his novels and was relieved to find someone with whom she could exchange ideas. They were intimate about their emotions, effusive about books they enjoyed, keenly interested in anything to do with contracts and royalties.

In her first letter Mary expressed the hope that he would agree with her 'that the chief pleasure of writing historical novels lies in the continuing tension between the particular – what is individual to the person, the society, the time – and what is universal, and the constant interplay of one through the other'.

He did, and extended the idea in his reply: 'There is another though, which is purely romantic – it is the pleasure of the theatre, in a sense of acting a part, of putting on a costume, of obliterating the present by an exertion of the imagination such as few modern novels require. And for me – as an American, at least – there's another, which is that in an historical novel I can make political comments which would be unwelcome in a modern novel . . . I think judging by your own treatment of Socrates, you must have felt this. Now that I know you are in South Africa, I wonder if it was more particular?'

Mary immediately responded that she 'was not without thoughts of our local government when I was writing about the manoeuvres of the Thirty; in the case of Anytos' views on Sokrates, I rather think the late unlamented McCarthy was uppermost in my mind.'

*

What Mary did not say was that these comparisons were beginning to look simplistic when applied to a country which was moving out of the realm of a limited parliamentary democracy into the darkness of a quasi police state. Having set up the legal framework of *apartheid*, the Nationalists were now vigorously enforcing it. One of Julie's African nurses was arrested with her husband and baby in the middle of the night because they were renting a room in an area classified as Indian. The baby had suffered an asthma attack when its parents were ordered out and interrogated in the darkened street.

In June 1958 Mary sold the second CAM property and they moved into the final house. Paul promptly went on a Sunday night drinking binge that ended in a brawl in which he was badly beaten. He was rapidly becoming a major problem. Returning home late one night, Mary and Julie found a rush basket in the garage stuffed with rolls of *dagga*, the local marijuana. They tried to flush it down the lavatory, but it began to swell and came frothing back out of the bowl. They transferred the soaking weed into buckets and buried it in the garden, where a few months later it was growing in profusion. Paul, in the meantime, had been terrified. He had been given the stuff by an Indian dealer and was now in fear of his life for having lost it. Mary was obdurate: no more brewing and no more *dagga*, or she would no longer pay his fines if he were caught.

He sulked a bit, then seemed to get over it, but not long afterwards the police raided his quarters and found two large buckets of *Shimmyan*, a dangerously potent brew, and took him away. The following day Mary was rung by someone at the court who asked if she could come round and pay a fine of £10, a good deal of money then. When it was pointed out that Paul had been warned he would no longer be helped, the voice at the end of the line gave her quite a dressing down: 'What do you mean you're sorry? You can't let a decent man like that go to prison. Do you know what prison's like? In twenty minutes' time he'll be gone and once that gate is shut he's finished.' They dashed to the car, and drove like mad into town, arriving at the court seconds before the prison van was due to leave. Paul was badly shaken and barely spoke as they took him home. Things were never quite the same again, and it was something of a relief when he found another job. They parted friends, but his departure severed one of the last links binding Mary and Julie to Durban.

There was, by this stage, only Julie's position at the hospital holding them back, though even that was looking increasingly fragile. The Matron had taken five months' leave without clearly indicating which of her four deputies was to be in charge. The result was administrative confusion on top of the upheavals caused by the implementation of *apartheid* and the promotion of staff purely on the basis of colour.

When the Matron returned from holiday, she found Julie organizing a staff protest and immediately banned all meetings in the hospital. At first the majority of the sisters were with Julie, but most of them had too many personal problems to risk losing their jobs and all save a few fell away, leaving Julie on her own. There was no option but to ask for an official inquiry, and a report was duly despatched to Pretoria.

While Julie awaited the outcome of all this, a means of escape was suddenly offered by a wholly unexpected source. *The King Must Die* was published in America in July 1958, two months before it appeared in Britain, and went straight into the best-seller lists. Within weeks, Twentieth Century-Fox had bought the film rights for $75,000. At a stroke, they were liberated, the days of financial struggle were over and, with only one house left to sell, they could leave whenever they chose.

*

While *Time* and *Newsweek* published major articles on *The King Must Die*, the British reviewers were no more perceptive than they had been before. Raymond Mortimer's lengthy review in the *Sunday Times* was one long hymn of praise and the anonymous reviewer in the *Times Literary Supplement* concluded that this 'new insight into the past' was 'triumphantly achieved', but only in America was there any realization that the book was more than an adventure story brilliantly told. The *New York Herald Tribune* devoted the entire cover of its Book Review section to an article by Moses Hadas, Professor of Greek and Latin at Columbia University:

> All of Miss Renault's reconstructions carry conviction because her imagination is informed by careful study, as a minor detail may show. Medea in her short scene calls Theseus 'Theseuss.' Euripides too made Medea hiss by making the s-sound prominent in her speeches. Miss Renault must therefore either be credited with remarkably careful reading or with even more remarkable imaginative power. Theseus' desertion of Ariadne and his failure to raise the white sail are puzzling blots on his chivalry; Miss Renault's rational explanation of both these derelictions as part of his campaign against the old order gives cogency to her entire reconstruction. Her narrative is not, nor does it claim to be, history; but it is a well-considered suggestion of how things may have happened, and for the personality and culture with which she deals we have nothing more plausible. Books from which we learn so much so agreeably are rare.

Although Hadas had understood the subtlety of language so important to Mary but rarely acknowledged, it was Siegfried Mandel, assistant professor at the Polytechnic Institute of Brooklyn, who recognized in *The King Must Die* a major shift in Mary's thinking. Of all her books, this was the one least concerned with the notion of sex as a primary cause of human action. Until Theseus, all Mary's leading characters had struggled against damage inflicted on them during childhood by warring parents or absent fathers. Theseus seems about to follow that line – his early story is a search for the father who abandoned him – but, as the book progresses, we realize that far from being preconditioned by an unfathomable psychological tic, he is actually motivated by a belief in his own destiny. He is not a victim of his childhood, but a man striving to come to terms with Fate as he sees it. As Mandel wrote in the *New York Times Book Review*: 'None of the dark complexes with which modern analysts like Carl Jung and Erich Neumann have saddled Theseus plagues Miss Renault's hero. Instead he enjoys life to the fullest and lets his spirit of independence carry him to triumph and tragedy.'

However, any pleasure Mary may have derived from such a perceptive comment was marred by a letter from Mark Longman, who wrote to say that he hoped she would return to writing contemporary fiction. As he saw it, her first historical novel had not been an outstanding financial success, and he held out little hope for the second; he wondered if she would consider writing a novel about a coloured lady librarian struggling against *apartheid*.

In her reply to Mark Longman, Mary set out her case firmly but quietly:

> ... I have really no desire to add one more to the many novels on the colour question. My bent is more for personal relationships and developments, and I have often seen the introduction of colour having a paralysing effect on character-drawing, when the author conceives each of his characters as if they were representatives rather than individuals, with whom everyone of that race must be able to identify without offence.

What this modest protest failed to reveal was the true depth of her feelings. In reality Mary was blazing angry – she even considered changing publishers and was restrained only by her concern that such a move might cause problems for John Guest. When Guest was told about the letter, he thought it tactless, but he was also aware that Mary's response was out of all proportion to the original offence. In any case, Mark Longman was proved wrong when the book and its predecessor became long-running money-earners for the company. When Mark Longman appreciated how seriously he had offended her, he tried to put matters right by promoting the book, getting his wife, who knew Princess Margaret, to give Her Royal Highness a copy, which was photographed with her as she boarded the royal train and given prominent space in the popular press. Mark Longman sent Mary the cuttings, but she refused to be pacified. His uncle Robert had always provided support and encouragement where the nephew seemed interested merely in money. As she put it to Jay: 'He might just as well be a self-made tycoon craving for stockbroker's Tudor and an electrically heated pool.'

John Guest insists that Mark Longman was 'the kindest of men' and that Mary's reaction was an example of her tendency to take an unbudging position over a quite minor issue. Guest admits to having been 'rather frightened of Mary, frightened that is of her certainties'.

The diffident young woman who had made her first, nervous visit to Robert Longman's office had become a figure to be reckoned with. Since the heavy cuts in *The Last of the Wine*, she had vehemently opposed any changes in her manuscripts, even to the point of forbidding Guest to alter her punctuation in any way. The greatest battles were fought over jackets, a highly sensitive area given her distress over the vulgarities perpetrated on her hospital novels. Because aesthetics concerned her less than historical accuracy, art-work flew back and forth as she lambasted this or that failure to use something from the right period, or castigated some error of dress or architecture which seemed to her to bear no relationship to what she had written.

To Guest and the others who dealt with her, she appeared to be utterly confident, but behind this façade was another, less secure reality. Mark Longman's letter had badly shaken her confidence, and the only thing she had been able to write since then had been *The Song of Troy*, a version of the *Iliad*, for the SABC. The long delay between recording and broadcasting suggests that it was not one of her livelier pieces.

What Mary could not know was the behaviour of her agent Spencer Curtis Brown, who, as the Longman Publishing Archives at Reading University reveal, was playing a curious game. Far from defending his author and promoting her interests, his confidential correspondence with Mark Longman shows a desire to please the eminent publisher at whatever cost to someone he was prepared to describe as 'difficult'. While Mary knew nothing of this, she must have felt a distinct lack of support from the one man who ought to have given it.

In a final attempt to repair the damage he had done, Mark Longman arranged to call on Mary during a visit to southern Africa which would be principally concerned with his company's extensive educational publishing interests. Mary duly gave a party for him and his wife, but she was not pacified and relations between them remained fraught. For Mary, the saddest thing about the whole episode was the strain it placed on her friendship with John Guest. For a time Mark Longman tried to deal with her direct, but gradually he realized that it would be better to let the two of them sort things out, which, happily, did eventually happen to the immense relief of both parties.

By contrast, the Wolffs in America were doing everything right. They had decided that Pantheon should bring out *The Charioteer* six years after its publication in Britain. Unaware of the earlier censorship, most reviewers simply assumed that Mary Renault, author of two successful historical novels, had now decided to write a book about the last war. The furore Morrow had feared did not take place, and the unrestrained enthusiasm of reviewers such as Richard Weston in the *New York Herald Tribune* testified to the success of the Wolffs in promoting Mary as a serious literary figure and not merely as a good historical novelist:

> Miss Renault is one of the major novelists of our time. Her insights are phenomenal, her reading of the fine print of psychological history extremely acute, her rendering of truth as she sees it forthright, courageous, informative and stirring. Moreover, she can keep several themes moving simultaneously, each reinforcing the other; and she knows from the beginning where her chariot is bound. In this earlier work her style runs occasion-

ally to preciosity; but this tendency is usually balanced by good sense, and is probably less the outcome of affectation than of the need to communicate intangible realities.

*

When Julie became aware that Mary was not writing, she suggested a holiday. At fifty-four, Mary needed a break from all the pressures she had been under and Julie proposed that they visit Rhodesia again. It was still nominally a British colony and might offer some respite from the political stresses of South Africa. They briefly considered settling there, but were swiftly disabused. They stayed with Mary's cousin Alan in Salisbury, but friction between the races seemed if anything more acute than in Durban, and they were glad to get home.

Julie was now faced with the board of inquiry from Pretoria. It found nothing wrong with her work, but she was told in future to stay away from the wards that had Black patients and nurses. She could have an office to sit in and she could continue to draw her salary, but she must remain inactive.

When Julie arrived home and told Mary, they both knew there was no point in hanging on. After more than a decade in Durban, they would move to the Cape at last. They made a brief, exploratory visit out beyond the city, on the road to the Point, where there was a series of small bays dotted with cottages at the foot of Table Mountain. It was so like Marathon there was no need to look farther. In Camps Bay they discovered a tiny sheltered cove called Glen Beach, where navy veterans had been allowed to build temporary wooden shacks on the slope leading down to the sand. Over the years, most of these had been bought and sold, and gradually transformed into charming clapboard cottages, though the one that was available, in the middle of the beach with its rear windows facing the mountain, was pretty run down and would need a lot of renovation. It was called Daisy Nook.

They sold the last Durban house and crated the animals to be flown to the Cape. Fortunately Mrs Messina seemed undisturbed and was perfectly calm as the three of them left by ship. Just before they closed the house, Mary received a letter forwarded by Longmans which seemed an omen of good things to come. It was from Kasia Abbott, her closest friend at St Hugh's, writing to say how much she had enjoyed *The King Must Die* and hoping they could get in touch again. It was impossible to do more than fire off a quick note, but as soon as they had settled Mrs Messina into the rented accommodation where they would all live while the workmen finished decorating the new house, she sat down and wrote Kasia a long résumé of her life during the ten years since she had left England. It was the beginning of a second rich correspondence, her only real contact with a past that, more than ever, seemed impossibly distant from her lost inlet on the southernmost tip of Africa:

> I think a lot of credit is given to S. Africans for being uniquely vicious when the truth is that the country is just backward in the march of civilisation. The Greek servant where we stayed in Athens was treated in a way no Zulu girl would stand for a week, nor would any normal white person expect her to; and we ourselves when we trained as nurses in the 1930s had worse hours, harsher discipline and less pay than the African probationer has today. I think things would improve with time, as they have done evidently for some decades, if the Nats don't get all our throats cut first with their absurd outdated chauvinism. But I am talking as if Africa were merely what most people in Europe see it as; the stage for a race-relations play. Of course it is a million things more, both the physical landscape and the human scene are immensely complex and interesting; and one thing it teaches you is the limited scope of what we understand by twentieth-century civilisation. What goes on here is still, very largely, the impact of the nineteenth century on the stone age. Very very few Afrikaaners, and those mostly men like Laurens van der Post who have spent most of their adult lives outside the Union, have emerged mentally from the epoch of the Boer War. You find here how constant human political and social behaviour remains through the ages, how completely Thucydides still makes sense. But I think it is only after you stop taking human goodness for granted that you realise what a miracle it really is and how inexplicable in rationalistic terms.

10

Delos

By January 1959, they decided that the cottage, even with the renovations half finished, had to be better than the run-down accommodation they were renting. As long as there was somewhere for Mrs Messina and Mary had a table for her typewriter, they thought they could manage. They moved in and formally renamed their new home Delos, in honour of Apollo and their blissful day on his island. However, the builders' work stretched on for months and came to dominate everything. Their neighbours were friendly and the woman next door recommended a maid, Katie, a Cape Coloured who, despite the distance she had to travel, had always worked in Camps Bay. At first she seemed rather dour, but they put that down to her German father and were soon very fond of her, and she of them. Still the workmen seemed no nearer finishing. The unpleasant green paint became a light Grecian blue, there were bookshelves in Mary's study, and the newly acquired gardener fixed up a little inner courtyard with seats made out of beach rock, where Julie planted flowers and Mary sat, staring out at the ocean, wanting to write, but unable to begin. She tried to put the best face on it, sending Kasia a happy picture of how they were settling in:

> The mountains you see in the beach picture are called the Twelve Apostles. Beyond the left of the picture they culminate in the sharp western edge of Table Mountain. When rain is coming, the famous tablecloth comes hanging down over the edges all along; a stream of white cloud like a waterfall, which melts into air a little way down the face, so that it is always the same depth at the hem. Bad news as it is, it's a lovely sight, and almost makes up for the drizzle it heralds. It is caused by the condensation of

the south-east wind as it goes across the mountain. The last few days have been wonderful; cool, brilliant, almost as sparklingly clear as Greece. (How lovely that you know Delos too. I got a shard at Phyle, and pictured Alexias and Lysis carrying up the water for the garrison from the spring in it; but my only keepsake from Delos is a bit of that sparkling rock you see everywhere underfoot.) Both in climate and landscape, this is very like the Mediterranean. The beach has a very friendly, easy atmosphere, everyone being on passing-chat terms without intrusion. All the people are English except for one Afrikaans old lady who is a perfect darling. (None the less she probably votes Nationalist at election time and really believes she is doing right. That's the tragedy of this country. How people in England over-simplify it all!)

So disorganized was *apartheid* at the Cape that the city authorities were trying to declare Glen Beach a 'Coloureds only' area, even though none but Whites lived in the wooden cottages. None the less, what Mary found most frustrating was that a city where the majority of people still lived in shanty towns had enough officious building inspectors to prevent her from finishing the internal reconstruction of the cottage. Her desire for a second lavatory was thwarted on the grounds that she might be trying to divide the space into apartments to rent out. And this when tens of thousands were crammed into tin shacks. In the end the work took over six months, due largely to official harassment. Mary complained about having no proper study in which to work, although the truth was that she had still not decided what she ought to be doing and was filling her time with other things. The local SABC commissioned a play, *The God of the Crossroads*, about Alcibiades, which Val Gielgud produced, and Mary spent hours answering queries about the script for the film of *The King Must Die*, until someone wrote to ask where bull dancers could be hired, and she gave up in despair. But it was the house more than anything that filled her days. She wanted to put in an internal staircase – the cottage was built on a slope – but was threatened with the full weight of the law if she did so. To add to her worries there were hints from America that Twentieth Century-Fox was

planning to turn her book into a full-blown Hollywood epic,
which, as she explained to Jay Williams, was the sort of bad joke
she enjoyed, but which she had no wish to be part of:

I have just seen, have you? a quite fantastic film about Hercules,
done in Italy and with dialogue, whether dubbed or not I
couldn't quite make out, of the most incredible banality. Hercules was a chap who has won a muscle competition for Mr
Universe. The sets represented every period you can think of
from late Mycenaean to – yes, really – black figure vase painting,
and costumes the same. The plot had Hercules running the
Argonaut expedition with Jason as a nice young lad he had
taken under his wing. Princess Iole was a lively teenager who
wore a hip-length white gym-slip throughout. No nasty Nessus
shirt business of course and *no* fifty virgins; Hercules carried
on like a youth club leader from first to last. Jason found written
in blood on the back of the Golden Fleece his father's last
message about who did him in. 'Forgive everyone,' said this
typical Homeric dad; 'there has been violence enough!' It all
ended with Hercules and Io sailing off on Argo into the sunset.
Oh dear oh dear. I was quite pleased afterwards to see *Quo
Vadis* again. It really does make an honest shot at the job, and
Leo Genn and Peter Ustinov give superb performances. No
more news of *my* film; and last thing I heard they are to start
shooting in July.

They did not. Fox had another epic in the making – *Cleopatra*
with Elizabeth Taylor and Richard Burton, which finally consumed such astronomical amounts of money they abandoned
Mary's book, much to her relief, since the last she heard was that
the script had been worked over by the same man who had done
The Robe, which she considered a 'tasteless, super-colossal stinker.
I don't know what part I loved more, the bit where the torch-
singer croons the Lord's prayer into an invisible microphone, or
where the reunited sweethearts have a good cuddle in a catacomb,
or where Victor Mature says to St Peter, "For all you've done for
me – thanks." '
Even without bad films, the distractions of Cape Town were

sufficient to keep her from her new typewriter. Leslie French turned up for what had become his annual season at the Maynardville Festival, bringing a new band of actor friends. Jim MacGregor, the doctor from their days in neuro-surgery at the Radcliffe, had settled near by and was working part-time at the Groote Schuur hospital. The dancer David Poole had come home from his stint at Sadler's Wells and joined the staff of the Cape Town Ballet School, where he was planning to launch a professional ballet company. Poole and his companion, Owen Murray, a fellow dancer, were to become Mary and Julie's closest friends, though they did not live in Camps Bay, to which many in Cape Town's artistic community had gravitated. It was a tiny enclave of liberal opinion whose inhabitants could safely fulminate across their dinner tables at the crudeness of the Nats in ghastly Johannesburg, and who were appalled when the hateful Heinrich Verwoerd finally became Prime Minister at the end of 1958.

Verwoerd moved quickly. His Homeland Policy cleverly promised separate homelands for Africans to justify dispossessing Blacks in what were now designated 'Whites only' areas. The opposition United Party, the preferred party of the English-speaking community, was unable to move too far towards siding with the Africans for fear of alienating its own White working-class support. In 1959 its moderate wing of eleven MPs broke away and formed the Progressive Party, which Mary and Julie and much of Camps Bay instantly joined. The party's platform was gradualist, advocating the re-enfranchisement of Coloured voters and educated Africans, followed by the setting up of multi-racial local councils. It was an attempt to offer the White community – the only voters – a chance to pull back from *apartheid* without the fear of being overrun by the Black majority.

Most Whites were increasingly apprehensive about conditions in the newly independent states to the north. Inevitably this was seized on and exaggerated by the pro-Nationalist press, but, even allowing for bias, the events in the Congo were terrifying and no encouragement to the White electorate to consider broadening the franchise. To Mary, someone like Kwame Nkrumah looked like the worst type of Athenian demagogue, and in that light the Progressive Party's policy that seats in Parliament should be limited to those with educational qualifications seemed reasonable to her.

As the 1960s opened, Mary found herself plunged into active politics for the first time in her life: canvassing from door to door, fund raising, attending meetings. From the start of the new year things moved so rapidly that it was impossible even to think of writing. In January 1960 Verwoerd announced his intention to make South Africa a republic, following a referendum of the White electorate. The Progressive Party opposed the move, not, as Mary was quick to explain to Kasia, because they were particularly against the idea of a republic, but because they hoped to make the issue a vote of no confidence in Verwoerd.

Early in the new year the author and journalist Rebecca West came out on behalf of the *Sunday Times* to write a series of articles on the political changes, and Mary invited her to Delos to meet Zac de Beer, the leader of the Progressive Party. 'My one attempt at being a political hostess,' she told Kasia, adding that the great lady had turned out to be very unpompous and had even struck a chord when she said she felt much modern writing was conditioned by the individual's sense of utter impotence to affect the society he lived in, control being so remote and elaborate. While Mary agreed that this was no doubt true in Europe or America, she claimed she had never felt so in touch with things as she did in South Africa. It was, she once told Jay Williams, 'like being in a city state where the people in control are personally known to the community'.

The party was a great success – the resulting four articles were highly favourable to Mary's party and were reprinted as a pamphlet, which she and Julie helped distribute. For a moment it looked as if reason and moderation might triumph after all; and, when the British Prime Minister, Harold Macmillan, arrived in Cape Town at the beginning of February and made his famous 'wind of change' speech, Mary felt elated, as if the leader of the 'old country' had come to say all the things that the Afrikaners had been trying not to hear. Mary thought Verwoerd's reply in the Cape Town Parliament crude and childish after Macmillan's urbane performance. It seemed hardly possible that anyone who heard them had not felt the same. She joined the massive multi-racial anti-republic march through Cape Town on Union Day, writing to Kasia to express her elation: 'It was meant to be very solemn though cheerfulness kept breaking in, it was so nice to be out in the open and to find that 11,000 other people were feeling the same way.'

Only in retrospect could she see how hollow her elation was. For too long the White population had deluded themselves into believing that politics came down to the struggle between Nationalists and Liberals, a simple contest between Afrikaans-speakers and English-speakers. Too few had any real knowledge of the seething anger within the Black townships, and even fewer knew of the potentially disastrous divisions among the Africans themselves, divisions initially fostered by Government action, which would eventually flare up in ways they could no longer control. The founding of the Pan-Africanist Congress (PAC) in March 1959 was the first straw in the wind; when its chairman Robert Sobukwe began calling for direct action against the Government, the more pacific African National Congress (ANC) was forced to counter this move by organizing massive demonstrations against the pass laws to be held on 31 March. Not to be outdone, the PAC decided to pre-empt this, calling for a demonstration of its own, ten days earlier, on the 21st.

Mary was also being drawn into literary politics in a way that would have been unthinkable even a year earlier. She had been telephoned by a local lawyer, Gerald Gordon, who was trying to contact writers in the province with a view to setting up a local branch of PEN International. Cape Town had had a branch of PEN, which had petered out just before the war, and a PEN centre still theoretically existed in Johannesburg, though it appeared to be moribund. Now that the Government was beginning to extend the censorship laws, Gordon and his wife Nancy were eager to see the local group revived. On his return from the war, Gordon had been an early member of Torch Commando, a veterans' group concerned with citizens' rights – a male counterpart to the Black Sash movement. A published novelist, he had combined writing with a legal career, and had already fought a number of test cases over book seizures by South African customs. In the revival of PEN he saw a useful way of continuing the anti-censorship battle.

Given his sincerity, it seemed to Mary that it would be churlish not to listen to his requests that she help in the relaunch. He had been approached by PEN International's headquarters in London to round up as many writers as possible with a view to holding an inaugural meeting. The British writer and critic Richard Church was due to come out to South Africa in March and would stay with the Gordons. As Church had been one of Mary's first reviewers and had given a very favourable notice to *Purposes of Love*, she knew she would have to take part. But when Gordon found he could not put up Church and Mary agreed to take him in, she became more deeply involved than she might have wished. There were certainly arguments against involvement: she had injured a tendon and a bungled operation on her foot had forced her to sleep in a bed downstairs; Mrs Messina would have to be kept out of the way of both guests and builders, and Julie would have to cook for any visitors Church might wish to see. Happily, he turned out to be a charming old man, rather conservative in his views, who seemed to have known everyone in the literary world for the past forty years, and Mary was soon won over. However, when Church pointed out that she was now one of South Africa's best known authors and ought to take an active part in the organization, she was appalled. She had never had any desire for a public role, and the idea of making speeches filled her with dread. Church was insistent. The work of PEN, he emphasized, was concerned with opposing censorship and furthering authors' rights, both of which causes were unquestionably worthwhile. Mary had already entered the public arena by working for the Progressive Party, and with Church so gracefully persuasive her resistance rapidly waned. By the time he left she had agreed to sit on the committee, on the clear understanding that people like Gerald Gordon would run the organization's day-to-day business.

It took the steering committee some months to formulate the rules and drum up enough potential members to make an inaugural meeting feasible. PEN centres are open to novelists, poets, playwrights, editors and essayists, but local centres are free to define their own membership requirements. Sensibly, or so it seemed then, Gordon and his colleagues proposed to adopt the rules in force at the English PEN centre in London, which meant that for the authors two published books were the minimum requirement for admission. The effects of this would become fully apparent only after the first meeting, by which time the rules were firmly in place.

The inaugural meeting was eventually held on 21 March in the Cape Town public library. The organizers had either overlooked the fact that this was the day planned for the PAC's mass protest against the pass laws or else had not thought this would amount to much. As it was, the later arrivals at the town hall were breathless with news, coming through on the SABC, that something had gone very wrong. While there had been non-violent protests across the country and most of them had been met with an equally non-violent reaction from the police, there had been one extremely violent confrontation in a so-called 'model' location, an African resettlement township in the Vereeniging area of the Transvaal called Sharpeville. Until that day the name meant nothing to anyone except the impoverished residents of the place, but since that morning, when the police had opened fire on the demonstration, killing sixty-nine Africans and wounding 180 more, the name Sharpeville had flashed round the world, becoming a synonym for oppression wherever the news was heard.

It was clear even from the earliest reports that South Africa's political life had plunged further down the path of racial violence, and it was with misgivings that the steering committee decided to continue with the meeting. The somewhat tattily typed minutes, riddled with spelling and typing errors, would look ridiculous coming from an organization pledged to the defence of literature were it not for the strain under which they were produced. As soon as the constitution was voted on and the first officials had been elected, the members hurried home to listen, like the rest of the nation, to the news. Robert Sobukwe and his fellow PAC leaders had been arrested. Like so many other momentous historical events, Sharpeville was an accident – no one had planned a massacre, the police had panicked – but this was irrelevant. Even as the committee members heard the first accounts, it was obvious to them that events had passed far beyond the possibility of peaceful democratic change. No sooner had they assimilated the first disaster than news of a second, smaller, but no less alarming incident came from nearby Langa, where two people had been shot after a massive protest meeting had failed to disperse, following an inaudible police request for them to do so. The Cape, which had seemed so liberal and calm beside the rest of the country, was being drawn into the same pit of violence.

Three weeks later, on 9 April, a White man shot Verwoerd in the head. Badly injured, but alive, his survival merely convinced him and his supporters of divine sanction for their ever more divisive policies. They were certainly undeterred by the growing disgust within the world community, a revulsion that earned their country pariah status and led to its isolation from most international bodies.

In a last desperate effort to resist this process, the country's embattled Liberals, Mary and Julie among them, devoted more and more time to fighting the forthcoming October referendum. They had almost no hope. Even while recuperating from the assassin's bullet, Verwoerd was preparing to ensure victory by announcing that a simple majority would carry the day, despite the fact that provinces such as Natal had originally joined the Union on the understanding that a two-thirds majority would be needed to change its constitution. This made the referendum a straight fight between Afrikaans-speakers and English-speakers, with the great mass of the population – African, Coloured, Indian – looking on, unable to participate in a vote from which they could only be the ultimate losers.

*

Meanwhile, there was ever worsening news from Joyce in England. Clementine was in great pain and needed constant attention. Joyce did not complain, but Mary could read between the lines and imagine how wearisome her sister's life must be with so difficult a patient.

Mary herself was feeling the strain of so much unaccustomed activity; at fifty-five she felt rather too old to be starting a new life as a political activist. She was often thoroughly exhausted, and as her letters to Kasia from the early part of 1960 make clear, when she was not out drumming up support for the party, she could do little more than sit by her window and stare at the view:

The South-Easter, or Cape Doctor (it would be the mistral anywhere else) is blowing this afternoon. A huge seething eider-down of cloud is lying along the tops of Table Mountain and the Twelve Apostles, the spray on the wave-heads is being blown furiously sideways, the beach is deserted because of the miniature sandstorm scouring across it. The sun is bright and hot and the sky, except where the Tablecloth covers the moun-tains, brilliantly clear. If one could slip one's body and blow about in it (a thing even the birds avoid) it would be beautiful. But everything flaps, pictures blow down and break, papers and dry leaves and bits of grass litter the floor under every door and window, which mostly have to be kept open for coolness (but, if you allow a real cross-draught, it wrecks the room). However, if a place as beautiful as the Cape didn't have some defect, it would be hubristic and unnatural.

To Kasia she revealed that she was re-reading Malory; to Jay that she was interested in the Knights Templar. But, if she were thinking of writing about the Middle Ages, her interest swiftly waned and she was soon on to other topics. She summed up her difficulties to Jay:

What with the new house, new place, new people (Cape Town has much more to offer than Durban both in scenery and society) and a tedious operation on a foot which would have been quite needless if an idiot doctor hadn't failed to detect a tendon injury and made me exercise it when it needed rest, work has not gone forward much this last year, but I don't feel too guilty, because I think one probably needs to shake off the unsettling effects of a book that has done better than one expected, let the fuss work itself to a standstill, and then settle down with one's eye on the ball. This is what I hope now to get down to.

She did not, however. South African politics proved as great a barrier to work as the war had done. When not handing out leaflets, she tried to keep up her reading, as if a break with Greece might somehow kick-start the cold motor of her inspiration. In July she wrote to tell Jay that she had discovered the works of Carl Jung, which had given her

> a most exhilarating peak-in-Darien feeling; in stature he seems to me Plato to Freud's Anaxagoras; one cannot exactly say he begins where Freud leaves off, because of course he begins where Freud begins, he only goes on and leaves him standing. He seems to have a so much more wide-ranging, uninhibited mind, prepared to consider all the facts of human experience, not just to explain away what he can't fit into his pattern, and ready to face the test of constructing a philosophy.

It is not difficult to see why she should instantly have preferred Jung to Freud; the former's interest in myth, philosophy and Eastern mysticism matched her own, but more than anything else there was the feeling that Freudianism had in part failed:

> I had always felt him to be uncomfortably dogmatic and narrow on great issues, however much he might in lesser ones preserve the forms of scientific humility. After all, the generation which was supposedly liberated from its taboos by Freud has now brought up *its* children, which ought to prove something, but they don't seem much better or happier than the ill-used Victorians; this seems to suggest he has missed something out of his equation. The idea that man evolved himself solely by tugging at his own bootstraps with his eyes shut has never carried total conviction to me.

What Mary found attractive about Jung was the liberating view that an individual's behaviour was not simply a matter of subconscious sexual drives but, more importantly, a question of what that person chose to do, his aims and hopes:

> Thinking all this I suddenly realised that without, so to speak, having a lesson in my life I had just written a hundred per cent

Jungian novel. What is Theseus, after all, but primitive man struggling to defend his new-found ego against the surrounding jungle of the unconscious; his kingship resulting from his first success and in its turn demanding greater efforts towards evolution? Of course by the end of the book he has not reached the point of reconciliation with his anima, and of course the tragedy before him is inevitable; you could call the rest of the tale THE MOTHER STRIKES BACK.

On 18 August, a fortnight after this letter to Jay, Mary received news from Joyce that their mother had died quietly at her home. Her inactivity had left her with little resistance at the end. Although Mary had expected it for some time, it was a blow, made worse by the feeling that her mother's had been a wasted life. In a unique moment of intimacy Clementine had once confided to Mary that before she met Frank Challans she had wanted to marry a complete waster 'without a brain in his head'. Her father had put a stop to it, which was, she thought, just as well, since the man had taken to drink and died from falling down in the street and catching pneumonia before anyone found him. To Mary there was something terribly sad about this solitary, fleeting moment of thwarted passion which helped redress her balance of judgement. As she revealed in a long letter to Kasia, her father had always seemed to her the more attractive of the two. He at least had been rational and logical, while her mother had seemed to view logic as a form of materialistic philosophy to be stoically resisted. It was a battle Clementine was never able to win, because her husband was cleverer than she, with a bitter tongue which won every argument. Now Mary could see that there had been nothing left for her mother to do except make every disagreement personal, though he could beat her at that too. Although Mary had been born within a year of their marriage, she could not remember a time when they seemed even to have liked each other. Now she perceived that a strange thing had happened to her since she had first realized her mother was dying: she would go to any lengths to avoid opening a door. She had not noticed this in Durban, because the house was very windy, and doors were often shut to keep papers from blowing about, so that it was easy to rationalize why she took a circuitous route from room to room. In Cape Town, there was no such excuse and she had to accept the fact that she behaved in this way because of the closed doors in Dacre Lodge all those years ago, behind which fearful rows were always in progress. Even now, fifty-five years later, she could not face opening one lest she find her parents there, locked in battle, breaking off only to draw her into their fight, making her the cause of their misery.

After the funeral, Joyce wrote to confirm that there was no inheritance for her. Mary had expected this; but, when she understood that her mother had not willed her so much as a trinket to remember her by, not even one of those 'nice' little objects on the polished side tables in her living room, Mary was deeply, if irrationally hurt.

*

When she wrote to tell Kasia of the death, Mary was still staring out of the window, not working:

It is a wet, windy, blustery day, but spring has arrived, and when you walk up the steps beside the stream at night you smell in the darkness a wonderful scent of wild arum lilies growing in the long rough grass. The Cape lilies are not little green ones like wild arums in England but the big white sort and they grow everywhere in the bush, on the edges of fields, or self-seeded in gardens. They don't take kindly to being planted and one just cherishes them where they appear as a gift of heaven. We have one big clump growing in our compost-heap, where we cut them for the house, and another in the garden which we leave to look at. Anemones are out too and stock and daffodils. Soon we shall be getting the high seas. The tide sets straight in to the beach in huge white horses which come rushing up right to the bottom of the sea wall on which we are built. All the inhabitants come out to watch them with respectful awe, wondering how high they will actually come, and neighbours tell newer residents like us about the year it came right up over the wall into the garden and Mrs Paarman found seaweed on her roof. It is a magnificent sight and sometimes you can even see a cat sitting amid the row of children perched upon the railings, inscrutably contemplating the sea.

She would watch these children growing up over the coming decade, children of the 1960s knowing no other world but the one created by that fateful election on the day she had arrived in the country. With her mother's death the peaceful enclave in Glen Beach became even more her only home. Though they lost money on them, the houses in Durban had been thought of as investments; Julie and Mary had moved as each in turn was completed and had sold them off without regrets; but Delos was different, a fresh start. Mary would love Delos as she had loved no other house before, adding to it over the years – a pretty fretwork balcony along the seafront copied from traditional Cape dwellings, practical sliding doors to give more room in her study, and frequent changes of colour, usually between books, to brighten life before a new task was begun. The sole constant was the splendour of the view: its sudden storms, the amazing play of light, the children cavorting on the beach as the dogs pointlessly charged the seagulls, who seemed to entice them like sirens towards the Atlantic rollers.

Mary wrote to ask Joyce to come out for Christmas 1960, offering to pay her passage and booking a cabin on the brand new *Windsor Castle* so that she could enjoy a taste of luxury after the rigours of nursing their mother and organizing the funeral. With that done, she was able to tell Jay she could now start writing again 'after too-long a break. One has to do it sometimes or one would ossify and have nothing to write about.'

Other letters reinforce the impression of someone trying to settle to a project for which she feels more duty than passion. What she could not tell Jay was that she had once again shunted aside the Middle Ages and intended to continue the Theseus story, in a sequel to be called *The Bull from the Sea*. She did, though, break her superstition about never revealing the subject of a work in progress to tell Longmans that she was writing another Greek novel, lest they send more silly proposals about librarians with colour-bar problems. But she was to regret this when things started to go wrong, and she came to believe that, by breaking the taboo, she had jinxed the book from the start.

Her intention was to run through the Theseus tale, episode by episode, from his return to Athens until his death – not an especially stimulating task, but, given all her other concerns, it was just as well that the plot was so easily taken care of. Her research, however, remained as fastidious as ever. She was writing to 'a nice American archaeologist from Pennsylvania' called Michael Jameson, who had published a report of a chariot burial which led her to ask about the nature of horsemanship in the Bronze Age. Jameson was then in the Classical Studies Department at the University of Pennsylvania; his replies and her subsequent enquiries plunged them both deep into the arcana of equine history. Mary's main concern was whether horses in the Mycenaean era were used for anything other than chariot teams before the invention of the stirrup made horseback riding easy. Some idea of the depth of detail she was prepared to wade through before committing herself can be gleaned from one of Jameson's answers:

I came across an article by Sinclair Hood, in the Annual of the British School at Athens, vol. 48, 1953, pages 84ff, on 'A Mycenaean Cavalryman'; it is a Late Mycenaean (1300 or not much later) figurine of a warrior on a horse found at Mycenae. He also refers to a potsherd found in the Levant, at Minet el Beida, the harbour of Ras Shamra, and shown in Furumark's *Mycenaean Pottery*, fig. 26, nos 2 and 5. There is some interesting discussion in Hood's article but I don't think he takes seriously the problems of riding small horses and fighting from them without saddle, stirrups etc. It could be done, of course, but chariots were easier.

What Mary could do with such dry stuff is little short of miraculous:

While I was there, Pirithoos showed me the Lapith riding-tricks; spearing a trophy at full gallop, snatching a ring from the ground; standing in the saddle, or shooting from it with the short bow they use. He could ride two horses standing, with a

foot on each. His people swore that Zeus had taken on the
likeness of a stallion to beget him. He had been riding great
horses at an age when I was still standing on tiptoe to give them
salt. I never had his style; but before I left, I could keep along
with him more or less. A horse is not so hard to stay on, after
the bulls; and sooner than give him the best of it, I would have
broken my neck.

The book broke down into a series of separate episodes, each
scarcely more than a catalogue of Theseus's adventures, allowing
her to turn out sections between other calls on her time.

Already Cape Town PEN was showing signs that it might be
more trouble than its founders had bargained for. The two-book
membership rule was lax enough to let in a gaggle of amateur
authors dealing with such local interests as Cape history and wild-
life, but stringent enough to ensure that aspiring African authors
were excluded. Efforts had been made to attract Black and Coloured writers, but the only one who had joined was Richard Rive,
the most famous of the country's Coloured authors. Rive was a
poet and the biographer of Olive Schreiner, but his close connections with Oxford University and his identification with English
literary life meant that he could hardly be seen as representative
of the radical Black writers who were beginning to attract attention
outside South Africa. After an initial flurry of activity, the committee seems to have accepted its failure to widen the membership and
to have concentrated on fighting the Government's new censorship
laws.

Hitherto the only books subject to censorship had been
imported works, which could be seized by customs officers at
docks and airports. Judgements were often based on the cover
alone, leading to classic howlers like the banning of *Black Beauty*,
presumably because it was thought to be about African women.
However, most serious books, no matter what their subject, could
usually get through. The new rules were intended to extend censorship to books published within the country. The underlying
aim was further control of political literature, but the promoters
of the law raised a smoke screen about fighting the Communist
conspiracy and wiping out pornography. The test case was Wilbur

Smith's *Where Lions Feed*, seized because of references to oral sex. Gerald Gordon fought the case three years before the refounding of Cape Town PEN and hoped that now the organization would challenge such bannings collectively. He felt the first step should be through letters to the newspapers, alerting the public to what had happened. Gordon drafted the letters and took them to Mary, who tried to strike the right balance between Gordon's legal niceties and the punch she knew was needed to arouse popular indignation.

One effect of this rising tide of protest was the revival of the Johannesburg PEN centre on the initiative of the novelist Nadine Gordimer, who had been born and brought up in the city. She had known Cedric when she was younger, and he had introduced her to Mary during a visit to Durban in the early 1950s. At that time Gordimer had published several short stories, but had not yet written a novel, while Mary was just finishing *The Charioteer*, and their first meeting was no more than a pleasant social encounter. Over the following years both had achieved considerable international fame, while their political views had diverged. Gordimer had become a prominent White spokesperson for the Black cause, adding her voice to those who supported the African National Congress struggle against the White minority Government. Both women were aware of their differences, but neither believed that these need affect the work they were doing to oppose the censorship laws. Indeed, in the early days of the struggle, Gordimer's views on PEN were remarkably similar to Mary's. That the organization was dominated by so many part-time writers had worried Mary from the start, and, when the Johannesburg centre was relaunched, Gordimer expressed exactly those sentiments in a letter to her. Gordimer wrote that if she were expected to take up arms alongside a doctor who happened to have published a thesis on prostitution or a woman who wrote school primers – these were she said the actual qualifications of two of the members of Johannesburg PEN – then she felt she might 'just as well join forces with the gas workers union or something like that'.

In another letter Gordimer listed the only writers left in South Africa whom she regarded as suitable to join: 'Alan Paton, Harry

Bloom, Uys Krige, Daphne Rooke, Hans Hofmeyer, Ronald Byron, Tom Hopkinson and Geoffrey Jenkins.'

Mary replied that these were hardly the *only* authors in the country and put forward one or two names of her own, though in truth she felt a good deal of sympathy with Gordimer's point and willingly signed the anti-censorship petition she had launched.

The referendum on the republic was held in October, with Mary and Julie working flat out in the days leading up to the vote. They lost. A narrow 3% of the White electorate voted to sever the residual links with Great Britain and its monarchy. The Afrikaners had, in Mary's choice words, 'outbred us, having, as a rule, fewer competing interests'. The sequal was equally galling. The new republic was obliged to leave the Commonwealth, a move deplored by Mary, as it played into the hands of the most segregationist Afrikaners and seemed to her to be against the silent wish of the majority, who, if they had been allowed to vote, would have opposed the republic and, by extension, have shown their desire to remain within the Commonwealth.

Her best guide in all this was her dancer friend David Poole, whose contacts within the Coloured community were a direct line to the thinking of those now insultingly classified as non-White. Since his return, David had had to adapt his own thinking to a changed reality, starting with the word 'Coloured', which was increasingly resented by his people. Although he had been brought up in the desperately poor Woodstock area of Cape Town and had attended a Coloured school, the education had been no different from that at a White institution, but the recent attempts to redefine Coloured as a separate racial sub-group and to close down the few opportunities his people had had were causing bitter resentment. The formerly open city hall concerts were now segregated, with only a few back-row seats reserved for non-Whites who wished to attend performances of classical music. David's original intention had been to counter these measures by founding a Coloured ballet group, until it was made clear to him that such a move would be deeply resented by the very people he wanted to help. The Coloureds did not want to be put into a Coloured group. If their dancers were good enough, they should be able to join any company. Yet David knew that if he decided to found South Africa's first professional dance group, it could not in the present climate start off fully integrated, a dilemma that left him walking an impossible political tightrope. To his own people he appeared to be bowing to the authorities' desire for an all-White ballet and only a few friends knew his real hope was that, once it was founded, the ballet would quickly be open to all. To take such a gamble, at the risk of alienating one's own people, looked to Mary like true courage. David was an exemplar of what she most admired – the dogged attempt to sustain Western cultural values amidst the deepening gloom of philistine Afrikanerdom. She does not seem to have considered the possibility of an alternative culture. While Nadine Gordimer in Johannesburg was trying to promote township voices, to discover and encourage the embryonic talent of young African writers, Mary's concern was that European theatre should be nurtured in alien soil at all costs, even if only the smallest minority was willing or permitted to participate.

From this standpoint, her actor and dancer friends were a last bulwark against the encroaching tide of barbarism, a travelling cosmopolitan brotherhood, free from the fettered, tribal obsessions of the despised Afrikaners. She was fascinated by their craft and traditions, and admired the way they wore their homosexuality like a masonic badge. She felt comfortable with them. And they reciprocated, loving the way she played charades so badly – as an actress she was, in the words of one actor friend, 'sublimely rotten', acting out the chosen phrase or title with child-like enthusiasm and an intensity that made him gasp. He recalled how she had once interrupted an earnest explanation of Spartan military tactics, in order to take the floor to act out *Gone with the Wind*.

※

It had not been easy for Julie to give up nursing. To Mary this was something to be handled calmly. She felt that Julie ought not to have been forced into such an abrupt break from full-time work and into total retirement. At forty-eight she was too young to have nothing to do except her self-imposed tasks of running the home, and Mary was relieved when Julie began to find a niche among their actor friends, writing a radio drama series and adapting new novels to be read on air.

Mary was happy when her sister arrived for Christmas. Joyce was now beginning to live her own life. Just before leaving she had bought a little bungalow near the hospital at Newton Abbot. Joyce's visit helped lay to rest a few ghosts, although she and Mary did not have a great deal to talk about, having barely known each other since early childhood. Joyce, being no great reader, had simply taken her sister's success on trust. But Mary found it was satisfying to do something for her. If nothing else, it made the closed doors seem less threatening.

During Joyce's stay, Mary took a few days to canvass in a local by-election, though it was soon clear that the Progressive Party candidate was heading for failure. Poor Whites from both language groups supported the Nationalist programme. Mary deplored this, but understood the cause. These people had something real to lose if the Black population made any significant advances, while the Progressives she met were all middle-class people who asked her in for, as she put it, 'a nice cosy chat on the lines of "It isn't right, it really isn't, how would we like it if it was done to us." ' She wrote to Jay Williams that it was pleasant enough meeting them, but their vague liberalism was obviously hopeless in what was increasingly an extremist maelstrom. In the end her candidate polled only 23% of the vote, and that in the supposedly more humane and civilized Cape. For Mary the overall lesson was that one should not put faith in the majority, which was bound to vote in defence of its interests. When the counting was over, she summed it up to Jay: 'Everything decent and generous is done by the elite, everything mean by the masses. To believe the African would not do the same, you must regard him not just as an equal, but a superior race. That's why I go for a qualified franchise, and I think a lot of White countries would benefit from it too.'

Mary never tried to deny that this was a thoroughly élitist philosophy – indeed she believed in the idea of an élite – but, if there was any injustice to be fought, she would take action, even when she knew it would have little effect:

Yesterday, Saturday, I turned out with the Black Sash to do one of these things we do, standing in two lines on an island in the main street with placards protesting against Group Areas. I stood next to one of the placards, which read CONDEMN NABOTH'S VINEYARD LEGISLATION. This was certainly apt, but I thought as soon as I saw it that it was putting an undue strain on the average citizen's scriptural knowledge. From time to time someone would pass and say 'Excuse me, what *is* Naboth's Vineyard?' and of course we are supposed to stand silent and immobile; now and again one of the Sashers would hiss out of the side of her mouth 'Book of Kings'. But of course we had some more explanatory placards as well. I must say that when doing these stands I have never encountered any of the insults, etc., that integrationalists seem to have suffered at Little Rock; of course those could not happen in any large American city either, as I fully realise. Yesterday the worst that happened all the half-hour was a man reading out the words of the placard in a rather hostile voice. Often people have stopped by us and said 'Good show' or words to that effect.

Mary's real problem was a natural disinclination to accept any political line no matter how reasonable it might seem. When Nadine Gordimer stepped up the protest against the censorship laws, it was only to Kasia that Mary could express the feelings which, as a PEN committee member, she could hardly voice in public:

Censorship is a great problem. The stifling of thought is such a tremendous evil that one tends to feel one *must* be absolute about it, leave no chink for oppression to creep through. And yet, you do seem to come at last to places where the line must be drawn. The corruption of children? Anti-Semitism? Suppose, for the sake of argument, some crank printed a book of health hints which if people took its advice would cause countless deaths? Have you ever read an American novel called *The Bad Seed*? It contains not a word of obscenity, in fact sex hardly enters it. It is about a little child who commits several horrible murders. At the end it emerges that unknown to everyone, she is the granddaughter of a famous murderess. It is a sensational book with no literary value. It appalled me to think that this book had sold tens of thousands of copies, each of which would tend to set up in people's minds a prejudice against children of unknown parentage. How many children are growing up in orphanages because people who might have adopted and loved them took fright after reading this book? Of course there was never any question of banning it. That sort of thing is kept for earnest social tracts like *Lady Chatterley*, or *The Well of Loneliness*. But had I had it in my power to ban *The Bad Seed*, I know without doubt I would have banned it. Of course I would never ban *Chatterley* or even *Lolita*, disgusting as I thought the latter. But I have admitted the principle, you see. And where do we go from there? The only moral seems to be that men should be better and wiser so as to know where to draw the line and draw it justly. Which seems to be asking for the moon.

The leaders of the Coloured population called a general strike in protest against the first annual Republic Day, the moment when South Africa would leave the Commonwealth. Mary and Julie arranged for Katie, their maid, to have three days off and gave her a letter saying she was on holiday in the event she was picked up by the police. The tension was so great that it looked as if the protests might lead to violence. The word 'revolution' was being bandied about, and Mary frantically tried to finish her novel in case things got out of hand and they were forced to pack up and move. All about her she could see a bizarre mix of the deadly serious and the hilariously inept. On the one hand, the Government was rounding up its political opponents in a manner reminiscent of Communist Europe; on the other, the petty restrictions of *apartheid* were so ramshackle as to be laughable. At some point a 'Whites only' sign appeared on their tiny beach, but Mary simply waited until it was dark, then went out with a screwdriver and took it down. At least PEN's campaign against the new censorship legislation was successful, though, as Mary perceived, this was probably because the Government did not care enough to force it through and was happy to buy off a few noisy liberals rather than generate more opposition at a volatile moment.

Republic Day came and went. The revolution had been a chimera. It passed, leaving a greater sense of helplessness in its wake.

October 1961 brought the first general election since the founding of the Progressive Party; it was a rout. The United Party recaptured all the breakaway seats with the sole exception of Helen Suzman's in Houghton, Johannesburg, which would be the only Progressive toehold in Parliament from then on.

*

When *The Bull from the Sea* was finished and despatched to her agent, Spencer Curtis Brown in London wrote to say that he had decided to hand her over to a younger colleague, Juliet O'Hea. Juliet would prove as sensitive and sympathetic as Spencer had seemed irascible and awkward. She had no sooner taken on the task than she was plunged into a battle. Mary had just received the American paperback of *The King Must Die*, the cover of which showed the bull dance fresco from Knossos at the top and beneath a full-blown orgy. There was no orgy in the book, but what really upset Mary was the fact that such clothes as the orgiasts wore were Classical Greek when they should have been Mycenaean.

As John Guest had observed, Mary's anger could be awesome, and Juliet and Naomi were given to understand that this was the last time she would tolerate such nonsense. From then on both agents were quick to let publishers know that, if they wished to retain this best-selling author, they had better ensure Mary approved any ideas for art-work before jackets advanced too far.

For Mary, it was a good time to take stock. *The Bull from the Sea* would be published early in 1962, but it did not entirely satisfy her. As she wrote to Kasia, it was not as good as *The King Must Die*, mainly because the legends based on Theseus's life had little unity.

Actually the book is too short; before the end I was tiring of the Mycenaean Age and looking rather longingly at better documented periods. However I did want to complete the Theseus story. It now seems that every American publisher (the English ones are much less extravagant) who brings out a publication on the Mycenaean or Minoan Age sends it to me, which has enriched my library with some splendid books but makes me feel rather a fraud!

Even in remote Camps Bay the launch of a new book was bound to bring its crop of well-wishers trying to persuade her to socialize. Where a letter of praise from a writer such as Jay was always welcome, the garbled platitudes of people who wished to be near her only because she was famous, embarrassed her. The thought of half-baked interviews with local journalists, who would have read nothing more than the cover blurb, was too much to bear. Besides, she needed a break and a chance to find something to rekindle her imagination in the way Knossos had done.

It was a good excuse to travel up the West African coast for the first time, especially as South Africa's increasing isolation meant that many of the newly independent countries might soon be out of bounds to her. By this route she could see Spain and Italy before travelling on to Greece.

They planned to leave in March and be away for almost four months, too long for Katie and her husband, who usually stayed in the villa to take care of the animals when they were travelling. Fortunately they found a mother and daughter who needed a place for that length of time, while Mrs Messina, who was now very frail, was again put into a nursing home where she could be properly looked after. If she understood any of this, she seemed not to mind.

The reaction from England was less pleasing. As soon as they heard that she was planning to leave South Africa, Longmans assumed that she would be travelling to London to help launch the new book, and only with great difficulty accepted her refusal ever to return to Britain. Cedric Messina, who was by then a successful BBC radio drama producer, was equally surprised that she had no wish to savour the success she now enjoyed in her homeland. To Mary, that was precisely what deterred her. The thought of having to cope with fans and the obligation to visit family and friends was daunting, especially when added to all her usual complaints about the English weather and her grim memories of what life had been like when she and Julie were nurses.

Cedric, confronted with her absolute refusal to come to

England, announced that he would fly to Naples to meet her. She had no sooner digested this, than Pantheon cabled that they would have someone senior in the company fly out to Greece, omitting to explain why, which left her puzzled. What she failed to grasp was that she was no longer the unknown author who had once made a peaceful, uninterrupted progress across islands rarely disturbed by visitors. She was now famous, and Greece was a tourist trap. She might avoid her English fans, but there would be others waiting for her in Athens. She had corresponded with the classical scholar Kimon Friar, whose translation of Kazantzakis's *Odyssey* she had relished and who was in turn a devoted admirer of her books. Friar was eagerly awaiting her arrival. There were others she wanted to see, like Sinclair Hood of the British School in Athens, whose work had been important in her research. But the thought of coping with so many new people was worrisome. She wanted to let Greece work its magic. All she could hope was that these people would come and go quickly, leaving her to the solitude she craved.

The trip began badly. The travel agent failed to book their passage as planned, and the only way to keep anywhere near their schedule was to take a Portuguese ship, even though it would not call at the places they most wanted to see. Then, just before they were due to sail, Mary was entering the living room, carrying two glasses of lemonade, when she slipped and struck her throat against a marble-topped side table. The swelling was ugly and painful. Julie rang the doctor, but it was Saturday and he asked her to treat it with a cold compress. While this brought down the swelling fairly quickly, her voice was gone for weeks, and she was still in pain when they boarded the ship.

I I

Apollo

Nursing her throat, Mary was ill-disposed to enjoy the Portuguese liner she had been obliged to take. She disliked the
food and the company – there were only five English-speakers on
board, none of whom she found particularly interesting, especially
as she was unable to communicate in anything above a croaking
whisper. She found sitting on deck impossible because of the ill-
behaved Portuguese children and preferred to spend her days in
a remote lounge playing Scrabble with Julie.

She longed for the voyage to be over, but there were what she
called 'meaningless stops in Portuguese places'. Luanda stank of
urine and seemed hopelessly mismanaged and filthy after the civic
order of British colonies like Kenya and Rhodesia. She found
Madeira a complete waste of time.

It rained solidly in Lisbon, and the train journey across Spain
was freezing cold. The travel agent had booked them into modern
'luxury' hotels, which turned out to be expensive and soulless. It
was dawning on Mary that at fifty-seven she was no longer of an
age when the new was automatically appealing. It was raining so
heavily in Madrid that she confined herself to the Prado until she
took a slow train to Barcelona to catch the boat to Italy. This
small ship chugged round the Mediterranean under pewter skies,
depositing them in Naples, where Cedric was waiting on the dock.
With three days to kill, they went to Paestum, with Cedric passing
the time by telling them about his life as a successful radio producer and his affair with the actress Coral Browne. The following
day they went to Pompeii, where an irritating guide tried unsuccessfully to shock them by pointing out the cruder obscenities.
To Mary these were simply further examples of the pettiness of

men, continuing with their foolish obsessions in the shadow of deadly forces they could not control.

Modern life showed hardly any improvement – a dustmen's strike had left Naples as filthy as Luanda, and countless sardine tins bobbed in their wake as they sailed for Greece. Determined to make an early start, Mary went down to his cabin to rouse an unwilling Cedric, so that he might share her favourite first glimpse of Piraeus when they steamed in with the dawn.

Even in the half-light and from out at sea, it was not the place they had known before. High-rise concrete apartment blocks and hotels ran along the front, there were cars in the streets, and a proper customs shed; and, as they set off for the city, they saw that the roads had been remade. Only the accommodation was much as before. They had booked a holiday flat and, as soon as they opened the door, they saw that the owners had simply departed, leaving dirty sheets on the beds and left-overs in the fridge. They dumped their bags and went in search of a taverna and a meal.

Mary was awake all night with diarrhoea and abdominal pain. It was a bad attack of traveller's tummy which Julie could treat with the right medicines, but the most important thing was to move the patient to somewhere more salubrious. Julie went to the British Embassy to seek advice, and was delighted to see Mary's novels on sale in the pavement kiosks, nestling among the street maps, guide books and postcards of explicit vase paintings.

The consular staff was unhelpful, but the doorman directed her to the El Greco Hotel which had recently opened on Athenas. The rooms were modest and clean, and there was a café. Julie and Cedric ferried Mary by taxi across to the hotel; she went to bed and stayed there, unable to do more than scribble postcards.

It was two days before Mary felt well enough to risk a stroll down Athenas to the Agora. The changes were remarkable. There was a general air of bustle and business, with people far better dressed and shops and stalls laden with goods. There were also many more visitors, but she thought it selfish to carp. 'For every ten dim-wit travel snobs there is bound to be someone deeply moved and changed,' she wrote to Kasia, having talked to a young American girl in the arcade of the Stoa of Attallos, 'so unassuming, intelligent and nice', who had dropped out of her group in order to stay behind and 'get the feel of the place'. This was exactly what Mary hoped to do – find an isolated spot near the Temple of Hephaistos, where she could look up at the Acropolis and daydream.

A postcard having identified her whereabouts, John Guest, her editor, cabled to say that Mark Longman wanted to come out to see her. Cedric proposed a quick trip to Crete before he arrived, but Mary still felt unwell and had no wish to spoil her one brilliant memory of Knossos. When Cedric departed on his own, she decided to contact her correspondent Kimon Friar. As a leading scholar, there would be doors open to him which were locked to her. What she did not expect was someone who would cheer her up so enormously. Friar was jovial and enthusiastic, and openly delighted to meet someone he obviously admired. He promptly whisked her away to a night club frequented by *Efzones*, the highly decorative ceremonial guard who parade before the tomb of the unknown soldier. Off duty they were not wearing their white kilts and pompomed shoes, but they were very handsome. Mary reckoned they must be the only true descendants of the Greeks of the classical era and wondered, in a letter to Kasia, if the recruiting officers had to scour the remoter islands to find them.

What most impressed Mary about Kimon was the way he had survived a home life that made her own seem placid. His father insisted he join the family business and, if he caught him with a book, would beat him so badly the neighbours had to call the police. Yet here he was, 'warm-hearted' in Mary's words, and eager to show her a facet of Greek life she would never have encountered on her own.

The following day he took her to a christening in a little church on the outskirts of the city filled with garlands of wild flowers. The baby boy was surprisingly large, but, as Kimon explained, his parents had not wished to go to the expense of buying the richly embroidered robe he was wearing before being sure he would survive.

They left for a wedding reception, another delayed event, as the bride had had to wait till her fiancé's sisters were married off before he could wed; she was, by this time, well into middle age and not especially alluring in a hired gown which had seen better days. As if this were not bad enough, her big day was ruined when a man came to demand its return, and she burst into tears.

Kimon proved most useful to Mary when he persuaded the authorities to let her visit the parts of the Acropolis Museum which were not yet open to the general public. When she arrived she was dismayed to find that he had invited other friends, among them the American poet James Merrill, but was relieved when she was expected to do no more than shake hands before being left to stare in solitary rapture at the Blond Ephebe, which she had loved since she first saw its copy in the Ashmolean when she was nineteen. She described to Kasia 'that brooding aristocratic face with its faint, disillusioned smile – the face I imagined for Phaedo in *The Last of the Wine.*'

But it was the newly found Apollo of Piraeus, 'the most truly Delphic of all Apollos', that absolutely stunned her. The whole group gazed silently at 'his stern, enigmatic yet (as it seems to me, though not everyone agrees) profoundly benignant face'. It was an archaic face, so much more haunting than later, classical interpretations of the god. This Apollo had been found near the harbour at Piraeus in the course of digging a drain and had probably been part of a shipwreck. The hoard had also included an Artemis and an Athene, lovely fifth-century works, still in the Piraeus museum, at that time awaiting full restoration, their bodies slightly flattened from being buried. From the split in one thigh the Apollo, too, must once have been slightly squashed, but to Mary he seemed perfect:

He is pure copper and is now a wonderful shade of antico verde. The eyes I expect were originally inlaid, with whites; but it is a wonderful good fortune that their essential character has been preserved. He is life-size, or a little over; god-size I suppose, for they are always supposed to top their votaries by a head or so. I cannot tell you how beautiful the hands are; every attribute of the god seems to be effortlessly expressed in them, they had such sensitivity and yet such strength. An archer's and a musician's hands, among other things.

Gazing into that face produced the *frisson* she had hoped for, a sensation akin to that which she had experienced at Knossos. Further letters would keep referring to it for months after her return home, and it is clear from the varying descriptions that the face of the Apollo changed as she reflected on it, much as if it were a tragic mask subtly altered by the words pouring from the open mouth. She had to have something to remember it by, but all Friar could find was a postcard photograph.

Now, even more than before, she longed to go to Delphi, home of Apollo's oracle, site of his most famous temple. They left the next morning, planning to stay overnight to give them the whole day to cover the extensive ruins. It was late April and, as Mary reported to Jay, the weather was sharp and sunny:

We drove to Delphi, which although sublime in the daytime seems to distil its real mystery at night, with the mountain smells, huge spaces full of moonlight falling away to the sea below, and the soft-harsh tinkle of the donkey bells, sometimes across the mountain and sometimes right under your window, sounding as they move about and graze. The donkeys themselves seem particularly vocal in Delphi, every so often even in the depth of night one will suddenly give a bloodcurdling cry full of tragedy and defiance; perhaps they have discovered the cleft from which the vapours of madness and prophecy escape since the earthquake closed the one used by the Pythoness, but will utter oracles only for one another; the lot of Greek donkeys is not such that one can suppose they have much love of mankind.

To Mary the most unexpected thing about the site was the dominant position of the theatre, its tiered hemisphere looking down over the ruins of Apollo's temple and beyond into the great sweep of the valley. As she followed the Sacred Way eastward towards the stadium, she looked back to take a photograph, already aware that this was the one image she would need to recall in detail.

*

Back in Athens once more, Mary awaited the arrival of John Guest in some trepidation. When he rang, she invited him to dinner at the El Greco, but with her memories of England and the English firmly rooted in the pre-war world, her first concern was whether he would wear a dinner jacket and whether she ought to put on a long dress. She settled on a silk skirt in green and peacock blue, and was much relieved when he arrived in an ordinary suit. Had she but known it, he was as nervous of her as she of him. With an image of this rather fearsome author, with her stern views on punctuation and book jackets, before him, it was a relief to find that she was human after all.

They were just settling into their dining chairs when they were approached by a young man who turned out to be another of John's authors, who happened to be staying at the El Greco. He was introduced as Colin Spencer, travelling with a friend, Billy Favell, who, it later transpired, was a vicar. Guest had published Spencer's first novel, *An Absurd Affair*, the previous year, but was undecided about the manuscript of his second book, *Anarchists in Love*, because of a largely autobiographical bisexual element, and a character who was a rather brutal male tart. Back in England, John would decide against the book, which was published elsewhere, but at that dinner the matter still hung in the balance.

Mary was very taken with Spencer. His looks were in his favour, but he was also something new – her first encounter with 1960s liberated man – he was married, but travelling without his wife. Having so recently agonized over the correct dress for dinner, it was quite a jolt for Mary to discover how much things had changed in England since she had left. That someone as young as Spencer could be so open and frank about his sexuality was a revelation in itself. Moreover, the fact that he was enthusiastic about her books was the first proof she had had of how much she meant to a new generation.

Spencer had been sketching at the temple at Sounion wearing

sandals, and his feet were painfully swollen with sunburn. While Mary was counselling him to put something at the bottom of the bed so that he could sleep with his feet in the air, he was concentrating more on her face than her advice, finding her 'incredibly handsome with a patrician head out of antiquity'. He broke off the conversation to go to his room to fetch some of his sketches, architectural line drawings with no shading, one of them a view from the Agora looking up to the Acropolis, which exactly corresponded to Mary's own favourite perspective. She offered to buy it, and their friendship was sealed. After the meal Guest slipped away, leaving Mary encouraging Spencer and Favell to visit Delphi.

The following evening Guest brought round the novelist Robert Liddell, another of his authors, who had been head of the English Department at Athens University since 1951. Mary had been familiar with his books since 1948, when *The Last Enchantments* was published, and she had often used his *Aegean Greece* for her research. As a young man in England, Liddell had known Ivy Compton-Burnett and Margaret Jourdain, and had been party to some of the more intimate gossip surrounding 'the Row', which he was happy to reveal to a fascinated Mary over dinner in a rooftop taverna in the Plaka. After the meal, Liddell suggested they should go and hear Theodorakis, as Athens was 'throbbing to his music'. But the place they went first said to try somewhere else, a procedure repeated in several bars until Mary suddenly grew bored and proposed that they abandon Theodorakis in favour of a night club she had heard about. Liddell looked puzzled and, when he managed to speak to Guest on his own, suggested they should deflect Mary from her plan because the club was notorious and hardly the place for women. Mary was insistent and neither man felt inclined to enlighten her. A taxi deposited them at the end of a dark passage. Liddell went on ahead, to see if everything was all right, then returned to lead them to a room loud with pop music and filled with beautiful boys dancing together. Mary beamed with delight. Even the waiters were beautiful. She was received royally, her hand was kissed, her chair wiped before she sat down, and some very rough *retsina* exchanged for a superior brand. Guest recalls being in fits of laughter the whole time they were there, especially when Mary announced that she found the club 'very relaxing and wholesome'.

They were much amused when a tall, epicene youth called Basil leaped on to their table to dance for them. He had stuffed a pair of socks up his shirt to give himself breasts, a sight which prompted Mary to expound her theory of male sexuality – all men, she declared, should love someone of their own sex until just over twenty, when they should marry and raise a family. They should, however, return to their own sex in middle age. It was not lost on Liddell that she had no corresponding theory for women.

After more dancing and laughter, Mary and Julie were escorted back to the El Greco. How Mary had known about the club was never revealed.

*

Guest returned to London, and Cedric came back from Crete. They had a final day in Athens, photographing each other against a backdrop of the Parthenon, before he, too, departed.

The changes in Cedric's life brought home to Mary how much she had changed in the past twelve years. While she had lived in Durban, she had still been able think of herself as a traveller who would one day move on. The Cape had altered that. She had definitely settled there. This may have been why her attitude to Greece had changed. On her first visit she had been a wanderer without roots, at home anywhere; this time she was a visitor, like all the other tourists, with a place of her own waiting for her return.

Trying to recapture something of her former freedom, she and Julie set off on a tour of the nearby islands in the Saronic Gulf, but as soon as they landed at Aegina they realized they were not going to find the wildness they remembered from Samos. Its artists' colony gave the harbour a slightly raffish air, but there were none of the casual taverna friendships which had sprung up so easily before. The one bright spot was Hydra; in a shop selling cheap souvenirs Mary picked up a pottery bull and laughingly pointed out that its horns were back to front. The indignant owner piped up that he had made it himself and that he knew it was right because he had read it in the book of the famous English expert Mary Renault.

Everywhere else she felt shut in. In Athens the novelist Robert Liddell had arranged invitations to a British Council reception for visiting authors, along with Barbara Pym and Elizabeth Taylor. But the writers had so little in common that the encounter was meaningless. Pym noted, rather tartly, in her diary that 'Mary Renault arrived all in gold lamé. Miss Pym (a failure) in her simple black.'

The arrival the following morning of a representative from Pantheon cleared up the mystery of why they were so keen to have someone fly out to meet her. As soon as the man had introduced his wife – neither Mary nor Julie remembered their names – he began to unveil a complicated story of the internal politics within his company. Mary knew that the Wolffs had left Pantheon in 1960 and was aware the break had not been friendly. What she did not know was that the Wolffs had joined Harcourt Brace and that most of their authors were moving with them, hence this man's rather desperate attempt to win her over. He insisted on taking her for a drive to a mountain-top restaurant outside Athens, thus wasting an entire day. The last stages of the journey were up a twisting road through what Mary knew had once been a sacred olive grove. The thought of it being desecrated merely to make a road to a restaurant only added to her distress, none of which permeated through to her host, who never stopped talking until they arrived at 'a hideous cantilevered ferro-concrete monstrosity' with a barman waiting on the veranda with a tray of martinis. At a table nearby a rather bored-looking couple sat languidly playing patience. Mary fixed a polite expression on her face, toyed with her food and tried to hide her relief when it was time to leave.

Back at the El Greco she promised to reflect on all he had said, but fought off an invitation to dinner and spent the evening with Julie in their room. They had hoped for some peace, but from Omonia Square came the unmistakable sounds of rioting. Discontent over the previous year's election was still provoking serious student unrest. When they leaned out of the window, they could just see what Mary described as 'a laager of police trucks' in the square:

> Like some old Afrikaans folk-tale all the students were chanting slogans in an intoxicating rhythm which might, I felt, as well have been '*euoi, Iacchos, euoi!*' Bits of paving stones were flying, wounded policemen being patched up in the hotel; finally, although on the seventh floor, we had to shut the window on account of the tear gas. I do not think anyone was actually torn asunder; next morning the catharsis seemed to be over and everything went on just as usual.

There was one last public engagement: a party in her honour given by Robert Liddell, which turned up one opportune guest, Sinclair Hood, the director of the British School of Archaeology, whose work on Knossos Mary keenly admired. He found her a 'very impressive person', having once sat up all night reading *The King Must Die*, which he found extraordinarily true to the facts 'such as are known'. He invited her to visit the School and introduced her to his colleagues, then took her on yet another tour of the National Museum, where he noticed that, unlike most visitors, she 'knew how to look'.

It was by now almost the end of May and time for a final outing in the Peloponnese, starting in Corinth and ending at Epidaurus. It was a fitting conclusion to sit in the finest surviving classical theatre, with Mary speculating on what a Greek actor would have seen from inside his mask, what awareness of the audience he might have had and how such stage effects as the god-hoist, the thunder board and the acoustic cave must have worked. It is joyful to think of her striding across that broad stage in her purposeful way, endeavouring to experience the sensation of making a vast audience weep for Agamemnon's daughter or howl with laughter at the phallus-bedecked clowns in the more ribald comedies, then listening to the imaginary applause thundering down from the high stone tiers.

*

They sailed for Italy in the first week of June, but any hopes of repeating their magical arrival in Venice were dashed when torrential rain engulfed the ship as they approached the Grand Canal. Mary tried to make the best of it, describing 'the rough green waves' in a letter to Colin Spencer, with 'the spray bursting up from the *vaporetti*, and an amazingly Guardiesque scow being poled along by a timeless figure in a red cap'. Once ashore, optimism deserted them. No one came to help, the hotel staff were on strike and, as they waited, everything they owned was soaked by the incessant rain. When they eventually dragged their bags to their hotel, there was no one to work the lifts and they had a three-floor climb, hauling the dripping cases after them.

Once inside their room, reception rang to say that a Signora Naomi Burton had arrived. Mary was astonished and delighted. She had not seen Naomi since the beginning of the war, and although they often corresponded about business, she was longing to see her friend and hear all her news. Julie was less enthusiastic. Watching Mary and Naomi together, deep in conversation, Julie felt increasingly irritated. Naomi, it transpired, had become an ardent Catholic, even to the point of wearing the scapula, a revelation which persuaded Julie that she was trying to convert Mary.

In a way she was, but not to Catholicism – Naomi was planning to leave Curtis Brown to join a New York publishing house and had flown to Venice in the hope of persuading Mary to move with her. So famous an author with her level of sales would be a great coup. Mary listened to her arguments, but was unconvinced; there had been too much said on this subject already. She decided to stay with Pantheon, more out of weariness with the issue than any feeling of loyalty to the company; that had ended with the departure of the Wolffs.

However, none of this affected Mary's pleasure at seeing Naomi, who accompanied them on all their trips around the city. Julie felt Naomi was monopolizing Mary and was sure that her friend would be glad to be free of her for a time. On their last day Julie offered to take Naomi for a walk while Mary went back to a shop they had seen earlier where there was a gold necklace she wanted to buy.

Left to herself, Mary decided to settle the hotel bill and gave the receptionist the last of her traveller's cheques, receiving a wad of Italian currency in exchange. She sauntered off to the shop and returned a little later, fingering the delicate gold chain, to find the two women waiting for her. After saying their goodbyes to Naomi, Mary and Julie waited for the hotel to send its *vaporetto* to ferry them to their liner – and waited. If Julie had not been so obsessed with keeping Naomi out of the way, she might have reflected on the folly of letting Mary deal with financial matters. It was only when their boat was due to sail that she realized something was wrong and rushed to the reception desk, where she was told that Mary had picked up all the currency and walked out without paying the bill. Until it was settled, they would not send the *vaporetto*. There was just enough left from the purchase of the necklace to settle the account, barely time to get to the boat before it put to sea. Boarding the liner with only minutes to spare, they stood, shaken and breathless, watching Venice disappear. It was Mary's last sight of Europe.

*

They arrived home to find Mrs Messina in a state of deep distress. The nursing home had not only refused to follow Julie's carefully set out list of her dietary needs but had also pressed its regular meals on her, and, when she stoically refused to touch them, had actually held her down and force-fed her, inducing a severe cardiac condition. Even then, they refused to call her doctor, bringing in their own, a stranger to the poor, frightened woman.

They brought Mrs Messina back to Delos at once, but the damage was done. She could not sleep and began to get up in the night and amble about. Two nights after their return, she opened a wardrobe, thinking it was the door to her room, and began to strike matches inside, trying to see where she was. After that, it was clear she might harm herself, and Julie sat up with her for part of several nights until she was sure she had fallen asleep.

In the midst of all this anguish, Mary unpacked her treasures and arranged them along the top of the bookcase in her study – a replica of a chariot trophy vase, a small head of a Polykleitos athlete and the photograph of the Piraeus Apollo – and went on what she described to Jay as 'a reading jag, long overdue, before rolling up my sleeves again'. She was re-reading Plato, but concentrating on the later life, happy to leave the Bronze Age to the archaeologists. Greece had engendered a number of loose ideas, which had not yet gelled into a single theme.

Two weeks after their return Mrs Messina's condition deteriorated; she was only semi-conscious when she had to be removed to a nursing home. A few days later she died.

Mary's surviving correspondence makes no mention of the death or the funeral, which is odd since she always exchanged a good deal of personal information with Jay and Kasia. But of Mrs Messina she said nothing – taking her in had been a personal and private offering to some goddess of family which Mary seemed to consider of no interest to even her closest friends.

Cedric did not return for the burial, and Mary's main concern was that Julie should not be too depressed by the sudden absence. She had always seen to the old lady, meticulously preparing her trays, buying her cigarettes, arranging her room and, in the end, nursing her. For Julie, the house now seemed unnaturally empty and Mary promptly decided it was time to redecorate. They would have a fresh colour, terracotta pink à la Pompeii, and the empty upstairs room with its stunning view of Table Mountain would be transformed into a study for Julie. She was a healthy woman in her early fifties, yet small things seemed to drag her down, anything from minor setbacks in organizing the house to the eccentricities of some of their friends. Mary had only to make a mild complaint about something or someone for Julie to take up the issue, as if it were a cause. Mary's letters hint at the problem: Julie has been ill and is finding it hard to pull herself together; there has been a visitor at the villa, and Julie is furious at having had to drive him back into Cape Town; the cooker needs repairing, and Julie is distraught. With her own study, Julie could settle down to something serious.

Julie tried. She decided to write a play based on the life of a local eccentric named James Barry – *not* the man who wrote *Peter Pan*, as she had to keep explaining, but a woman in nineteenth-century Cape Town who dressed as a man and managed to gain a position as an army surgeon. Barry was more than a transvestite, she was a zealous campaigner who reformed the city jails and lepers' quarters. The irony was that, while Julie was typing away upstairs, Mary was still staring out at the ocean or watching children and dogs gambolling on the beach.

It was in this frame of mind that she decided to accept a proposal from Harper in America that she write a children's book on some aspect of Greek history. As she told Jay, she felt she ought to. He had been sending her his children's stories as they appeared, and it looked to her as if she had a duty to help out, to do something worthwhile for young people. It was a highly romantic notion, and one she was shortly to regret. She had thought it would take three months and help to clear her thoughts for the adult novel that was proving so resistant. In the end, it took nine months and became a torment.

She chose to retell the story of the Persian Wars under the title *The Lion in the Gateway*, but soon realized that she could not think herself into the young reader's mind. When she had been a child, she had read either adult cowboy stories or Kipling. All she seemed to be doing was watering down Herodotus, and the only section that pleased her was the embassy to King Amyntas of Macedon, where the insolent Persians call for the royal ladies to join the supper, treating them like *hetairae*, and the young Prince Alexander smuggles them away, dresses seven of his young bodyguards in their clothes and has all the Persians massacred on their supper couches. It worked, as she told Jay, 'because it reminded me of my unregenerate youth when I would climb with two pistols to the top of a wardrobe or whatever, and utter through clenched teeth, "One more step, Mr Hands, and I'll blow your brains out." '

Several times during the writing, she considered abandoning the project, but felt constrained by her contract to continue. Even when she sent off the finished manuscript, the irritation continued. Her editor, Walter Lord, was the author of *A Night to Remember*, the story of the sinking of the *Titanic*, and he began pestering her with time-consuming questions and requests for reading lists and other subsidiary material. She grudgingly complied until he wrote to say that he felt she should provide an introduction. She did so:

AUTHOR'S FOREWORD

Dear Reader,

The Publishers of this book have asked me to write a preface, to tell you what it is about. But I have said in the book what it is about. Besides, when I was your age I never dreamed of reading prefaces, nor I am sure do you; in fact if you have read this far I shall be amazed. What is more, though now advanced in years I still do not read prefaces, so often do they consist of things the author felt he ought to say, but which are not interesting enough to be in the book. So I have decided to be kind to us both and let you off a preface; and now you can get on with the story.

This was the end of the matter. She wrote to Jay that her copy lay on her desk 'as wet as a kitchen dishcloth', and that she couldn't wait to get on with work begun before she had let herself be side-tracked. It was late 1963. Over a year had drifted by since she had last attempted to write a serious novel, more than two years since she had completed *The Bull from the Sea*, and even that had been largely a stop-gap, a means of keeping her hand in until she found a more inspiring subject. None had suggested itself. She had had silences before, most painfully at the end of the war, but that had been the result of war fatigue. This time there was no easy excuse; if anything, the problem was self-inflicted – each time she could have got down to work, she let something else prevent her.

In 1964, she agreed to become president of Cape Town PEN, and while she asked for assurances that this would be purely ceremonial, she must have known that even an honorary role would eat into her time. What she had not bargained for was the acute discomfort she would experience. The monthly lunches at a Cape Town hotel were a great strain: the idea of people staring at her was unsettling, as was having to worry over what to wear now that she was accustomed to the easy-going beach life at the villa. Although the chairman and his deputy undertook the basic administrative work, she was occasionally expected to make a speech and discovered she had no talent for public oratory. She loathed it all the more because she knew she wasn't good at it.

Her concern about clothes seems to have dominated her thoughts when she was asked to be one of two authors to front yet another protest. The country's writers and artists had been invited to sign a petition opposing the formation of a new censorship board with wide-ranging powers. The petition would be jointly presented in Parliament to the Minister of the Interior by an Afrikaans writer and an English writer; when Mary was offered the latter role, it was an honour she found impossible to refuse. She instantly regretted her decision when everyone told her she would have to wear a 'parliamentary hat', which was, as described to Kasia, 'a grotesque creation, unique to the Republic and already a great Cape Town joke, looking somewhat like plates of rice pudding with a dash of fruit-salad and meringue, worn mainly by the wives of nationalist ministers who would sit in the gallery watching their husbands deliver interminable speeches on this and that, their broad Dutch faces peeping out from under these amazing constructions.'

In the end she dressed 'as for Matins', in a black coat and discreet beige silk turban, but she still felt peculiar when she arrived early in the morning at the house of one of the organizers, a painter, to meet her counterpart Bill de Klerk. Her chief difficulty, as she explained on their drive to Parliament, was her inability to speak Afrikaans, but he assured her that the Minister would be far too gentlemanly not to address her in English once he knew she was not bilingual. He was wrong. After an interminable wait in an ante-room, they were ushered into the presence of what Mary described to Jay with memorable vehemence as a 'fat stupid slab-faced old geezer' who talked 'endless politicians' crap in Afrikaans'. This left her free to admire the ministerial office with its wall-to-wall carpeting 'in what Tottenham Court Road calls Autumn tints and the real hand-painted landscape done in pink and blue mud'. The Minister was also called de Klerk – 'they only have six surnames for the entire race' – and Mary could not but feel sorry for her colleague, who was clearly having a hard time. Mary knew that there was nothing the Government could do to harm her, but Bill de Klerk was forced to write for a limited local language group and, if his books were not bought by the state schools, he would be in deep trouble. Yet there he was,

MARY RENAULT

courageously defying his main source of income while she was
powerless to help him.

Not until they were ushered to the door did the Minister deign
to notice Mary, offering a curt goodbye in English. Unwilling to
be so easily snubbed, she said, 'Mr de Klerk, we are both of
Huguenot descent, our forefathers left France to preserve their
liberty of conscience, and I think we should try to be worthy of
them.' As she reported to Kasia, the Minister then 'inclined his
head with an indulgent smile as if to say: "Get back to your
kitchen, little woman" and added: "You shall have it, never fear".
Which of course meant nothing.'

She was furious but at least had the satisfaction of knowing that
with so many authors and painters signing the petition the Minister
was in for a humiliating rebuff when he attempted to get anyone
important to sit on his board of censors. Yet when she was back
at Delos and the rush of adrenalin had died away, it was hard to
remain convinced that any of it really mattered. The political
struggle had moved so far from those days when it had been
possible to believe it could all be contained within the scope of a
White parliament. There no longer seemed to be any point in
continuing to protest about legal niceties. What did an irritant
such as censorship matter when set beside the increasing violence
in South Africa, much of it inflicted by Africans on other Africans?
Her accounts to Jay show a marked weakening of sympathy for
the protesters, and her distress at what she saw as a slide into
anarchy:

The Paarl mob surged forth in the night towards the police
station, but in the meantime stoned cars, set petrol pumps alight,
and generally alerted the neighbourhood. When they got to the
station, not unnaturally it was full of police who opened fire
(low) as they charged. One or two were killed but it was in no
way a Sharpeville and there is no doubt the lives of the police
were actually threatened. After this they ran away into the
streets and split up. One lot of them then ran riot in an ordinary
suburban street where they attacked several small houses and
started to batter in the doors. A young schoolgirl of seventeen,
terrified by the din, jumped out of a window and found herself

236

in the middle of the mob outside. They hacked her to death with cane knives and whatever weapons they had. A lad of 23 heard her screams and very bravely ran out to defend her only to be sliced up in turn. (The man in whose garden she actually died, though he had a gun which the boy hadn't, was afraid to go out.) An elderly woman was also beaten up, but recovered. This is the incident about which the Commission of Enquiry is being held.

If the choice were simply between the boorish White tribe of Afrikaners and Black mob rule, where was she supposed to situate herself? It was all there in Plato, of course, the distasteful reality set against the desired ideal. When Plato's beloved pupil Dion had brought him to his native city, Syracuse, to help create the ideal republic, even the noble philosopher had failed. After all that had happened in the Athens of his youth and the bitter failure of his theories in Syracuse, it was easy to see why Plato advocated the prudent rule of a philosopher-king, the good man who, restrained by philosophy, would govern justly, preparing the people for the day when they, too, would be ready to participate in the affairs of their city. It was a paternalistic view of politics Mary found increasingly easy to translate into her own context:

Quite honestly the best thing that could happen would be to get rid of every kind of theorist from the Government and be run on a system of humane laissez-faire with adequate security. The Africans who are evolved would then be integrated into industry as big business is dying to do both for labour and consumer reasons; a settled middle class would emerge, aspirations would be satisfied, and meantime of course the primitives would be relieved in hunger and sickness and given the educational opportunities to catch up. In fair competition the white man has so little to fear that you would think he would be ashamed to have his job protected; but to keep the poor-white vote the Govt. will ensure that the most slovenly drunken white worker will get skilled work before the most intelligent African. The trouble is with the Nationalist Afrikaaner, he seems to have vanity but no pride.

237

This was what she ought to be writing about, and she knew it. It was the logical sequel to *The Last of the Wine*. The Theseus books had been an escape into mythology. If she were consumed by political concerns then better she should do something effective through writing rather than through direct action, the effects of which she now doubted. The face of the Piraeus Apollo had stared down at her for too long, waiting to be brought back to life. She had a superstitious regard for his powers – even admitting to Jay that she occasionally felt his presence guiding her. Now it was time to follow the advice and get back to work.

12

Another Country

There were obvious parallels, it seemed to Mary, between 1960s Africa and the accounts she found in Plutarch of the tyrannies and despotism of the fourth-century Greek world. A man like Dionysius I, tyrant of Syracuse, held on to power in his city-state by the same police state methods employed by modern African despots – though what most fascinated Mary was not so much the terror and death as the nobility of those who attempted to rise above it. It was Dionysius's son-in-law, Dion, who held her interest and propelled her towards the new novel.

Having studied under Plato, Dion persuaded his teacher to visit Syracuse, hoping that he would lead the tyrant towards a knowledge of the Good. It was a visit doomed to disaster. Dionysius had the philosopher deported and sold into slavery – fortunately he was bought and freed by an admirer. But Dion yearned to make an ideal Athens in Syracuse and, when Dionysius died, he convinced Plato that he should return, try once more with the son, Dionysius II, and thus prove to the world that his theories of good government could work in practice.

Plato agreed, only to discover that the boy was weak and already corrupted by power. Dion was expelled, and Plato barely escaped with his life. For Dion long years of exile followed until the actions of the debauched Dionysius proved too much even for family loyalty. Having raised an army, Dion returned to Syracuse, where he overthrew and exiled the loathed dictator.

Tragically, the cycle of tyranny and demagoguery could not be broken by one man, no matter how honourable. Dion tried to set himself up as a benign monarch – the philosopher-king advocated by Plato – but he discovered the bitter truth that some people will always reject the Good, and that to deal with them requires base methods, which reduce even the loftiest ruler to their level. It was a grim tale, a sharp riposte to those idealists who believed there was a ready-made theoretical solution to the age-old problems of human greed and lust for power. It ended with the murder of Dion, and his city's ruin and oblivion.

Such a challenging mix of action and debate would require skills that had lain dormant during the story-telling period that had produced the Theseus books. Mary's first challenge was how to recount the history at one remove from its historical characters. If the narrator were someone close to Plato, Mary would have been placed in the invidious position of having to invent a large amount of dialogue for the great philosopher, a challenge she found too hubristic to consider. In *The Last of the Wine* she had resolved this by running a fictional story parallel to the historical action. To use this technique again called for someone well-travelled, who could have been in all the right places at the right times, but for his own separate reasons; someone who could weave in and out of the main story as required, but who would be distant enough to avoid the need to invent dialogue for Plato. She had tentatively invented a fictitious narrator, but was beginning to find he bored her. She considered having Dion narrate the story, but this, too, was abandoned when she wearily acknowledged that he was a somewhat humourless figure unlikely to win the reader's sympathy. However, recognition of this fact in turn suggested a solution of sorts: with so many heavyweight philosophers in the story, it would do no harm to introduce a more frivolous character as a counterbalance. She described to Jay how the answer to her problem came 'with a snap, as if the spine of the book had been shoved into place by an osteopath, whereupon it got up and walked and in no time it was running'.

It was the memory of Delphi and Ephesus which provided the solution. Since her return, she had been reading all she could on classical theatre: Margaret Bieber's *The History of the Greek and Roman Theatre*, T. B. L. Webster's *Greek Theatre Production* and A. Pickard-Cambridge's *The Dramatic Festivals of Athens*. What provoked the 'snap' was her discovery that during the upheavals of the fourth century BC actors passed freely between cities, even those at war, and were often used to carry messages and, on occasion, to act as ambassadors. It was possible to imagine an actor who had been witness to the events she wished to describe without his having been too close to the participants. Better still, where the philosophers were serious, even dour, he could be as camp as most of her actor friends, for there was no doubt he would share their sexuality. She already knew from her reading that although the theatrical conventions were utterly different – acting in masks, men playing the women's roles, the use of the chorus – the ways of actors had barely changed at all. She had already been intrigued by the account of an actor called Polos, who, when he was given his dead son's ashes in an urn just before going on as Electra to mourn the death of Orestes, brought it on stage for the speech. Polos is said to have given such a moving performance that he brought the house down.

The voice range of an actor like Polos must have been extra-ordinary. Hidden behind a mask, deprived of facial expression, the male actor was expected to use sound and gesture to create several roles within the same play. It was this three-actors rule that interested Mary; it required that whatever the apparent cast of a classic drama, it had to be acted by just three men supported by a 'mute' extra, who wore the principal's mask, while that actor changed for another role. She wrote to Kasia of her astonishment when she realized how great a speed was needed for the actor playing Phaedra in the *Hippolytos* to get into his Theseus costume and back on stage within minutes of leaving it. She was equally intrigued by how the god-hoist had been used to fly in the actor playing the deity without it looking like a modern pantomime.

All her regular correspondents were drawn into these specu-lations. She wrote to Cedric, by now a television drama producer, telling him of her ideas on what the theatre must have meant to a fourth-century Greek:

Barring a sprinkling of intellectuals, the whole vast audience believed the whole thing had actually happened. They might be highly sophisticated and critical about the way the story was rendered, but they believed not only that Oedipus really did put out his eyes in Thebes (and perhaps he did, who knows?) but that, for instance, Achilles was the child of a man and a goddess, that Orestes was pursued by visible furies and rescued by Apollo, that Herakles went down into Hades. So that as well as the aesthetic appeal of the plays, they appealed to the ordinary people in the same way as Cody's Wild West show must have done to an audience who remembered Custer's last stand as recent news. And then behind all that, was an immemorially ancient folk-memory of masked rituals going back, probably, tens of millennia to some horned shaman in a cave; there was magic in it.

Mary called her fictional actor Nikeratos – Niko – an Athenian whom the reader follows from his childhood where he mutely plays bit parts with his actor father. After years of struggle in second-rate travelling companies, mastering his craft, come his first successes in the great drama festivals, winning all the major contests and touring the Greek world as a leading actor-manager. Niko's suitability as a narrator at one step removed from the historical figures is obvious, but Mary goes beyond this elementary device to create two surprisingly *similar* worlds, in which both sets of protagonists are struggling against the decline of the age. Where Dion, through Plato, sees himself as the inheritor of the fading traditions of the age of Pericles, Niko operates in a theatrical world which is thought decadent when set against the fifth-century glories of Sophocles and Euripides. These are symbolized by an old mask of Apollo, which Niko inherits and which seems to him to embody all the old virtues he tries to maintain. Although no longer fashionable, the mask is still an awesome object, kept first as a talisman, but later as an oracle, when he realizes that through it he can divine whether or not the god approves his actions. Its strange, archaic features are a constant reminder that, even in a lesser age, he is the representative of a noble tradition:

I remember the first time I unpacked the hampers, at Eleusis, and saw it looking up at me. It gave me a start. It was a face, I thought, more for a temple than a stage. I know I sat back on my heels, among all the litter, looking and looking. Meidias was right in calling it old-fashioned, one must allow him that. No one would say, as they do before a modern Apollo, 'Delightful! What a nice young man!'

Demochares, whom I asked about it, said it had been left to Lamprias by some old actor who had thought it brought him luck. It was supposed to have been made for the first revival of Aischylos' *Eumenides*, where the god has a central role. That would be in the great days of Alkibiades and Nikias, when sponsors were sponsors, Demochares said.

The mask is, of course, the Piraeus Apollo, staring down at Mary from the photograph on her bookcase, which sometimes seemed to communicate with her as the fictional Apollo did with Niko. She even told Jay that the new novel 'seems to come as a gift from Apollo, some fluke shows what you need. I offer him a pinch of incense for you . . .'

Romance aside, the device provided the necessary bridge, crossed when Dion goes backstage to congratulate Niko after a particularly hair-raising performance in which a jealous actor has tried to kill him by tampering with the god-hoist, nearly causing him to fall to his death. Dion admires his courage for having carried on until safely lowered to the ground. For his part, Niko worships the grave and beautiful Dion from the moment he sets eyes on him and will support his cause, no matter what personal risks are involved. Niko is well placed to carry Dion's messages as he plots first to convert the tyrant's son, later to supplant him. But the fascination of the novel lies in the subtle way the fictional narrator moves centre stage, until we gradually come to see that Niko also represents a kind of heroism. Initially his camp, theatrical world seems bright and superficial beside the weighty statecraft of the Academy – until Mary points up the fact that even the would-be philosopher-king is also acting out a role. When Niko last sees him, Dion's face is a tragic mask; he is *playing* the doomed and suffering king. The book gives form to the Socratic injunction 'Be what you want to seem.' Niko aspires to this each time he gazes into his mask, readying himself for his role. The book's underlying theme is that art alone survives; the great battles of the age and shifts of power all recede to the level of mere tribal squabbles, surviving at best as the subject matter for a dramatist, so that some future Niko may give them life once more.

✳

By mid-1965 Mary was able to write to Kasia that she was well into her new novel. It would be entitled *The Mask of Apollo* and she gave Kasia an unaccustomed clue to its subject, sending her a photograph of a portrait statue of Plato, in which:

> the head and body have fairly recently, I think, been brought together by a German scholar called Hekler. I found it in Gisela Richter's three-volume *Portraits of the Greeks*, which sells at the frightful price of 25 gns., but in my job I couldn't really afford not to have it, and it was worth the money, as far as I was concerned, for this alone. I think perhaps you could enrol him among the sad captains, so long as sadness doesn't imply defeat. Few men surely can have weathered so much tragedy with so much physical and spiritual courage. I feel for him a tremendous personal loyalty, like you. The fascination of the Sicilian affair to me is the constant interplay of the great ethical and political issues with human character; it must be one of the most perfect demonstrations of the fact that you cannot have such a thing as a universally valid political theory. Not of course that Plato ever supposed you could, but a lot of people do today.

Richter's book was merely one expensive volume in what she had made the best private classical library in sub-Saharan Africa. Whereas *The Last of the Wine* and the two Theseus novels had been based on a small number of key sources, fleshed out by recent studies of the historical sites referred to in the stories and illuminated with visual details from pottery and sculpture, she was now doing original research. What had begun as a novelist's interest in the technical aspects of ancient theatre, its construction and the techniques of the participants, had developed into an obsession which would make her a leading expert on classical drama. Until *The Last of the Wine* she had boasted that she could carry on her trade anywhere, that all she needed was a table on which to set down her portable typewriter. Now she had numerous notebooks in which she jotted down discoveries, while she constantly cut out snippets from the newspapers flown in from England: the *Sunday Times*, *Observer*, *Telegraph*, the *Times*' supplements, *Spectator*, *Apollo*, *Punch*, *Illustrated London News* as well as *Archaeology* and a whole range of specialist journals. She cut out photographs of archaeological digs and newly restored artifacts but, while she would always remember the clippings, she could not always remember where she had put them, so Julie spent much time gathering up these bits and pieces to be sure they were on Mary's desk when she needed them. Her notes were meaningless to anyone else. Perhaps as a result of her medical background, her handwriting was as illegible as any doctor's. It is fortunate that most of her correspondence is typed; the rare handwritten letter is impenetrable and must have been largely meaningless to its recipient.

More copious notes went into exercise books and were cross-referenced on a card-index system. Anything with pictures might prove useful – when Kasia sent her a collection of photographs put out by Swan's Tours to accompany one of their lecture tours in Asia Minor, Mary promptly wrote back to say that she was filing it in her 'Topography Section'. Her love of technology was almost fanatical: she wrote to Kasia with childlike enthusiasm about her new photocopier or the amazing functions of the latest electric typewriter. Her handwriting might be sloppy, but her working environment was as neat and as mechanized as a Swiss bank, occasionally submerged under a blizzard of notes and clippings.

Towards the end of 1965, one year into the book, life and art collided with the decision of the South African Government to segregate theatres. These moves were followed by public announcements from prominent playwrights in Britain and America that they would no longer permit their work to be staged in the Republic. Mary's opposition to both segregation *and* the subsequent boycott was the beginning of a lonely and often misunderstood position. As she wrote to Kasia, leaving aside the morality of the boycott, its efficacy was open to question:

The writers most insistent on the ban are the ones with a message. To me this does not make sense. If one is a writer, one must surely stake enough confidence on one's work to hope it may influence people one thinks misguided or wrong, not treat it like a bag of sweets one takes as a punishment from a naughty child. And I think this is all tied up with this other subject of the blight. They not only don't believe any longer in their work influencing anyone for good, they don't even try. I find this deeply depressing.

It was well into January 1966, when all the annual 'summer' visitors to the Cape had receded, before she was able to return to the task of finishing the book. By June, she was laboriously typing out the fair copy, though having a photocopier meant she no longer had to fuss about with carbons. Whatever tedium was involved – and the smallest typing error was likely to mean an entire page being redone – was eased by the satisfaction of knowing that the story worked. As she would agonize later, in her letters to Jay, there were one or two moments when the device of having an off-stage narrator made the action wear a little thin – the death of Dion, all in reported speech, did not entirely please her. But overall the novel's 'split personality' held up, largely because of her finely honed skill as a painter of an entirely plausible historical world imbued with her instinctive sense of how its inhabitants must themselves have seen it:

Ask some poet to describe the awe of Delphi, and some philosopher to explain it. I work with the words of other men. I looked back down the valley, the olives winding and falling mile on mile to a rock-clipped blink of sea. Beyond a vast gulf of air were the highlands of Mount Korax, cloud-patched with sun and gloom; westward the iron cliffs of Kirphis; above us reared Parnassos, more felt than seen. Its head was hidden by its knees, the rock-towers of the Phaidriades, which themselves seemed to gore the sky. Truly, Apollo is the greatest of all chorus-masters. The town, with his temple in the midst, is tiny as a toy in all this vastness; yet all those titan heads seem to stand around that and look towards it. They are the chorus round his altar; if he raised his arm they would sing a dithyramb. I don't know any other deity who could bring off such a show. At Delphi, you don't ask how they know it is the centre of the earth.

The voice is that of Niko, her most fully rounded character to date mainly because he suffers least from her authorial desire to make her creations adopt a moral stance. Niko is her first self-admitted homosexual. His deviance is not a stage in his development; it is his nature. He is as likely to chase after a pretty face in some foreign town where he is playing as any of her real actor friends would have been. He is 'married' and is loyal, after his fashion, to his boyfriend Thettalos, a younger actor whom he has trained and launched, and who later becomes a prize-winning performer. Niko and Thettalos have a convincing homosexual marriage because of the infidelities and tearful reunions, not because they are trying to invent a childless facsimile of heterosexual family life. They get by as real people in an imperfect world, making such accommodations as they must and hoping to see things through as honourably as possible.

With Niko, Mary brings an end to the critical, detached view of homosexuals that divided the characters in *The Charioteer* into the camp set, all silly talk and vicious behaviour, and the good guys who stayed together no matter what. *The Last of the Wine* came close to advocating chastity, though few of her gay readers seem to have noticed this, preferring to regard Alexias and Lysis as representatives of an ideal homosexuality to which they believed they themselves aspired. Part of Mary's increased tolerance must surely have come from her role as confessor figure to many of her readers, even one of her publishers turned to her when his lover of many years ran away with a friend made on holiday, driving the betrayed man to unburden himself to that remote yet understanding figure in distant Cape Town. She wrote back at once, not offering meaningless advice, but recounting her own feelings when Julie had gone off with the schoolteacher a lifetime ago, describing the desolation she had felt before it all ended a week later with Julie's return.

One correspondent was a young sergeant with the American forces in Vietnam, where he and his dog Fritz were serving as advance scouts for troop movements in the Central Highlands. He poured out his heart to her when Fritz died and was buried 'as befits a soldier', averring that Lysis was his 'model for conduct'. Later, after being invalided out of Cambodia, he wrote from San Francisco to say that his copy of *The Last of the Wine* had been captured from the man to whom he had loaned it. 'It can be assumed,' he wrote, 'that somewhere deep in the untenable Cambodian jungle a young Communist is wondering about the matter of Socrates and the soul of ancient Athens.'

When the House of Representatives in Cape Town established a commission to consider widening the scope of the Immorality Act to create even greater legal restraints on homosexuality, Mary tried unsuccessfully to involve Black Sash in the protest. They refused, and she had to be content with making her own representation to the commission in a letter warning that the way it intended collecting evidence would only confirm its own prejudices:

The promiscuous homosexual, who, like the equivalent type of heterosexual, relies for his sex life on casual or mercenary contacts, usually lives alone. Relying on the immunity offered to persons who testify, he can safely describe events of his past life, since they have no links with his future; if the Act as it stands becomes law, he will no doubt plan to evade it, assisted by the kind of racketeer the Act would call into being, as the liquor prohibition act did in America.

The respectable and domesticated homosexual, however, is likely to have found himself a permanent companion, with whom he lives, often without mixing at all in an exclusively homosexual set. If such people want to testify, they have to state their intention in writing, which will presumably remain on file, and when the Committee, or Commission, is dissolved, will pass into the keeping of some Government department. Immunity offered by the Committee covers the present and the past, but not the future. The implications are too obvious to need labouring.

I have no doubt that some homosexuals of this kind will take the risks of coming forward, from a sense of social duty. Many others, however, will inevitably be deterred by considerations of their families, their companions, or their careers. This cannot but lead to a false estimation of their numbers, proportionately to those of more promiscuous types.

The qualities of intellect and character, and the idealism often shown in their attitude to their relationships, which these men displayed, are such that I should deeply regret seeing their case go by default, owing to the fact that the present conditions of testimony must appear, to them, to threaten them with tragedy and even ruin, should the Act become law.

The bill was eventually quashed on the ground that homosexuals could not help themselves, though, as Mary explained to Colin Spencer, 'We weren't too delighted at being relegated to the ranks of morons and screwballs . . .'

Her use of the word 'we' catches the attention, and it is only in the few letters she wrote to Spencer that there is some sign of a belated acceptance of her own lesbianism. Perhaps she felt obliged to reciprocate his openness over his own sexuality and the way in which he had transformed it into *Poppy, Mandragora and the New Sex*, his latest novel, which became a *succès de scandale* of the Swinging Sixties – a phenomenon Mary could but dimly perceive through his letters to her.

When the British press threw itself into the debate on homosexual law reform in the wake of the Wolfenden Report, Mary wrote to the *Spectator*, complaining about the apologetic way people were defending homosexuals, when they ought to proclaim 'that under conditions of population explosion it is a healthy human reaction which ought to be encouraged'. She did, however, add a rather touching rider to her letter to Colin Spencer reporting this, saying she hoped that her last surviving Baxter aunt, then nearly eighty, would not see it.

The proposed action against homosexuals in South Africa was fought off, but Mary was left dissatisfied with what she saw as a failure of nerve on the part of Black Sash. She made one last attempt to persuade them to extend their area of interest beyond African civil rights, writing to the Cape Town committee to urge it to protest against the suffering of farm animals transported by train in scorching weather across tracts of veldt to the slaughterhouses. Their reply was a rather terse list of the organization's aims, clearly intended as a brush-off for someone regarded as being wilfully out of touch with political reality. Mary took this as another example of the moral failure which had infected even supposedly liberal South Africans, and fired off a final broadside: 'We are often told that the present distrust of the young for their elders' aims leads to drug addiction and violence. Much as I regret these outlets, I can understand the disillusion.'

At sixty-one her own sense of disillusion was leading to a gradual disengagement from the seemingly intractable problems of her adopted country. In September 1966 she wrote Kasia a long letter which barely touched on the assassination of the once-hated Verwoerd, as if this momentous event had failed to arouse her interest. She even called his death a tragedy, noting how he had moved from the wilder shores of extremist theology – forced by experience to 'deepen his thinking' – to a point where the unreformed fantasists in his own party had begun to think of him as a dangerous liberal.

That it might be she who was less liberal and not the late leader who had become more so does not seem to have crossed her mind. In any case, it was hardly the crux of her letter, most of which was devoted to an elegiac description of her immediate world, by this stage the only one that fully engaged her attention:

It is spring here and the beach is full of young surfers with their almost inarticulate jargon and beautiful expressive bodies. It is so wonderful that they are able to have this instinctive relationship with the sea which they find so satisfying, instead of hanging aimlessly about being exploited by mass entertainers and other time-wasters. Though it's a social sport it's an individual thing too; no two surfers can meet the same wave in the same way. Someone was remarking to me lately how mountaineers tend to be intellectuals, surfers not. I don't know why this is. Mountaineers would fit into your idyllic picture of summer Shakespeare in the ruins of castles; the surf boys would just kill time till the next good day. But what a good thing they have the sea. Sometimes at sunset I see two or three who have made a little fire on the beach and squat round in the gathering dark, deep in esoteric talk. I don't know what they talk about but they look wonderfully fulfilled. They are all boys. The girls are there; but only to fag for them and admire from a respectful distance. I don't think they have much time or energy for serious sex. They get terribly battered and bruised and stiff; the boy next door recently broke his neck, but is now back on his board again as keen as ever. They have strange fashions of their own; just now, of all curious things (for they are not in the least effeminate) they are all peroxiding their hair. Some of them look very odd, but it is the symbol of their cult and they do it devoutly.

For Mary the neighbouring children, grown and transformed into young gods of the beach, seemed to offer an antidote to the political poison that had infected so much of life. Later that year she and Julie drove to Durban for a short break, and, as they crossed one of the new 'Bantu homelands', Mary spotted a young Xhosa, whom she described to Kasia as a Bronze Age prince

striding along beside the road with his hunting-dog running ahead, dressed in a chalmys of burnt-sienna draped from one shoulder, over a very short sky-blue kilt which showed most of his legs; Praxiteles would have been delighted with them. He had a wonderful buoyancy and zest, an absolute harmony with his environment like a hunting lion. I don't think I have ever seen a more beautiful human creature. On the road it is only expected, really, that women will greet women, one does not greet men, though if they are with women they will respond too. But though this young man was alone, I could not keep from smiling from sheer delight at the sight of him, and he gave a radiant smile back before the car went past him. I hope that, unlike Hippolytos who prayed in vain for it, he will end as he began, and grow old as a respected elder with good wives, fat cattle and strong sons.

Even girls' bodies, as she told Jay, seemed to have become more beautiful:

It comes of stripping them. Living on a beach you see it. When first we came here, the place was full of awful fat teenagers with carbohydrate faces and spots; they usually had on a bouffant skirt and over it a cardigan, they looked like tents with a camel inside struggling to escape. Now they all feel they will die if they cannot be seen in a bikini, and the change is miraculous. Every fine weekend the place is full of these simply magnificent boys and girls (the boys get that way through surfing, which also has its aesthetic standards, and they have to be real, like those of the palaestra). It really is most heartening. If only they can be encouraged to develop their mental sinews and realise that nothing in this life is ever to be had for nothing, nor for wishing either, however altruistic the wish; nor for kicking someone else in the backside and urging them to go on and do it instead. Then their faces may look as good at 40 as their bodies are looking now.

She hoped his daughter was wearing the new mini-skirts she had read about and, at a safe distance, thoroughly approved of. Young people irritated her less than their parents, and they reciprocated, no doubt finding her inability to dissemble – which led her to discuss Aristotle with shopkeepers – attractive when compared to the normally patronizing attitudes of their parents. Surprisingly, Mary liked girls more than she had ever liked women of her own generation, although she found reports of the burgeoning feminist movement less pleasing, no doubt because she still found most women slightly pitiful, especially married ones, most of whom seemed to end up with what she described to Jay as

this terribly stunted look . . . I've never been a feminist, simply because all those years my inner persona occupied two sexes too indiscriminately to take part in a sex war . . . I do have sympathy for the *early* feminists, because they were then subject to rigid apartheid and job-reservation, unable to show what, as individuals, they could do. But immediately it became a Cause people felt justified in saying quite idiotic and untrue things, like how women had never produced a Shakespeare or a Beethoven or a Michelangelo because they had been kept at the kitchen sink (as if you could keep Shakespeare at a sink, if she was Shakespeare she wouldn't let you) and doing totally unjustifiable things like chucking themselves under horses in the Derby – what had the poor horses done to her, two or three of them might have had to be shot; or the jockeys either? Even *now* they keep subjecting boys and girls to these idiotic IQ tests which always flunk the potential (and practising for that matter) artists in favour of the computerised types who dream them up. Whereas the truth obviously is that Shakespeare and Beethoven & Co do seem to have, as men, some extra reserve of neural strength, some capacity for sustained intensity and inner drive, which women do not possess. I will believe otherwise when given evidence.

That said, she spared no effort, encouraging individual girls to break through any barrier they might encounter. She told Cedric, when he was still in South Africa, that she hoped he would go on using a young actress, Judy Henderson, whom she much admired. Later, when he was in London, she wrote to recommend Sue, the daughter of her old friend Dr MacGregor, who had been working on the SABC's version of *Woman's Hour* and wanted to try her hand with the BBC.

However, it was still men, preferably good looking and gay, who most easily claimed her attention. Unfortunately, with so much modern drama forbidden in the Republic, new actors were becoming rarer. While British Equity was unable to force an outright ban, it put increasing pressure on its members, so that little new talent came to the Republic, save that brought by the tenacious Leslie French for the annual Maynardville Festival. Early in 1967 he brought out a young English actor named Michael Atkinson in a production of *Macbeth* which greatly pleased Mary for the way the protégé created a full-blooded villain in his own right, not a mere weakling manipulated by his ambitious wife. Leslie played 'a sweet old Duncan' and doubled this with a clowning porter, who stumbled on with one boot off, making erratic attempts to get his foot in it. Mary told him he *must* get it in for the very last night, because everyone would expect it of him.

Happily, some of these fresh arrivals were less transient than earlier actor friends. Michael Atkinson settled in Cape Town when CAPAB, the Government-funded Cape Performing Arts Board, got under way, and he introduced Mary to a young South African actor, John Whiteley, who would become one of her closest friends. Many of these new friends came to live in Camps Bay, which was more than ever an isolated enclave of well-off Whites with artistic leanings, decent to their servants and despairing of their Afrikaner co-citizens. Mary was fond of telling the story of one of her author friends, Theo Aronson, who found himself at an official function seated next to Mrs Diederichs, wife of the State President, who said to him: 'I hear you write books?' and on receiving an affirmative, held out her open palms like a fisherman describing the one that got away and exclaimed, 'My husband reads books – books as big as this.'

When Theo Aronson and another young writer, Brian Roberts, arrived at the Cape, Brian brought an American edition of his book on Cecil Rhodes to show to Mary. What followed was the sort of social nightmare that might have floored someone less witty than Mary. As they were talking, one of the dogs quietly chewed the book to shreds. 'Ah, well,' said Mary, 'he clearly couldn't put it down.'

With that behind them, they could get to know each other, an especial pleasure for Mary, who had few author friends to share her interest in historical research. Brian had met Theo, who was South African, in London, where the success of his first book *The Golden Bees*, a study of the Bonaparte family, had enabled him to give up a job in advertising and become a full-time author. Before long, the two young men were being invited by Mary to dinner as well as to more general parties and would often spend Christmas at Delos.

Of all these fresh faces, the one who became closest to Mary was David Poole's friend, the young dancer Owen Murray. Owen was dyslexic and read Mary's books with the greatest difficulty, which may partly explain why she so enjoyed his company: he obviously liked her for herself.

It is strange that as Mary was turning away from the progressive ideas being thrown up by young people around the world, she should have found most pleasure in the company of a new generation. They seldom called unless bidden, aware that entry might be blocked by an ever-vigilant Julie, if work were in progress; but every one had good reason to love Mary – some for her sympathetic ear, others for a discreet loan at a difficult moment, all because she was genuinely interested in them.

*

The British newspapers reviewed *The Mask of Apollo* in mid-October 1966. Reactions were tepid. On balance *The Times* was for, while the *Observer* and *Sunday Times* were marginally against. Though no one had any specific criticisms, they all left a vague impression that the book did not quite match its predecessors. The usually sanguine John Guest felt obliged to explain that it was a feature of British journalism first to build up a writer, then, success achieved, to gnaw away at the edifice.

It was a relief when the American reviews appeared, and the book was lavishly praised by Rex Warner and Dudley Fitts, both classical specialists. Despite the British critics, the book was an instant best-seller on both sides of the Atlantic, but the sniping had hurt and marked the beginning of a low period in Mary's life.

Walking to the hairdresser in late April 1967, Mary stepped into the road and found herself staring up at the sky. She had been hit by a motorcycle messenger and had a scalp wound, a cracked rib and a damaged hand. As she waited at the hospital, she felt curiously detached, telling the young radiographer precisely what treatment she should be given. She was so poised that as soon as they had patched her up, she was sent home. The rib healed reasonably quickly but was followed by an especially vicious bout of gastric flu. As she convalesced, she re-read Malory, though this seems to have been more a longing for familiarity than a serious resurgence of interest in the Middle Ages. For once she had no doubt where she would look next for a subject. She had been toying with it as far back as *The Last of the Wine*, which had ended with a note that Alexias's memoirs had been discovered by his grandson, who was 'Phylarch of the Athenian horse to the divine Alexander, King of Macedon, Leader Supreme of all the Hellenes'.

The Mask of Apollo also ended with a reference to Alexander.

When Niko travels to Macedon to perform Achilles in *The Myrmidons*, the young prince comes backstage to congratulate him:

> He came up and touched my flimsy stage armour to see how it was made. On his arm, half-covered by his big gold bracelet, was a thick scar one would have thought had been got in battle, if he had not been so young. His face was a little longer than the sculptors' canon; just enough to make the canon look insipid. His skin was clear, with a ruddy, even tan; he was fresh, yet warm. A sweetness came from him; not bath-oil, but something of himself, like the scent of a summer meadow. I would have liked to draw him nearer, to feel the glow from him; but I would as soon have touched a flame, or a lion.

Judging by her letters, this fictional attraction to the young hero was an expression of her own feelings. She had already written to Kasia about a photograph of the Acropolis Head of Alexander, which had joined her bookcase treasures, and which had given her

> an almost physical sense of the presence of Alexander like a blazing sun below the horizon, not yet quenching the stars but already paling them. I was all too conscious of my inadequacy even in such a minor essay at presenting him at fourteen. His face has haunted me for years; the amazing eyes, the way his hair springs from his brow, and what must already early in his twenties have been his weather-beaten beauty, his skin burnt almost black and his hair almost white with sun. 'There is no part of my body' he said to somebody, 'free from scars. Anyway, in front.'

There is the same sense of physical pleasure she had found in the surfers and her Xhosa 'prince'. Indeed, the book she would write, *Fire from Heaven*, is almost a love letter to the boy hero, covering only the first twenty years of his life and stopping just short of the great conquests. The story concentrates on his struggle to shake off the baleful inheritance of a tug-of-love childhood between his bisexual father Philip II and Olympias, his possessive, sorceress mother. We are back in familiar Challans territory, with echoes of Theseus, even down to the way Alexander fights harder than his companions to compensate for his small stature. But any lingering Freudianism is soon dispelled when the boy shows that he is master of his fate and not its victim. In fact, the book is as much an exciting story as a complex psychological drama. The fact that it ends before Alexander's life takes on its heroic dimension shows that Mary wanted the novel to be a fascinating, if somewhat ignored piece of history brought vividly to life. Had she begun with the intention of writing the tetralogy she eventually produced (three novels and a scholarly biography), the decision to end Book One at the point where the hero becomes King of Macedon would need no explanation. But, when I interviewed her, she insisted that, as with *The King Must Die*, there had been no thought of a sequel, let alone two. *Fire from Heaven* was meant to stand on its own as a book about joyful youth casting aside the old order and challenging the world with its own romantic vision. In a way, she was writing her cowboy novel again – not least because her interest in ancient equestrianism had become as much of an obsession as classical theatre had been. The section where Alexander claims the unridable Bucephalus (Boukephalas) sings with the rich detail of horse lore and, but for the absence of guns, the skirmishes in the Macedonian back-country are conducted by the teenage Alexander like a sheriff and his posse tracking down cattle thieves.

Mary continued her research throughout the latter part of 1967 and well into 1968, then spent the rest of that year writing. As the work progressed, she became as possessive of her young hero as if he were a son to be shielded from unsympathetic neighbours. The fact that heroism itself was unfashionable was sufficient to stimulate a slightly perverse desire to raise him even higher. She was defying a world that sees Alexander in the same mould as Hitler or Stalin, emphasizing the death and mayhem brought about by the conqueror rather than the glory and honour which clearly thrilled her. Even a supposed admirer like the classical scholar W. W. Tarn seemed to her to have but feebly defended him. She despised the way Tarn had set him in the mould of a good Victorian public school man, a rather priggish figure, little better than the vicious conqueror Alexander had become at the hands of a whole horde of compulsive denigrators. To Mary, both sides were guilty of judging him by standards that did not exist in the ancient world.

In late 1969, when the book was finished, and she was free to reveal its subject, she tried to communicate to Jay the fascination that had driven her to surrender herself to so unfashionable a subject:

> I have become fascinated over the years by the aseptic, book-bound seclusion in which all these historians seem to have lived who write about Alexander. They say again and again how he was enigmatic and complex and contradictory; yet the little that Plutarch has space to say about his youth, is enormously significant in itself, and very much more so if one takes the trouble to line it up against contemporary history, so that one knows, for instance, what his father was doing at this and that time of his life, why Aristotle (who had not then become at all famous) was picked to be his tutor, things like that. Did you know that when he tamed Boukephalas the horse was only a year younger than he was? So it must have been a fully-trained war-horse. Why was it so unmanageable when it was shown, how did Alexander, who was about thirteen at the time, get it in hand so easily? How did Hephaistion become so irreplaceable that Alexander nearly went mad when he died, and only survived him by about three months? I may have got the answers all wrong, but I have never studied anything more interesting.

Up to this point, no one but Julie had known what she had been writing about. Her young friends came to visit at agreed times, when they knew she would have stopped work. With their interest in writing and history, Theo and Brian might have seen the mass of books on the subject lying around the villa and deduced the historical era with which she was concerned, but, if they did, they knew better than to ask; Mary liked her friends to distract her, not carry work over into drinking time.

In December 1968, half way through the book and needing a

rest, she began to plan a special Christmas party. Even with Katie away for the holidays, which meant they would have to do all the work themselves, she was looking forward to it and therefore was doubly upset when it turned into a catalogue of mishaps.

These began on the morning of Christmas Eve, when Julie woke and told her that she had dreamed she was having an operation and had opened her eyes to find herself feeling her left breast. There was a lump in it, but, as there was no possibility of treatment until after the holiday, they decided not to cancel the party. Having forty people at the villa took their minds off the problem – so much so that, with all the jollity, they failed to hear the thief who broke into Mary's room and stole all her Greek rings, including an especially beloved Minoan sealstone of about 1600 BC, which she had bought from a visiting archaeologist to help raise money for his next dig. She ought to have been distraught, but set beside her concern for Julie, the matter seemed almost irrelevant. The day after Boxing Day they drove to a new clinic, where, two days later, Julie was operated on. An immediate biopsy revealed that it was not cancer, and most of the breast was spared, with only a very small scar. To add to their relief, the nextdoor maid was seen handing things out of a window to a strange man and, when the police were summoned, Mary's missing rings were discovered under a pile of clothes soaking in a tub of dirty water. The only long-term effect of this unpleasant affair was the mistrust it left in a place where people had always gone to the beach without locking their doors. Mary was, however, determined not to be downcast; when she wrote to Kasia to tell her about Julie and the theft, she pointedly added that her spirits had been lifted by the news that the Apollo spaceship had taken the Americans to the moon:

A friend of ours was complaining about the flight on the lines of 'Could not this have been sold for a hundred pence and given to the poor?' Which is reasonable in a way; but I think humanity desperately needs to know there are men capable of this transcendent courage, determination, character and skill. This friend said [Dr] Chris[tian] Barnard was more worth while, and it is true people are alive owing to him who would be dead; but through these men everyone is a little more alive, and I think there is room for both.

*

Mary sent *Fire from Heaven* to Longmans and Pantheon in June 1969, hoping that in the interval before proofs arrived she would have time to start on a new book. It was with mixed feelings, therefore, that she learned that the American Book of the Month Club wanted to distribute *Fire from Heaven* provided publication was brought forward. She was pleased to be chosen, but exhausted by the unseemly rush as they attempted to correct the proofs by transatlantic telephone at a time when international telecommunications were still in their infancy and callers wasted a great deal of time listening to their own voices echoing at them.

Mary had decided as she wrote *Fire from Heaven* that there would have to be a sequel and had even included a long note at the end of the book outlining the whole of Alexander's life. This was to cause considerable hilarity when the critic on *Newsday* reviewed the book, having read only the note. After saying that 'as a rule historical novels put me to sleep, but this one was really readable', he went on to talk of Alexander's marriages and the dramatic funeral of Alexander's friend Heephestion (*sic*) even though these were mentioned only in the note and not dealt with in the novel.

The other reviews were fine, but, as Mary made clear to Jay, she was feeling rattled:

Reviews have been what one must I suppose call good, in the sense that they haven't panned the book and on the whole seem to recommend it; but it is quite amazing (unless I've been more obscure than I thought) how few seem to have the foggiest idea what it is about. Even Rex Warner, who had quite obviously read the book carefully, and is a classicist, and was very generous to it in view of the fact that he didn't agree with all its theories, says that the coming tragedy of Hephaistion throws no shadows before; yet I plugged it in at least four places.

The underlying problem was the lack of serious attention paid to the historical novel, a genre often despised by historians and literary critics alike. One attempt, by Peter Wolfe, an American academic, to examine her work seriously had not pleased Mary when it was published in 1969, and among her papers is a reply to a proposal from a potential PhD candidate, discouraging him from making her his subject, on the grounds that he, like Wolfe, had shown no sign of a correct approach to what she was trying to do:

> Peter Wolfe's book turned out a perfect example of how not to tackle a historical novelist. He failed to ask the most important question of all, and the first one that needs asking: 'How far is this writer concerned with historical truth?' If the answer is 'All the way,' which is true of me, then the book really should be set against the sources by a critic who has read them, not necessarily in the original Greek, but read them anyway. Plato himself can only be understood against his historical and social background; without this it is impossible to speak the truth about him, as I quickly found. One cannot simply extract it from his writings, which are invariably rooted in his own society and its values and moral norms. He is often critical of these, and has to be read in the context.

It sometimes seemed to her that only Jay understood this, until towards the end of 1969 an American publisher sent her the proofs of *Master and Commander* by Irish author Patrick O'Brian, asking her for a quote for the jacket. Normally, Mary fought shy of such gestures because the books were nearly always hopeless. She had even had the crippling embarrassment of having to refuse to comment on a rambling, semi-autobiographical novel by Naomi Burton, whose religious obsessions had spilled over into fiction. But, as Mary recognized at once, O'Brian's approach to research and reconstruction was as deep and serious as her own. Even before she was half way through the book, she despatched a glowing quote to the publisher and as soon as she had finished she wrote to O'Brian, who was then living in Spain:

For years and years I have been saying that nothing, not even Zoe Oldenbourg's *The Cornerstone*, has ever quite equalled Rose Macaulay's *They Were Defeated* for that real empathy with the life-style of a period, which is the result of applying imagination, and a deep humanity, to a knowledge of the sources so thorough that it merges into instinct. This book of yours equals if not surpasses it. I can't express to you the excitement and delight with which I have been following characters so real in universal humanity, drawn with so much sympathy totally without softness, so individual, and at the same time perfectly men of their age. So real do they become that one never conceives of their not continuing to exist when the last page has been turned; and thousands of readers will pay you the supreme tribute of slight resentment at your ceasing to recount their lives.

To Mary's delight, O'Brian did not cease recounting, and *Master and Commander* was only the first of a series which continued throughout the rest of her life. As each book appeared, it was greeted with praise from Mary. She was even involved with the fourth book, *The Mauritius Command*, when O'Brian asked her to help with details of the Cape, and she responded with picture postcards covered with scribbled information about which parts of the landscape would have been visible from a sailing vessel. When the finished novel arrived in 1977, it gave her 'the sensation of stepping on to a very sumptuous red carpet which has just been unrolled in front of me.' She had opened it to find that O'Brian had dedicated the book:

TO MARY RENAULT
γλαῦκ᾽ εἰς Ἀθήνας

The Greek 'An owl to Athens' means, in effect, coals to Newcastle.

*

Mary continued her defence of Alexander in another letter to Jay, which gives a rare insight into how she saw the second book developing:

Often I think far less enduring evil was done in the world by the great conquerors of earlier ages, who felt no need of any moral justification to go forth and take for themselves the lands of other rulers (it would be anachronistic to talk of taking them from the *people*, a concept which no one, including the people, entertained). Feeling their right to be conquerors self-evident, they had no need to work up hatred against the enemy or to make out the population was sub-human. Of course they caused immeasurable agony and bloodshed, as all wars do, but provided they were not oppressive to the conquered lands they did not leave behind this terrible legacy of Us and Them. Alexander was almost uncannily aware of this factor, in ways that are in advance of anything today. Realising the Persians would never take seriously a Great King before whom they did not prostrate themselves in the traditional way, he tried to persuade the Macedonians, with considerable tact on the whole, to take part and not make the Persians feel humiliated by doing it alone. But all he got was to be accused of hubris, the Macedonians not, of course, being willing for a moment to forego their superiority to the grovelling orientals. In spite of his natural disinclination to marriage he married three different women in the cause of racial unity, winding up with this tremendous mass wedding in which he got all his friends and high-ranking officers to marry Persians too. As some historian remarks, they dropped all these wives as soon as he was dead; but at least he tried.

What she could not tell Jay was the way she planned to portray this racial union. She had seized on an idea from Curtius's account of the death of Darius, where he states that the Great King's murderer Nabarzanes, 'having received a safe conduct, met him [Alexander] bringing great gifts. Among these was Bagoas, a eunuch of remarkable beauty and in the very flower of boyhood, who had been loved by Darius, and was afterwards to be loved by Alexander.'

From this slight reference, Mary created *The Persian Boy*, the second book of her Alexandriad. Bagoas is her most unusual historico-fictional character – a Persian eunuch was hardly the most obvious narrator for an epic tale of war and conquest – but, as she explained later during our interview:

> I wanted Alexander seen through Persian eyes, not through the eyes of a Macedonian who would just have all the Macedonian prejudices against the Persians. I wanted to have some of the prejudices the Persians had against the Macedonians to see how Alexander overcame them, because he did in a most astonishing way. I mean there was a whole body who wrote legends about him in Persia after he was dead and this is what fascinates me about Alexander, you know, the legends he left behind, the enormous love and admiration he inspired. I don't know of anybody who has left a legend behind like this in the land that he conquered.

Given the geographic scope of *The Persian Boy*, it is small wonder Mary had little time for anything else. Her main sources were Herodotus and Persian art, though the travel writings of Sir Richard Burton were useful, especially about the sexual lives of eunuchs, not the easiest subject to research from the fastness of Camps Bay.

The reading and note-taking were this time on a scale to match a story that covered two continents, whereas before she had concentrated on not much more than a cluster of islands. She would mention to Julie, almost reverentially, that she felt she had somehow become one with Alexander, so totally was she absorbed into his world. And, indeed, the other world of South Africa recedes from her letters. There is the occasional flash of distress over the horrors of the Zanzibar revolution, a sudden resurgence of interest in the fighting in Rhodesia, a brief mention of the mass murder in Uganda, but these seem more and more like distant intrusions from another world.

Her letters to Kasia at this time make frequent references to their old teacher Tolkien, from which it is clear that Mary empathized with the hermetic universe he had created. His books seemed to transcend fiction by becoming the historical record of a perfect alternative reality.

In following Alexander and Bagoas on their gruelling journey across Asia, Mary, too, had slipped into a parallel world. She was, in effect, living in another country. Even her rare references to the 'real' world convey an image of utter detachment, as if she and Julie, and Alexander and Bagoas, and the surfers in the bay are all that remains of any significance:

> Just before sunset we were eating supper in the window, and looking out, and listening to the last movement of Franck's Piano Quartet, which as Socrates would have thought, must surely be remembered from heaven. There was one boy on a surf-board, floating like a nautilus on the glittering sea. Just as the music was running up to the coda, he caught a wave, and stood up on the board, and came plunging and skimming in with the music. The low sunlight shone green through the wave he rode on. On the wet sand, which reflected the yellow sky, some gulls were standing in silhouette. It was all so beautiful.

For someone in her mid-sixties it might have been enough to sit back and enjoy such loveliness, yet she had never worked so hard on a book before. Alexander's travels took him from Pella to Persepolis, to the endless 'Stream of Ocean', to the very borders of India. That she should withdraw into herself was only to be expected.

Julie allowed nothing to disturb this tranquillity. The opening months of 1970 passed peacefully. The 28th of April was sunny and clear, and for some reason Julie remembers that Mary was wearing white slacks as they walked the dogs on the beach. When they returned to Delos, Mary went to the bathroom, but came back a moment later and said she was passing blood. It seemed best to go straight to Dr Sonnenberg's surgery, and he advised her to see a specialist at once. The conclusion, that she needed a hysterectomy, was irritating, but nothing out of the ordinary for a sixty-five-year-old woman. Neither she nor Julie was too concerned when it was arranged for her to enter hospital the next day to have an operation early the following morning.

It was while Julie was waiting to hear how it had gone that she overheard the surgeon briefing Dr Sonnenberg and learned that they had discovered a cancer, which had been removed.

Julie interrupted them and demanded an assurance that the

operation had been successful. The surgeon said he thought it had; Mary would need prolonged medication, but he had no reason to believe the cancer would spread. Julie's relief was tempered by her concern at how her friend would react to the news – Mary's experience when nursing her father had given her a horror of a lingering terminal illness. Julie recalled that when they had nursed cancer patients, they had agreed it would be better to live out what remained of life in ignorance of the nearness of death.

With all this in mind, Julie asked the two men not to tell the patient what had happened. She would, if need be, tell Mary herself.

13

To be Loved by Alexander

Why did the daughter of a doctor, herself a trained nurse, not guess? There were sufficient signs – her recovery was slower than was normal for a hysterectomy, and six months after the operation Mary was still writing to Kasia of her weariness and the difficulty she found in getting down to work. The British publication of *Fire from Heaven* merited only a passing comment, and she seemed more pleased with a letter from an Oxford postgraduate telling her that he had dedicated his life to the classics after reading her books.

Julie lived in constant fear that her friend would realize something was wrong and ask the fateful question. If she did express any doubts about what was wrong with her, Julie's stock response was, 'Would I lie about a thing like that?' But that was precisely Julie's living nightmare – as she put it: 'I *was* lying to Mary, not only in words, but in every possible way, and I used our relationship to lie to her.' Her difficulty was that, as time went by, it became impossible to backtrack and tell the truth, for how would she ever be trusted again?

Mary continued receiving medication well into 1971, with Julie ripping open the packets to remove anything that might give a clue as to their real purpose. But so much deception was taking its toll. She felt frantic and sometimes found herself standing alone in an empty room, staring at the wall, appalled at the web of deceit in which she had enmeshed herself. She was brusquer than ever. It was sufficient for Mary to express a mild dislike or moderate disapproval of someone or something for the over-zealous Julie to make a battle of it.

One day Mary showed her a letter from her schoolfriend Beryl, written in a shaking hand and addressed from a hospital. That in itself was disturbing – Beryl had always given the impression of indomitable strength. Her husband had died and she had lost a son, killed by a car while coming home from school on his bike, yet she had soldiered on, taking in refugee children and occupying herself with local causes. Now she had sent what seemed to be a cry for help. Mary wrote at once, but her letter crossed with one from Beryl's daughter, telling of her mother's death from leukaemia – she had been receiving treatment, secretly, for two years and had told no one. Only at the very end had she given in and written to her oldest friend.

*

By mid-1971 Mary felt strong enough to pick up the pieces of the second Alexander book. As she explained in a later letter to Patrick O'Brian, she found writing hard after a long break: 'It's not so much that one forgets what one was going to say, as that the vein of imagination breaks and the flow stops. The best cure, I've always found, is to go over the part one's already written and do some general titivating till one is on the go again.'

She had decided before her illness that Bagoas ought to look like the head of a slave by Michelangelo, a copy of which she had first seen in the Ashmolean. She had bought a print of the original from a shop near the Uffizi during her stay in Florence. And, as if to confirm her vision, an Iranian ship docked in Cape Town harbour, where she saw some of the sailors on shore leave, describing them to Kasia as 'amazingly distinguished, handsome and aristocratic . . . like princes out of the Arabian Nights . . . the same race that attracted that unprejudiced elitist, Alexander.'

Alexander was seduced by the grace and culture of the Persians, and they by his courage and mercy to a defeated enemy. Had he lived, he might have unified eastern Europe and western Asia, and Mary brilliantly prefigures this in the love of Alexander and Bagoas. The plot itself is a seduction – the first third taken up with the slow advance of Alexander, beginning as a rumour, then as a threat, lastly as a saviour, as he advances from Greece into Persia, while Darius, along with his catamite Bagoas, flees before him. Alexander advances like a lover, courting the object of his desire. When Darius is murdered and Bagoas is brought before

Alexander, there is no question of his simply taking this slave as one of the spoils of war. Alexander needs to be loved, and in a deftly handled scene Mary shows how the boy seduces Alexander by letting him believe that it is he who is doing the seducing. As Bagoas describes it:

> He really wanted love from me. I could not credit such fortune; nobody ever had before. In the past, I had taken pride in giving pleasure, since it was my skill; never had I known what it was to take delight in it. He was not quite so ignorant as I had supposed; it was just that what he knew had been very simple. He was a quick learner, though. All I taught him that night, he thought that by some happy harmony of our souls, we were discovering together. So, indeed, it seemed at last even to me.
>
> Afterwards, he lay a long time stretched out as if he were dead. I knew he was not asleep, and began to wonder if I was meant to go. But he drew me back, though he did not speak. I lay quiet. My body echoed like a harp-string after the note. The pleasure had been as piercing as the pain used to be before.

Their love is as glorious and brief as Alexander's life, ending with his death in Babylon, still young, like his hero Achilles having traded long life for lasting fame. Mary was writing a hymn to the best, the favoured, the outstanding, believing such heroes to be the means by which the species evolves. Alexander set the standards of his own day. Beside the tribal lords he conquered, he was compassionate and loyal, and without a hint of racial prejudice, qualities expressed in the book by the sheer sensuousness of the love-making between Macedonian and Persian. Nothing in Mary's earlier books quite prepares the reader for these moments, which culminate in the disturbingly voluptuous scene where Bagoas lies down beside the dying Alexander:

> I drew close and whispered, 'I love you, Alexander', and kissed him. Never mind, I thought, from whom his heart accepts it. Let it be according to his wish.
>
> My hair had fallen on his breast. His eyes opened; his hand moved, and touched a strand, and ran it between his fingers.

He knew me. To that I will take my oath before the gods. It was to me that he bade farewell.

*

Even with Julie guarding the door, it was too much to hope that the outside world could be held at bay forever. Mary's chief contact with life beyond Delos was the equally hermetic world of the theatre, though that was about to prove a poor refuge from the tribulations of the *apartheid* state. Initially, there had been a great deal of excitement among Mary's theatrical friends when the Government, after years of neglect, decided to do something positive about the cultural life of Cape Town. This had begun with the setting up of CAPAB, the Cape Performing Arts Board, to promote and fund theatre, ballet and opera in the province, and it provided work which kept friends of theirs like Michael Atkinson at the Cape, and offered David Poole the opportunity to set up his ballet company. But CAPAB's work was severely limited without a permanent home for its various groups, and the Government's grandest scheme was the building of a large theatre complex near the centre of the city. Thus 1971 saw the opening of the Nico Malan Theatre, named after an Afrikaner politician whom nobody in Mary's circle could recall, but whose shadow was to fall heavily over the enterprise when he agreed to accept the dedication on condition that the place be kept for Whites only. At first this was not taken too seriously. The Cape had a long history of ignoring segregationist moves from Pretoria, and with luck the Coloured population might be eased in, if no one made too much fuss. It was when the liberal English-language press took up the issue that the whole matter blew up. A campaigning United Party councillor organized a petition and threatened a boycott, whereupon enraged Nationalist Party officials insisted that the letter of the law be enforced. The effect on the artistic community in Cape Town was more dramatic than any play destined for the new theatre. People took sides for or against the boycott with a vehemence that set friend against friend.

Friendship led Mary to oppose the boycott, prompting her to support John Whiteley and Michael Atkinson, who would be in the opening production, and David Poole, whose dream of professional ballet in Cape Town would have collapsed if he had withdrawn. His decision to go ahead with a theatre his own mother would not be able to attend, in the hope that it would one day be desegregated, was enough for Mary, no matter what opprobrium it attracted. Her determination arose in part from her disgust at the whole concept of a cultural boycott. That an organization such as British Equity could blacklist South Africa, she found utterly indefensible, especially when what the country needed was increased exposure, not less, to contemporary drama. Equity was attempting to ban the export of television programmes, a move that would become completely effective by 1976. The union's attempts to dissuade its members from appearing in South Africa was less effective, though actors who did perform in the country were usually subject to considerable and often acrimonious criticism upon their return to Britain. Indeed, it was on this issue that Mary was most at odds with the liberal consensus of her day. Most British writers and actors were firmly convinced that they should show support for the oppressed Black population in the only way they could, by refusing to allow their work to be seen by White audiences. Their strongest argument for this was that the leaders of the African freedom movements wished them to do so. The counter-argument, supported by Mary, was that in keeping out Western culture, the boycott helped achieve everything the Nationalist Government desired. By withholding BBC television programmes, Equity ensured that nothing challenging or progressive was seen in South Africa, and that its people, Black and White, could be fed a diet of cheap trash bought from less scrupulous sources along with local news carefully adjusted to toe the Government line.

To Mary's chagrin, PEN was drawn in when Theo Aronson and Brian Roberts proposed support for the boycott on the ground that segregation was a form of censorship. Theo and Brian left for Europe while the issue was still being debated, but, when they returned, they found a letter offering PEN members concessionary rates for tickets to the Nico Malan Theatre. They assumed that Mary, as president, must have known and approved of this link-up. They both resigned, and there was a bitter row in which the word 'Fascist' was bandied about, so that they parted with small chance of a reconciliation.

The atmosphere in Camps Bay was electric. If anyone so much as hinted to Julie that they were for the boycott and thus at odds with Mary, they were cast into outer darkness. Where Mary had made her decision on the lesser of two evils, Julie saw it in terms of plots and enemies. She was to find ample evidence of both the following year, when David asked Margot Fonteyn, an old friend from his Sadler's Wells days, to dance at a special gala at the Nico Malan. Politically naive and apparently unaware that any criticism might come her way, Fonteyn accepted, though even David Poole could not have foreseen the furore that ensued when the world's press heard of the visit and decided to make it a *cause célèbre* in the anti-*apartheid* struggle. Well before she arrived, Fonteyn was put under intense pressure to withdraw, and she cabled David to see if the theatre could be desegregated for her performance. When the Government refused to budge, she asked him to lay on a special matinée at another theatre for a Black and Coloured audience only. Predictably, this caused a second firestorm of criticism, whereupon a rather desperate Fonteyn suggested they hold yet another free show for sick Black and Coloured children from local hospitals.

Fonteyn flew to Cape Town hoping to have fudged the issue. She danced for her Whites only audience. No one now doubts that her presence gave an enormous boost to the company and was probably the single most important event in its early history, but, in the wider political sphere, the visit was a débâcle. Most Coloureds chose to ignore the special performance at the Three Arts Theatre, and the majority of the audience were White ballet-lovers who had blacked-up to get past the reverse boycott.

While all this was going on, Mary and Julie fled town, preferring the calm of Ceres to the cultural battlefield of Cape Town. However, the Nico Malan affair took a long time to fade and, even when the theatre was desegregated a few years later, the bitterness remained. Theo and Brian went off to settle in England, still angry over Mary's failure to support them. They were not alone, and from then on many people saw her as just another reactionary, a judgement that took no account of her earlier political activism.

*

Mary was surprised when *The Persian Boy* became her most

immediate best-seller. *The King Must Die* would outlast it, with major sales continuing to this day, but nothing made a greater impact on first publication, in 1972, than the story of Alexander's love for the eunuch Bagoas.

Mary appears to have anticipated the same reaction as had greeted the publication of *The Charioteer*, two decades earlier. She even wrote to Jay to explain that she would not be sending him a copy because she did not think he would approve of its subject matter, and was amazed when he promptly wrote back to say he had bought the book and had been deeply moved by it. Nothing better illustrates her isolation from the experience nowadays labelled 'the Sixties'. Even her correspondence with Colin Spencer and her devoted reading of the British press had given her only a distant appreciation of the extent to which attitudes towards sexuality in Europe and America had changed during that decade. The publication of *The Persian Boy* came five years after the Sexual Offences Bill decriminalized many homosexual practices in Britain, and three years after the Stonewall Inn Riots in New York marked the beginning of Gay Liberation in America. From that perspective it is not hard to understand why the book was seized on by a grateful public. To Mary it was a puzzle. What she heard of the Gay Liberation Movement made her feel uncomfortable. It was mass action again, something she always distrusted. She told this author that she disliked 'sexual tribalism', having always pictured human sexuality as a line along which people should be free to move as they chose. The sight of people digging themselves in at any particular point on that line struck her as foolish.

Because she so seldom gave interviews, none of this was known to her millions of gay readers, who continued to look upon her as an apostle of the sexual revolution. While she loathed the hijacking of the word 'gay', her gay public revered her. *The Last of the Wine* was a rite of passage, *The Persian Boy* a gift for young male lovers. Gay bookshops in San Francisco had prominent 'Renault' sections. There was even talk of filming *The Persian Boy*, with the would-be producer launching a press campaign to find an actor to play Bagoas on the lines of the famous search for an actress to play Scarlett O'Hara in *Gone with the Wind*. Many were the beautiful, willowy youths who hopefully sent in their photographs; one even managed to get through to Mary, offering to have 'the operation' if it would guarantee him the part. 'That', she replied, 'would be gelding the lily,' and she advised him to think again.

One result of the Gay Liberation Movement in America was the spread of Gay Studies, with Gay Literature, including Mary's work, as part of the curriculum. Inevitably, someone tried to prove that the idol had feet of clay. In *The Homosexual as Hero in Contemporary Fiction* (1980), Stephen Adams criticized the party scene in *The Charioteer* for the way the 'manliness' of the main characters was contrasted with the behaviour of the effete homosexuals with names like Bunny, Toto, Bim and Sandy, who are 'hysterical, neurotic, lecherous, malicious and above all *loud*'. Adams angrily concluded that Mary was clinging to the discredited notion of homosexuality as a handicap, like Laurie's damaged leg. It was only after Mary's death that a more balanced view began to emerge when Claude J. Summers's *Gay Fictions: Wilde to Stonewall* (1990) devoted a chapter to *The Charioteer*, putting Mary at the heart of post-war homosexual literature, on a par with Vidal, Baldwin and Isherwood.

*

When Mary opened the first copy of *The Persian Boy* airmailed out to her, she was horrified. It had been published by something called the Longman Group. On inquiring, she discovered that without warning, she had been transferred to Allen Lane, the hardback division of Penguin. She had known there would be changes after the death of Mark Longman, and had been aware that his daughters had no wish to continue the family business, but she had not expected to be passed on like a chattel.

She had admired Robert Longman and been proud to be published by a company dating back to 1725, especially as she had been with them for a seventh of their existence. Now she was livid and in her fury decided to accept a proposal from a packager, George Rainbird, who wanted her to gather together all the research she had done on Alexander for an illustrated biography.

Rainbird had been trying for some time, without success, to

interest her in a project and had even written to ask if she would consider a life of Pericles. When this was cursorily dismissed, Rainbird, in Mary's words, 'had the almighty gall to turn up here'. She swallowed her anger and invited him to dinner, though, as she reported to Jay, the encounter was less than successful:

> He is one of these Food and Wine kings. Food is nice but to make a career of it is a bit much I think. He sniffs a lot. It was a tacky evening, I can tell you. He greatly approved Julie's cooking & suggested she should open a branch of the Food & Wine Society here! The food *was* nice, but we could never decide if this was just another bit of sucking-up.

However, with Longmans' cavalier treatment still rankling, she decided to overlook the tackiness and agreed to write what she decided to call *The Nature of Alexander*, wishing more to present a defence of her hero than to compete with the recently published biography by Robin Lane Fox, which she admired unreservedly.

To distance her book further from a straightforward 'life', Mary decided to make it a piece of historical travel writing, each chapter advancing with Alexander across his world: Macedonia, Troy, Persia, India, Babylon. Rainbird's task was to heighten this material with photographs, some reproducing the art of the period, but most being specially commissioned from Christina Gascoigne, who travelled as far as the Hindu Kush in the wake of Mary's hero. There was some talk of Mary accompanying her, which would have been a thrilling experience, but as she was approaching seventy, such an arduous voyage seemed impractical and was reluctantly rejected.

For the present there was no new novel in view. Alexander had exhausted her, and the most she could consider was the possibility of trying her hand at writing short stories. When she was asked to contribute to a celebratory publication honouring the fiftieth birthday of the Duke of Edinburgh, Mary, knowing the Duke's passion for horses, composed a terse account of the first meeting of Alexander and Bucephalus, crammed with all the fascinating minutiae of ancient horse lore she had been gathering for more than a decade. As she put it to Kasia: 'I suppose a polo pony must need some of the nippy qualities of a Greek war-horse, and some of its nerve.'

She decided to make use of some of the other material that had fascinated her during her various bouts of research but did not seem to merit a full book. She was intrigued by the theory of Celsus, an eclectic philosopher of the second century AD who held that Jesus of Nazareth had lived and worked in Egypt as a young man. It was a theory not entirely incompatible with the New Testament, if one accepted that the Holy Family had remained in Egypt after the flight, with Jesus going to Galilee as a young man. The only event of Jesus's childhood that required an earlier visit was the presentation at the Temple, which could have happened on a holiday, as it were. It was a slight matter, but one with fascinating possibilities as the basis for an 'entertainment' in the Graham Greene sense. Another was the story of Harmodios, the beautiful Athenian youth pursued by the tyrant Hipparchos, who was in turn slain by Harmodios's lover, Aristogeiton. The Athenians had raised statues to the two lovers in the Agora, honouring them as liberators. These were despatched to Persia by Xerxes during the Persian invasion, but found and returned by Alexander, who saw something of himself and Hephaistion in the loyalty unto death of the two young men.

Mary was about to start writing when a series of troubles intervened, making all thought of work impossible.

*

Her problems began in early October 1974, when she was taking the dogs – a young labrador and an old Scottie – for their walk in the 'Glen', a stretch of open ground surrounded with trees at the back of Camps Bay, where the foothills of Table Mountain begin. She tried to go down a slope which turned out to be too steep, stumbled and fell. Her foot turned, she felt the bone snap and knew at once that it was a bad break. A group of picnickers were able to look after her, while Julie phoned for help.

At the hospital they found her leg broken in three places just above the ankle, a serious matter for someone of her age. Because the skin was cut, the doctor thought it best to let any chance of infection pass before operating and took the extraordinary decision to let her go home, in the belief that Julie was the best person to take care of her. Only Julie's air of bustle and confidence can have led him to consider this wise, which it certainly was not. For a week Mary was totally helpless, returning briefly to hospital for the setting, then back to Delos in plaster, where she was bedridden for almost two months. Even with the plaster removed, she remained in bed for a further week, and it was another month before she was fully mobile again.

Julie should never have been burdened with such a task, though not even Mary was fully aware of the stress she was under. All the strain of the accident had come on top of her permanent anguish at having lied about Mary's cancer, which in turn had been exacerbated by the Nico Malan crisis. No one knew what Julie had been going through, how she sometimes tried to work off her guilt with manic bouts of housework until she dropped with exhaustion. Unable to explain why she was so tired, she lapsed into long periods of silence.

By February of 1975 Mary had progressed from crutches to walking sticks and had even found a way to propel herself around the villa on the swivel castors of her typing stool. But such fun was short lived. They were having breakfast one morning when the whole situation came to a head. Julie was reading the newspapers. As usual, the news was bad, but that morning she burst into tears. When Mary tried to comfort her, she pulled away, racked with sobbing. Mary had seen this sort of behaviour before in tuberculosis patients, an illness that can lie dormant a very long time. Horrified, she summoned Dr Sonnenberg, but he saw at once that the problem was not physical. Julie was suffering from depression, and at first the pills Sonnenberg prescribed seemed to help. They left her slightly dazed, but her condition was stable. Mary took care of her, an air of normality was maintained, and no one but the doctor was aware of what was really happening.

What finally triggered Julie's collapse was ludicrously unimportant. She had been manically cleaning again and had switched off the fridge, only to find that she could not get it started again. Next she tried to use a new dishwasher they had ordered and could not understand the instructions. It was intolerable. She went to Mary and asked her to telephone the police because she had failed to look after her; she had made a mess of the household accounts, and she ought to be punished.

This time Dr Sonnenberg insisted she have treatment, though it took some persuading before Mary agreed to commit her friend to a private clinic. Fortunately, once there, she was taken in hand by an elderly doctor. Over the next ten days she was given seven electric shock treatments. They left her unsure where she was, but she was calm; she was allowed home on a course of medication which kept her pleasantly sedated.

There was no ultimate cure, and Mary knew that all she could hope for was a slow return to something approaching their former lives. She encouraged Julie to see a psychiatrist, if only to escape from the villa once a week to talk to someone else. By the end of September, with Julie still on tranquillizers, Mary felt they could risk a short holiday at Ceres. Away from everything, Julie relaxed at last, though there was still the touchingly comic situation of Mary watching Julie watching Mary in a tender hall of mirrors.

Back home, Mary decided they should redecorate, even though there was no real need. Colours were chosen, workmen hired and, as soon as they appeared, there was Julie chasing after them, supervising everything, determined to see it was all done properly without Mary's work being disturbed. There would be occasional relapses, but they were now forewarned, and at the outset of a bout of depression Julie could quickly enter the clinic for medication and psychiatric care, which helped shorten the attacks, even though it did not prevent them.

This series of crises caused Mary to consider putting her affairs in order in the event of her death. She was worried lest the inevitable sorting-out rest too heavily on Julie. She wrote to Juliet O'Hea, her agent, and obtained her agreement to be joint literary executor, so that Julie would have someone to lean on if she needed advice. Financially, there was no cause for concern. All the historical novels were in print and some, like *The King Must Die*, were still best-sellers years after publication. There were numerous translations, and there were even occasional revivals of interest in the early books, though Mary was never very encouraging, as she could hardly bear to think about them.

Being so preoccupied with each other's well-being was, in other ways, rather relaxing. Mary wrote to tell Kasia that life had become 'practically animal-centred'. Following the death of the Scottie, they had acquired Mandy, a labrador bitch, as company for the male labrador Coco, inducing love at first sight, with affectionate romps in the surrounding greenery. When Mary and Julie ventured out to the ballet, for the first time in ages, they returned to find that the two lovers had spent a jolly evening, playfully shredding Michael Holroyd's life of Augustus John.

*

In the midst of such events work was inevitably patchy. *The Nature of Alexander* was published while the crisis was at its height and, though Mary was pleased with Christina Gascoigne's photographs, she was far too preoccupied to give them more than a passing glance. After the trip to Ceres, she could risk longer sessions in the study, but the thought of anything as all-consuming as a novel was beyond her, and her first attempt back at the typewriter was one of the ideas for a short story she had been toying with earlier.

According to Celsus is an amusing conceit, intelligently crafted. A Greek *hetaira*, mourning a young lover who has squandered his inheritance and committed suicide, goes to the Jewish quarter in Alexandria to beg a carpenter she had once helped to make a coffin for her beloved. Only by slow stages does the true identity of the carpenter dawn on the reader. When she enters the workshop, he is putting newly forged nails into a box. When he greets her, he offers her wine. He mimics his mother, expressing her displeasure at his habit of revealing that he was born in a stable and recalls how his father saved for years to send him home for his *bar mitzvah*. He is about to go to Galilee for good, but, yes, he will make the coffin, even though her lover is being embalmed according to the heathen rites of the Egyptians. The subtle twist is that the story is not so much about Jesus as about Alexander and his multi-racial city of Greeks, Romans, Egyptians and Jews. If Celsus was right, then Jesus was originally as much a Hellene as a Jew, and the story ends cheekily with the grateful woman making a secret vow to make a votive offering for him at the shrine of Hephaistos, the artificer's god, who would 'surely favour an honest craftsman; and he would be none the wiser'.

279

An account by John Guest of a visit he made to South Africa in 1976 gives the only intimate description of Mary's life at this time:

> Delos was crammed with a fascinating collection of *objets*, fragments of carving, semi-precious stones, things collected on their travels, little pictures, all personal and unusual, and flowers in abundance from the crowded garden. Julie was the one who ordered their lives, leaving Mary to concentrate on her work. Both were keen on the theatre and ballet at the new Malan Centre in Cape Town. On these occasions, Mary wore magnificent embroidered kaftans and heavy jewellery. She looked, and was indeed, a person of importance in that *milieu*. But, as a whole, their social life was happily self-contained and quiet. Mary enjoyed the visits of the many actors, producers, writers and ballet-dancers who came, with permission, to call on her.

This was published in *Books & Bookmen* in 1984 as part of a posthumous tribute, from which Guest deleted a description of a metal statue of Hermes, which he had noticed as soon as he arrived. It was standing in the garden, and Mary had explained how it had at one time modestly sported a fig leaf. This had irritated her, so she had called in a metal-worker to remove it with a hack-saw:

> Unfortunately, as might have been expected, there was nothing underneath. So Mary commissioned him to fashion, and to attach in the proper place, a new 'set' (if that is the word) of pudenda. The metal-worker was no doubt competent at his trade, but could hardly be classified as an artist. The result was that he fashioned and attached organs of a scale that was twentieth-century South African rather than Attic! This story was told with much laughter.

While they clearly had a thoroughly enjoyable time during his visit, Guest was aware that Glen Beach did not please Mary and Julie as it once had. Their secluded, almost private cove was taken over in the summer months by day-trippers from the city, with all the inevitable noise and mess. Worse, the occasional oil tanker would illegally flush out its residue, with disastrous results for the nearby beaches. Mary, Julie and the dogs would often find themselves with tarry black stuff on feet and paws. Since her accident, Mary was increasingly wary of the steps down to the villa, especially if they were wet and slippery. The problem was how to find sufficient money to buy a house that would provide the same degree of isolation they had once known.

When Guest left, Mary began work on a second tale, the story of Harmodios and Aristogeiton, only to find her interest shifting away from the two lovers towards Simonides, the poet who had been in Athens at the time of the assassination and whose later record of the event is one of his rare surviving works. Poets travelled the ancient world as actors did, and it must have seemed to Mary that she had stumbled on another Nikeratos, as she explained to John Guest:

> I've often wondered what it was like to be a court poet when they seldom wrote anything down and knew the whole of the *Iliad* by heart as well as their own compositions and those of other famous bards, and the 'tyrants' were starting up everywhere in the general ferment. Simonides lived to be 86, he saw everything right through the Persian Wars and died when Pericles was already 30. But I have just taken him up to the conspiracy of Harmodios and Aristogeiton. Of course it won't sell like the Alexander novels. Alexander has been strong magic in his own right for two and a half millennia and still going strong. But one has to break fresh ground sooner or later.

The ground was not, however, quite as fresh as all that, the format having much in common with *The Mask of Apollo*. But whereas the story of Nikeratos was a fiction, played in tandem with a dramatic historical moment, *The Praise Singer* had only the story of the Pisistratid tyranny to underpin it, a part of Athenian history far less gripping and important than the struggle of Plato and Dion in Syracuse. Worse, there is just enough known about Simonides to keep a stickler for truth like Mary fettered to historical details and unable to make the imaginative leap that might have brought the novel to life. Despite this, the poet is one of her most sympathetic characters, quite different from any other in being both thoroughly heterosexual and famously ugly. Perhaps this is the 'new ground' about which she wrote to John Guest, though it is odd that Mary should have shunned the very elements that had created such a large and loyal public. The fact that the ancient poets were essentially singers made Simonides an even stranger choice. All her musician friends, including the conductor David Tidboult in Durban and the pianist Lionel Bowman at the Cape, agreed she was not musical. As Julie put it, 'She liked Mozart and so on, but that was all.' When she was asked by Sir Michael Tippett for permission to use some lines from *The Mask of Apollo* for his *A Mask of Time*, she was flattered but could not make much of the resulting composition. Her interest seems to have been purely intellectual. When the SABC adapted *The Mask of Apollo* as a radio series, she became friendly with a young composer, Michael Tuffin, who taught at Cape Town University. Tuffin introduced her to the few surviving fragments of Attic music and aroused her interest in what little was known of composition and performance in the ancient world. Just as one can use the story of Nikeratos as a textbook on Greek theatre, so Simonides provides a course in lyric history; nevertheless, even though it is one of her shortest books, we are clearly left with a story stretched to a novel. Only at the dénouement, the kernel of the original tale, when Aristogeiton kills Hipparchos, does the book really take wing.

None of this was apparent to Mary, who wrote to Patrick O'Brian to say she had not yet decided whether she would go on with Simonides. A second book would have taken her up to the Persian Wars, but the thought of the research this would involve, at a time when there were still upheavals on the home front, seems to have gradually dampened her enthusiasm for the project.

*

The solution to the house problem came almost accidentally, when Mary discovered that, under instructions from her New York agents, her publishers in America had been withholding a large part of her royalties in order to minimize her tax liabilities and she was now able to withdraw all of the outstanding monies without incurring punitive payments.

They found their new home by another stroke of luck. David and Owen were looking for a place and had discovered an unusual house overlooking Camps Bay farther up the foothills of Table Mountain. It was white, modern and uncompromising – Julie thought it was a block of flats at first. When David and Owen decided to look elsewhere, they too hesitated. The square house on Atholl Road was as different from Delos as it was possible to imagine. Theo Aronson had thought the wooden cottage almost 'the perfect writer's house', whereas this had been built thirty years earlier by a German architect in a style that was still fairly adventurous. The house had three floors with the entrance at the rear on the middle floor and a bottom section farther down the slope overlooking a dismal, unloved garden. But there were compensating advantages: a garage on the same level as the entrance plus a modern kitchen and a large downstairs study for Mary. Best of all, there were huge picture windows offering a spectacular, uninterrupted view of the Atlantic.

To the surprise of their friends, who had pigeon-holed them neatly into the old-world charms of Delos, they took it. By the end of 1977, they were settled into what was effectively a whole new life. More than ever Mary's study resembled a modern bank; it is bizarre to think of her sitting there lost in the sixth century BC as *The Praise Singer* entered its final stages. She would wake at six to read and make notes. Dressing took a long time now; she liked to prepare herself slowly for the day and hated any morning arrangements that might force her to rush. She could be a good hour washing, dressing and tidying her room. The new maid, Maggie, would say, 'I never saw her nightie,' though, as Julie knew, it was a question of surfaces – Mary liked an image of tidiness, while there could be chaos inside drawers and cupboards. What she really hated was the sight of feminine things, stockings and so on, trailing about. At around 8.30 a.m. she and Julie would stroll out with the dogs, up to the 'Glen' where Mary had had her fall three years earlier. She was at her desk by 9.45, but would appear for a huge mug of tea sweetened with honey, which she would take back with her to sip as she worked. While she was in her study, Julie occupied herself with the house above. They always had a full lunch, with Mary appearing at 12.30 for a beer before they ate. After lunch they would sit and read the English papers and magazines. Then Mary would return to the study. Julie gave the dogs their evening walk, and Mary joined her for a drink before supper.

Mary had had to become less fanatical about her correspondence – she had tried a secretary, but the woman wanted to improve her grammar and had to go. Next came a dictating machine, but that defeated her, and she abandoned it. In the end, time and age took care of the problem. Her correspondents were also growing older and no longer replied with the same alacrity as before. Over the past two years her correspondence with Jay had become less frequent. He had recently moved and was preoccupied with the business of setting up a new home and adjusting to a new community. In July 1978, while on a visit to London, he was running for a bus after an evening with friends when he suddenly dropped dead from a heart attack. He had not been ill, and the news was a great shock to Mary, who wrote at once to his wife Barbara to say how appalled she was. Although she and Jay had never met, and everything she knew of him was from his books and letters, they had been very close.

Now there was no one but Kasia left. Only she could understand all the jokes. There is almost a shriek of girlish delight from the pages of a letter in which Mary recounts her astonishment at finding an article in *Encounter* by Joan Evans explaining the real origins of the apparition recounted by Miss Moberly and Miss Jourdain in *An Adventure*. Evans had discovered that Robert de Montesquiou, Proust's friend, had had an apartment adjoining the park at Versailles and was in the habit of throwing private parties in the grounds of the Petit Trianon. These took the form of costumed *fêtes champêtres*, with his male acquaintances acting out various roles, including that of Marie Antoinette. What was doubly amusing to Mary was not merely the obvious conclusion that the two English ladies had stumbled upon one of these charades, but also that the figure of a queen which Miss Moberly saw was exactly that.

There was one final, major upheaval in her life: the decision to move from Allen Lane and to find a new English publisher. With *The Praise Singer* completed, the time had come. Curtis Brown suggested two or three possibilities, but there was never any real choice. Mary wanted John Murray, because they had been Byron's publishers and were still a family firm as Longmans had been. Her sole regret at leaving her old publishers was the loss of her editor, so she was mightily relieved when Murray's decided to hire John Guest to edit her books on a freelance basis.

The Praise Singer was published in December 1978 in America and February 1979 in Britain. The reviews were respectful rather than enthusiastic.

Shortly before Christmas 1978, Mary and Julie were standing on the veranda of the new house when they heard fire engines below and looked down to see smoke and fire rising from Glen Beach. They got into their car and drove down to find Delos burning.

'It is a most curious feeling', Mary wrote to John Guest, 'to watch a sixty-year-old house, which one has occupied for a third of its life and quite a segment of one's own, with rafters flaring, the roof falling in, one's familiar bedroom window filled with flames . . . It's odd what a concrete existence Delos still has in my mind, as they say that amputated limbs do.'

*

At some time in mid-1977 Mary was telephoned, out of the blue, by a Johannesburg stringer for the *Guardian* newspaper in London. He wanted to know why PEN Cape Town had done nothing when 'a whole generation of Black writers was silenced in the 1960s'. It was such a peculiar phrase that Mary was left with the impression the man was quoting it, and her first thought was to wonder who was behind this mud-stirring. She was soon to find out.

A week or so later Gerald Gordon received a letter from PEN International in London, warning him that there was considerable concern among some national branches that the Cape Town centre was not sufficiently concerned about Black writers. Why, the author enquired, were there no Black members of the centre?

It was the initial problem returned to haunt them, though after seventeen years it would be hard to explain why there was still only one Coloured member and why no one since Richard Rive had been recruited. Over the past decade Nadine Gordimer in Johannesburg had successfully identified and promoted young African writers. That Mary did not share her interest was due to her deep dislike of politically motivated fiction, the main literary form among Black writers in South Africa in the 1960s and 1970s. Whatever Mary's personal feelings, the fact remained that there were Black writers who were not members of PEN Cape Town and, while this was more the fault of the executive officials than of the honorary president, Mary chose, somewhat unwisely, to adopt the same bellicose stance as she had done over the Nico Malan Theatre, seeing it as her duty to defend her friends from outside attack.

It was only gradually that Mary realized Nadine Gordimer was one of those behind the fresh assault. Gordimer had recently given a talk at a PEN Cape Town lunch, an occasion described with some pleasure by Mary in a letter to Cedric Messina, from which it seems clear that the two women were still on perfectly amicable terms. Had Gordimer raised the issue of the centre's lack of Black writers while she was there, Mary might have been prepared to deal with her criticism. But Gordimer had not done so, and the event passed, like any monthly meeting, with no hint of this difference of opinion.

It was only after the telephone call from the *Guardian* stringer that Gerald Gordon was able to piece together what had happened. Despite the fact that Gordimer had said nothing about Cape Town's membership during her visit, she had decided to tackle the problem at a higher level. Her own centre in Johannesburg was moribund, but she was by this time an international vice president of PEN and thus had a ready welcome at the annual conferences, the most recent of which had been held in Stockholm. While there, she had spoken with the president of PEN Sweden, Per Wästberg, and the Dutch and Hungarian delegations, all of whom began calling for Cape Town's expulsion.

When she learned what Gordimer had done, Mary was as furious as she had been over the Mark Longman letter. She felt personally betrayed and fired off a broadside to Cedric, who had, after all, first introduced her to Gordimer:

It rather gives me the creeps. I have never played literary politics, I have never sucked up to anyone to get my work promoted; so far as I have influenced PEN policy on behalf of
banned writers, I have always gone along with the direct
approach to the Minister, which has often achieved results,
rather than the self-advertising protest which hardens his attitude towards the writer while turning the limelight on oneself.
Naturally this does not get into the papers, but the writer
benefits, which is what PEN is supposed to be all about.

As her private correspondence shows, Mary had indeed preferred the quiet approach, taking food anonymously to the Cape
Town prison for the writer Alex Laguma when he was jailed in
the 1960s, but such self-effacing deeds did nothing to improve the
public image of the Cape Town centre.

As the PEN secretariat in London had advised Cape Town to
defend itself at the next conference, a large part of its funds –
formerly spent defending authors – had to be deflected to send
Gerald Gordon to Holland, where he successfully refuted the
charges in a speech which was enthusiastically applauded.

The accusation lingered and festered, however, and the matter
stretched on over the next three years, with Gordimer and others
continuing to attack the Cape Town branch whenever an opportunity arose. Things might have continued in this way, with
nothing more than a lot of ill-feeling on both sides, had it not
been for the capture and imprisonment, on charges of terrorism,
of the Afrikaans poet Breyten Breytenbach. When his case was
taken up by PEN International, the international secretary, Peter
Elstob, decided to visit South Africa to lobby the appropriate
ministers and to try to sort out the two warring camps. Before
setting off, he wrote to Mary to see whether there was anything
she could do to get more non-White members. Mary replied that
because the rules insisted on two published books as a minimum
standard for membership and no African with such a qualification
had ever asked to join, there was little she could do. Letters
were exchanged, but, while the correspondence dragged on, Mary
learned that Elstob had been writing, without her knowledge, to
the chairman of Cape Town PEN, Frank Bradlow, suggesting that

the centre should be less rigid in its membership requirements. From Elstob's point of view there was nothing underhand about this – as International Secretary it was perfectly proper for him to correspond with the executive chairman of a local PEN without reference to the honorary president. But Mary was furious and let Elstob know it. He tried to pacify her by pleading that he had simply been asking for tolerance for people who were born poor and Black.

The stage was thus set for another confrontation between Western attitudes, which had changed and adapted radically since the 1960s, and the essentially pre-war values which remained in force among liberals in Cape Town. Well-travelled and cosmopolitan in her thinking, Nadine Gordimer believed in adapting to local conditions in the way Elstob was advocating. In fact, Elstob was merely putting forward the view of International PEN that in Third World countries, where hardback publishing barely existed, the two-book rule, itself a Western concept, should be replaced and that anyone recognized as a writer 'by his fellow writers', in Elstob's words, should be allowed to join. Gordimer had done much to advance young Black writers from places like Soweto, speaking on their behalf at international gatherings to which they had no access. To those unaware of the size of South Africa, of the immense difference between Johannesburg and the Cape and of the cultural isolation of its ethnic groups, it must have seemed astonishing that two writers like Gordimer and Renault could hold such utterly opposed beliefs. From the standpoint of a radical, racially conscious European, Elstob's proposals were essentially practical and humane. To Mary, they were offensive, as her angry reply to his letter makes clear:

A double standard is essentially patronising, and is recognised as such by serious writers of any race or sex. Until fairly recent decades it was often extended to women, but I never knew a self-respecting woman writer who wished to exchange self-criticism for the facile self-esteem it offers. I would expect an ambitious Black writer to reject it equally.

She concluded: 'If genuine non-racialism is to be denounced as racism, we are moving fast into Orwell country. A central motif of *1984* is the suppression and punishment of moral logic by the promotion of double-think.'

At this point Elstob concluded that he needed to meet the antagonists and confront the problem face to face. He set off early in 1979, intending to do four things: plead the cause of Breyten Breytenbach, attempt another revival of the Johannesburg centre, persuade the Cape Town committee to take action over Black members and, finally, have a holiday with his wife.

Although she would be in France during the early part of their visit, Nadine Gordimer arranged for the Elstobs to use her house in Johannesburg. On arrival Elstob invited a number of African writers, mainly journalists, for drinks, and persuaded some of them to join a new Johannesburg centre. They were later joined by others, such as Winnie Mandela, who had written a couple of articles for the local newspapers and could at a pinch be described as an author. However, the treasurer of the old centre, Mr Suzman, a relative of the Progressive Party MP Helen Suzman, and a man of impeccable liberal credentials, cautiously refused to hand over the centre's remaining funds until such time as this new group had proved itself to be more than a chimera.

The Elstobs travelled to Cape Town in the second week in February and were invited to tea in Camps Bay. It was not a success. Mary flatly refused to consider lowering membership standards and, when Elstob spoke of the need to help Black people, Mary countered with her impressions of the recent violence in the newly independent African states. Elstob said that he considered her insistence on the two-book rule equal 'to the methods used by racists in the USA to deny Blacks the vote on the grounds of their level of education'. When he suggested that illiterate people possess an oral literature, Mary dismissed the idea as a contradiction in terms. The more Elstob pressed his case, the more stoutly Mary defended what she saw as an island of White culture precariously surviving amidst peoples who had not even had a written language when Dias first set foot at the Cape. She was angry, and to Elstob she appeared to be merely the type of bigoted White South African he had been warned to expect. Back at his hotel, he wrote in his day-book that she was an out-and-out racist who appeared to consider Africans a cruel and primitive people without writing and thus without culture. There was, he concluded, no point in expecting her to support the necessary changes; he would have to assume command himself.

With the help of Gerald Gordon, Elstob placed an advertisement in the Cape newspapers calling on Black and Coloured authors to attend a special meeting of PEN. Mary presided, wine was served and everyone grumbled – the existing members because they claimed it was up to the Africans to apply if they really wanted to, the Africans because they felt they had never been truly made welcome. But this was nothing beside the quarrel which broke out between Blacks and Coloureds, who, Elstob suddenly realized, distrusted each other more than they disliked the Whites. The meeting closed with a lot of ruffled feathers and not a single new member.

Elstob's account of his visit is refreshingly honest and makes no attempt to disguise his failure to appreciate the complexity of South Africa's racial problem. When he announced to the press that the main reason for his visit was to campaign for the release of Breytenbach, he found himself under attack from the ANC, who demanded to know why this PEN official was so concerned about one White prisoner when so many Black ones, including Nelson Mandela, were languishing on Robben Island. Elstob's only defence was to point out that Mandela was not an author as defined by PEN, the very argument Mary had been putting forward all along.

Elstob had one final misfortune while passing through Johannesburg on his way home. He was interviewed on television and used the phrase 'non-White' about the Black and Coloured population. He was accused of racism in some newspapers, and Nadine Gordimer had to step forward to explain that he had not realized the term could possibly give offence.

After his departure the new Johannesburg centre quickly fell apart when a group of African writers who had not joined accused those who had of being 'Uncle Toms'. At one point their animosity threatened to take a physical form. To save face, the Black members voted to expel all the White members including Nadine Gordimer herself – an act that contravened the very spirit of PEN

International, which forcefully rejected any such move, following which the Johannesburg centre ceased to exist from sheer inertia.

The sole observable result of the entire episode was that the once amicable relations between Mary and Nadine Gordimer were irreparably shattered. Even years later, in a letter to Kasia, Mary's burning anger remained undiminished:

> There's hardly anyone who knows her and likes her, and instead of ever asking herself if this can possibly be because she is a bit of a bitch, she always attributes it to political martyrdom. Alan Paton has been every bit as outspoken as she has, and everyone respects *him*. I could write you chronicles about her, the only writer I've ever known to go in for calculated intrigue in the world of letters. But, as Jane Austen very properly says, let other pens dwell on vice and misery.

※

Mary's reasons for deciding to write one more book about Alexander – this time the *dead* Alexander – are not immediately obvious. The novel is a remorseless crescendo of violence, beginning with the despair of his companions at his death and leading on through treachery, deceit and murder to ultimate tragedy as his family and friends are each in turn cut down when they attempt to seize some portion of his power, and all, with one exception, ultimately fail. The book's working title, *Hot Embers*, better conveys a sense of this burned out, yet still dangerous world than the more elegiac *Funeral Games*, which she finally settled on. It may be that Mary had decided to complete the Alexander story for the same reason she wrote the second Theseus book – to keep her hand in. Or she may, like Tolkien, have come to inhabit her own fictional world so thoroughly that it was impossible for her not to see it through to its conclusion. The novel is the ultimate expression of her distrust of the human lust for power. As she wryly described it to Patrick O'Brian, 'I fear it is a rather grim affair with few of the cast surviving; I must really do something more cheerful next time' – which scarcely does justice to the horror and mayhem inflicted on her characters, all recounted with a bleakness new to her writing:

She moved to the space under the high roof-peak, and he saw her fetters. He wept again, wiping his running nose. The smell of his unwashed flesh repelled her as much as the privy. Involuntarily she drew back against the far wall; her head met the roof again and she had to crouch on the filthy floor.

'Please, please, Eurydike, don't let them beat me again.'

She saw then why he did not sit with his back to the wall. His tunic was stuck to his skin with dark stripes of clotted blood; when she came near he cried, 'Don't touch it, it hurts.' Flies were clustering on the yellow serum.

Fighting back her nausea she said, 'Why did they do it?'

He gulped a sob. 'I hit them when they killed Konon.'

A great shame filled her. She covered her eyes with her chained hands.

Eurydike, wife of Alexander's idiot half-brother, Philip Arridaios, is one of the rare female protagonists in the historical novels. However, Mary makes it abundantly clear that she has no time for a woman in a man's world. When Eurydike prepares to seize power by winning over the Macedonian troops at the great assembly summoned to vote on the kingship, we are left in no doubt that it is her very womanhood that renders her inadequate:

She would not, could not admit defeat. She would speak, it was her right; she had won them once and would again. Soon this old man would finish talking, and she must be ready.

Her hands had clenched, her back and her shoulders tightened; her stomach contracted, achingly. The aching turned to a cramp, a low heavy drag which, with dismay, she tried at first not to recognize. In vain; it was true. Her menses, not due for four days, had started.

She had always counted carefully, always been regular. How could it happen now? It would come on quickly, once begun, and she had not put on a towel.

She had been strung-up this morning; what had she failed to notice in all the stress? Already she felt a warning moisture. If she stood on the rostrum, everyone would see.

The Regent's speech approached its climax. He was talking

of Alexander; she hardly heard. She looked at the thousands of faces round her, on the slopes, in the trees. Why, among all these humans made by the gods, was she alone subject to this betrayal, she only who could be cheated by her body at a great turn of fate?

Beside her sat Philip, with his useless gift of a strong man's frame. If she had owned it, it would have carried her up to the rostrum and given her a voice of bronze. Now she must creep from the field without a battle; and even her wellwishers would think, Poor girl!

Antipatros had finished. When the applause subsided, he said, 'Will the Assembly now hear Eurydike, daughter of Amyntas, the wife of Arridaios?'

No one dissented. Antipatros' men were curious; her partisans were ashamed to vote against her. Their minds were made up, but they were prepared at least to listen. Now was the moment for a true leader to compel their hearts . . . She had come, the morning being fresh, with a himation round her shoulders. Now, carefully, she slipped it down to her elbows, to drape in a curve over her buttocks, as elegant ladies wore it in fresco paintings. Getting to her feet, taking care over her draperies, she said, 'I do not wish to address the Macedonians.'

All the women in the novel are dismissed as irrelevant or murderous. Alexander's wives and children, along with his mother Olympias, die hideously, at the hands of other women. Eurydike's humiliation is only the most extreme example of a tendency to marginalize her female characters which had grown as Mary's novels progressed. The early, English novels are unusual for having strong women at the centre of the action, though even the strongest, Hilary in *Return to Night*, is obliged eventually to accept that her life and career must be second to that of her lover. By the time she wrote *North Face* Mary's women were caricatures, and with *The Charioteer* she finally gave up the attempt and began to write about men who did not need women at all.

In 1979, before *Funeral Games* appeared, a lecturer at Columbia University, Carolyn G. Heilbrun, published *Reinventing Womanhood*, an influential study of feminine fiction, the third chapter of which, 'Women Writers and Female Characters: The Failure of Imagination', used Mary as a classic example of the way women authors refuse to grant their female characters the same freedom and independence they enjoy in their own lives. Heilbrun was not singling out Mary for attack; on the contrary, her thesis was that all female authors were guilty of the same thing:

> Jane Austen cannot allow her heroines her own unmarried, highly accomplished destiny. Women writers, in short, have articulated their pain. But they cannot, or for the most part have not, imagined characters moving, as the authors themselves have moved, beyond that pain.

Heilbrun saw no reason to doubt that Mary was speaking through Axiothea, the one female character in *The Mask of Apollo*, when she says of her gender, 'I must have done wrong in my last life on earth, and this is the punishment I chose when my eyes were opened. So I ought to bear it patiently, and hope for better next time. But, oh, it is hard.'

Of the handful of studies (all of them American) of Mary Renault's work, Heilbrun's is undoubtedly the most stimulating, though her assertion that the Alexander novels create an all-male world where women can be raped and murdered at will falls into the trap of seeing and evaluating the past through the eyes of the present, which Mary always opposed. Had Mary been confronted with such criticism, she would have responded that the Macedonians had a violent male-dominated culture, and it was no business of hers to pretend otherwise. Indeed, the degradation of women identified by Heilbrun is somewhat counter-balanced by the equally harsh treatment meted out to the men in *Funeral Games* who, when they are not fools, are certainly cowards and who meet deaths quite as vile as those of their womenfolk. It is significant that the only survivor of this bloodbath is the 'female' lover, the eunuch Bagoas, the Persian boy, who seems to represent for Mary a solution to the problem of gender by being, like T. S. Eliot's Tiresias, of neither, yet of both sexes at once.

Bagoas remains Mary's most intriguing creation. Gaunt and grief-stricken, forgotten in the confusion which follows his beloved's death, the boy remains in the tent, guarding the body. When the vast sculpted and gilded death carriage sets off across Asia Minor, the cloaked figure of the eunuch lover follows at a discreet distance. He alone knows that Alexander's step-brother Ptolemy plans to carry it off into Egypt, the portion of the empire he has reserved for himself, where the great tomb he will erect will legitimize his reign. Ptolemy was the only member of Alexander's family to establish a dynasty, which endured to the last queen, Cleopatra VII. Bagoas will live out his days in Alexandria, at the shrine of its founder, and it is his presence that makes *Funeral Games* more than a mere fill-in or mopping-up operation. Where Mary's first novel had been a gift to Julie in their earliest days, this hymn to homosexual fidelity was hers, too, in their last.

14

That Really Bucks Me Up

Late in 1981 Mary wrote to Cedric, telling him that *Funeral Games* was out in America and, although she had not yet seen any reviews, she had been told that *Time* was giving it a full page, which augured well. She added that, in order to please her British publishers, she had agreed to a BBC television interview, as she had no wish to appear 'bloody-minded'. This was a significant change of heart. She had recorded a radio interview with Sue MacGregor, the daughter of her old friend Jim MacGregor, while Sue was visiting him in Cape Town, and a journalist from the London *Times* had once flown out to talk to her, but a full-scale, filmed documentary was something new and not altogether welcome.

I had made the proposal while on a training attachment to the BBC arts programme *Omnibus*, feeling that a popular, yet serious writer had been unjustly ignored. Once the idea was accepted in London, I had to spend three frantic months begging and cajoling agents and publishers to get Mary to agree. The idea of linking the interview to publicity for the new book was a ruse, but at least she finally, if nervously, agreed.

From the 26th to the 30th of January 1982 I turned up every morning at Atholl Road with a camera crew for a day's filming. Mary soon overcame her fears and decided that I was not 'an omnivorous carnivore' and a later description to Kasia neatly sums up a memorably happy week:

For 5 days the house was as full of people as if we were giving a house-party. Though of course they didn't actually sleep here, they seemed to be here all day; Sweetman, the producer, a delightful woman called Jane Coles, and her assistant, a nice girl, Jenny Cathcart. On top of this there was the camera team, on contract from Johannesburg but run by an ex-BBC man; and the sound man, a cheerful Falstaff with a beard. By some miracle, or rather because they were all so gemütlich and got on together, we all seemed to find the same things funny, and we quite missed them when they went. Of course they take miles and miles of footage, and then edit about three-quarters of it out. They did me in my study and with Julie on the balcony and both of us with the dogs on the beach, and of course talking, which I had been terrified of, thinking I would be sure to seize up and become totally inarticulate, but I managed to run on somehow. I rather dread getting the film, which they have promised, since we have a video, to send me; feeling sure I shall look uglier than I ever guessed; but it was fun at the time anyway. It is coming on in a programme called *Omnibus*, provisionally on March 14th.

Mary was predictably chary of questions about South Africa but wandered off happily into the deeper recesses of the ancient world. Now that I realize how little I knew about her at the time, I am amazed, when I read the transcripts of our days of talk, how often my rather vague questions drew out something worthwhile. Although, as she said, only a fraction of any interview ends up on screen, the producer, Jane Coles, managed to achieve a rounded picture of Mary's life, work and general philosophy boiled down to broadcast length. By the end of our time I was simply having fun and wasted a good deal of expensive BBC film stock, asking questions I personally wanted the answers to:

DS: What sort of books do you relax with?
MR: Dick Francis.
DS: And television?
MR: *Dallas* – you have to know what ghastly things JR is going to do, and I keep trying to work out how Sue Ellen manages to expose her lower teeth all the time.
DS: I've been sneakily going over your bookshelves while we've been here, and I noticed a number of books on spiritualism – why?

MARY RENAULT

MR: I haven't got a commitment to spiritualism or anything like that, but I am very open to the supernatural – though I think that's an absolutely ridiculous term because nothing which exists can not be natural, it is just that we don't know about it.

DS: There are some who would suggest that your ability to look into Ancient Greece is evidence of some sort of psychic power. Do you ever feel that?

MR: No, I don't feel that; I think it is mostly hard work. But I read recently that just as you can have telepathy between people, you can have telepathy with the past. And you know sometimes I have guessed that something was so, and found the evidence later which proved it.

DS: Is that disturbing?

MR: No, I feel pleased.

There was one particularly memorable moment, when I asked her what she would like to be remembered for and she replied, 'As someone who got it right.'

At the end of our week together, I asked Mary where she might care to have a farewell dinner. She chose the Mount Nelson, a grand hotel in the British style, once used by the P & O liners en route for India, with a formal dining room and the type of solid British food one forgets still exists. As Cape Town is blessed with wonderful seafood restaurants, I gently enquired why she so obviously loved this curious place. Her smile was a delight in itself. 'Because', she said, 'they have always let us wear slacks and put us at Kipling's table.'

For Mary the low spot in the whole business came after the broadcast, when the *Daily Express* television critic described her as a 'sweet old thing'. It provoked a memorable outburst to Kasia: 'Do you see anyone saying that about a male writer? Feminists bore me, but sometimes I do see they have a point . . .'

Mary and I would occasionally write to each other, over the year following the programme, but it was when I made a film about the Duke and Duchess of Windsor that my status was assured in her eyes. Mary never forsook her golden first love and had stoically refused to admit the least criticism of the former

King. It is one of the strangest things about her. She was so fanatical about the truth, so furious if anyone tampered with facts, so clear-sighted about history, so uncompromising in her political judgements, yet over Edward, Prince of Wales, later Duke of Windsor, she was deliriously irrational. She loved him, and that was that.

*

The last letter I received from Mary was dated 2 April 1983 and came after a long silence on both our parts. Her reason for writing was entirely in character: she had come across one of my poems in an old copy of *The Times Literary Supplement* which must have meandered out by sea mail. She had immediately sat down and composed a letter full of congratulation, based on the kind of detailed analysis that is always so flattering and encouraging. She had also come across an article about herself which I had written for the *Listener* to coincide with another BBC radio adaptation of *The King Must Die*. In it I had wondered, rather tongue in cheek, what she would be writing next. She had, I opined, progressed from the Bronze Age through Socratic Athens to Alexander; could we now expect a book on Hellenic Egypt? Was it, I suggested, too much to hope that Mary Renault was going to write a novel about Cleopatra? That she would even consider writing about a woman, let alone one who had frittered away her chance of power for something as unworthy as sex, was a joke she might have resented. Happily, she took it in good part, but, as I might have expected, she gave no hint of what she really was writing.

Extraordinary as it is to imagine what was involved, she had, at the age of seventy-five, decided that the time was right for the novel of the Middle Ages she had been contemplating ever since her days at St Hugh's over half a century earlier. She was concentrating on the Knights of St John and their settlement on Rhodes, mixing chivalry with Greece and bringing in an echo of hospital life, since these knights belonged to a medical order. As she had always maintained that her first attempt at a historical novel had failed because she had written it blindly without doing any research, she was clearly going to have to begin yet another massive programme of reading and note-taking. She had been building a library of medieval studies over the years, but what she needed now were manuscripts and theses often available only from university photocopying services. She began work early in 1981, when *Funeral Games* was completed, but the going was slow, partly because it was new ground, but also because of increasing ill health. In December 1982 she wrote to tell Kasia that she was undergoing physiotherapy for a bad back, admitting that she was seeing a chiropractor, which she felt must have her father turning in his grave, so low were such people considered in his day.

While she rested, she re-read Malory for the umpteenth time, finding more details to enjoy. 'I like to read him in the original spelling, which brings out the full flavour. Once launched in, it seems quite natural, and one takes things like Powlis for St Paul's in one's stride.'

Early in 1983 she began writing in earnest, although she did not feel entirely well and could no longer keep to the hard schedule she had formerly set herself. Her last letter to me ended with the news that she and Julie had just been back to their beloved Ceres.

> In the evening the sunset dyes the mountains like the Tunis walls in your poem, and the colours are most dramatic, going from topaz to amethyst to ruby. It is now the done thing to build nice labourers' cottages in the Dutch style, and only poor farmers keep them in hovels today. One of the mysteries of this country is how the urban Afrikaaner has lost all the good plain taste of the otherwise backward 19th century Dutch, who built white farms which actually improve the landscape, white churches with a brilliant appreciation of light and shadow in a simplified Gothic which puts Ruskin to shame. Nowadays they have everything which is symbolised by the garden gnome. It is only the country farms that keep the tradition alive.

What she did not say was that Julie had wanted them to make the trip in the hope that it would restore Mary's spirits after a bad bout of flu she seemed unable to shake off.

By August 1983 she was admitting to Kasia that all was not well:

It was so sweet of you to find time to write me a lovely letter with all that you have to do. You are so loyal, and expend so much of yourself, the same self that goes into your poetry which is so valuable and which you are getting so little time for. It is true, too, that one does slow down with time; with, really, virtually no responsibilities other than work, because Julie runs the house entirely and we have 'help', I find it takes more and more of my breath to cool my porridge so to speak, and when my publishers say when will the next book be ready, I just say 'don't know', because the thought of all that machinery going into motion, and knowing as the time draws near that I'm not going to make it, makes my blood run cold. It is about 80% done, I suppose, but it's all that knotting-up.

It was true that the novel was effectively written, but she was still dissatisfied with the final chapter, and there was the last fair copy to be done, that essential drawing together of the much scribbled over manuscript which Mary always considered the most vital part of her work. The trouble was it seemed harder and harder to get down to it. The Cape winter was exceptionally wet that year, but she was determined to be ready for Owen's fiftieth birthday party on 29 August. Normally she loathed such crowded gatherings, but for Owen she would do anything and had already bought his present, well in advance. The wet weather continued into August, and with it came a cough. At first this was no more than a mild irritant, but it soon became a persistent, hacking attempt to clear her lungs and catch her breath. When Julie voiced her fears to Dr Sonnenberg, he arranged an x-ray, but they had no sooner returned to Atholl Road than he telephoned to say Mary must go straight to bed as the x-ray showed pneumonia.

Sonnenberg asked a mutual friend, Dr Slome, to call on Mary later that day, and he decided she would be better off in a nearby nursing home. For a week they tried, in Slome's words, 'to knock this thing out' with antibiotics, but he eventually conceded defeat and brought in a visiting British surgeon, who proposed a bronchoscopy under general anaesthetic. It was at this point that the truth dawned on Julie, though again she said nothing to Mary.

As Mary was wheeled out of the theatre, this time singing 'Pick yourself up, dust yourself down, and start all over again', the surgeon asked to see the family. Julie told him she was the family and listened as he explained that he had found fluid on the lung and had aspirated some of it: the cause was cancer. Once again she begged the doctors not to say anything unless Mary demanded to be told. The surgeon was doubtful, but Sonnenberg and Slome convinced him it was for the best.

Back home, Mary cheered up a little. Now that she was no longer full of antibiotics she could eat and enjoy re-reading Patrick O'Brian as she waited for his new book. Whenever fluid built up, Dr Slome came to the house to aspirate her. Between times she went on trying to finish the novel, making her way down to the study to work on the fair copy, though progress was painfully slow. Occasionally, Julie would take her for a drive around the local beauty spots on the road to Cape Point, which was tiring, but always raised her spirits.

She did not ask why she was not getting better. If she guessed, she said nothing. Old friends were still welcome. Julie invited John Whiteley, who was in Cape Town rehearsing a play, to come round. He was surprised to find Mary propped up in bed, but left without realizing how serious her condition was.

It was when August drifted into September that she began to feel too tired to see anyone apart from David and Owen. When Kimon Friar wrote to say that he planned to visit South Africa and would, of course, be coming to see her, she asked Julie to forestall him. She loved his company, but was too exhausted to cope.

By October Slome was draining off liquid twice a week and was by this time convinced that there was a pocket he could not reach. It was decided that oxygen might ease her breathing, and a cylinder was hired, which Julie dressed up in a kaftan so that the bedroom would look less clinical. By now the trips to the study were over. Mary was able to work only at a table in her room, and then rarely. It was when the typewriter broke and had to be sent for repair that the fragile thread finally snapped. The manuscript lay there reproachfully, the fair copy not started. Mary pointedly reminded Julie of an old promise that, if anything were to happen to her, all her unfinished work was to be destroyed.

*

Despite Julie's letter, Kimon Friar turned up at the house and Julie served him coffee, brandy and cakes in the Greek manner. The afternoon dragged on and only with great reluctance did the man who had once done so much to ease her stay in Athens accept the fact that he would have to leave without seeing her.

Mary wrote a last letter to Kasia at the end of November, no more than a note telling her that she had viral pneumonia and did not feel bright enough to work, though she had been able to listen to tapes of the recent BBC dramatization of the Theseus books, which had pleased her. She returned to the nursing home on 8 December. Apart from David and Owen, visitors were not permitted, but an exception was made for Theo Aronson and Brian Roberts, who were holidaying at the Cape. It was a necessary reconciliation now that the issues of a decade earlier no longer seemed as crucial as they had at the time.

Julie arrived every morning and returned in the afternoon and early evening, usually weighed down with library books, as Mary could still get through two novels a day. She much enjoyed Salman Rushdie's *Midnight's Children*, but, as she grew increasingly tired, she surrendered herself to old friends: *Treasure Island*, *Morte d'Arthur*, Patrick O'Brian. She was still longing for O'Brian's latest book, but there had been a mix-up with the post and another had to be despatched. He wrote her a separate note, which arrived on Monday, 12 December; she read it as soon as Julie brought it in:

We were in England last month and at a dinner party. I heard the man opposite me say your name: as soon as there was a pause I leant over and asked him what he had been talking about. A friend, he said, a friend with a merely scientific education who on meeting the Regius Professor of Greek at Oxford asked what he should read to gain insight into the Hellenic world. 'Oh Mary Renault every time,' said the excellent Professor. 'Mary Renault – perfect for historical accuracy, perfect for atmosphere.' I could hardly have put it better myself.

Mary lay back against the pillows. 'That really bucks me up,' she said. It was the last thing she read.

The two of them passed the day quietly. There was no longer any need to speak. Julie did not stay late – the doctors wanted to inject something new into the pleura early the next morning in the hope that it would help stop further fluid from forming. Julie had guessed that this was a 'last hope' move, but was calm about it. Mary always rang her at eight in the evening, before the switchboard closed down, and again at eight in the morning, as soon as it opened again.

Julie slept quite well that night, but, when the phone woke her, and she saw that the bedside clock said seven, she knew that it could mean only one thing.

*

Julie had always assumed that she would lay out Mary's body herself, but in the end she did not return to the hospital, did not see the corpse and left everything to the undertaker. She telephoned David and Owen, and then the *Cape Times*, who would see to it that the news became public. She phoned Joyce herself, but felt unable to contact all Mary's friends individually as there was much to arrange for the simple funeral service, which would be held in the Anglican Cathedral in Cape Town on Thursday. Mary's friends heard about her death in various haphazard ways. Michael Atkinson was directing a television play when the phone rang and a friend told him that he had heard the announcement on the radio. He was so overcome, he could not go on. John Whiteley had decided to walk to his rehearsal that morning, and it was only when he was sitting in the theatre café, having a late breakfast, that Owen came to break the news. Old friends like Kasia and new ones like myself read about it in the newspapers and were shocked, having known nothing of the seriousness of her illness and being unprepared for the jolt of seeing that strange, cosy photograph of a lady in a cardigan looming out of the obituary pages. Most writers praised a life dedicated to scholarship, and *The New York Times*, ever her greatest supporter, spoke of her love of freedom and her opposition to *apartheid*. Only *The Times* of London added a sour note of literary criticism, mentioning her flawed views on matriarchy in the Theseus books and the obituarist's belief that her lack of classical Greek turned away some readers. Later, the letters pages would carry a rebuttal of these inappropriate remarks, which at the time caused much distress to Julie and the friends who had loved Mary in life.

In Camps Bay most of their friends were surprised at how well Julie appeared to be coping. No one knew that she had already gone through the agony of grief a decade earlier, when she learned of Mary's first cancer. Grateful to have had thirteen more years, she felt no need for public tears. Under Julie's guidance, David arranged the pall-bearers, among whom were John Whiteley and Owen, Michael Atkinson, Theo and Brian. David also drove with her to the cathedral, where the coffin was waiting. She had brought roses to lay on it and ordered a vase of Mary's favourite St Joseph's lilies to be placed near the altar to represent her many friends abroad who could not be there.

The service was short. David gave an inspired eulogy, quoting from Patrick O'Brian's letter. They sang 'Immortal, invisible, God only wise', the hymn Mary liked best. The brilliant African sun lit up the stained glass windows, and Julie remembered morning chapel at the Radcliffe and the curious probationer with her ill-tied 'Sister Dora' cap.

*

Julie laid her roses on the coffin, which was taken, unaccompanied, to the crematorium. The acting contingent made their farewells, hurrying off to rehearsals, knowing that Mary would have approved. David took Julie home to Atholl Road, where they had tea.

In the days that followed Julie had much letter-writing to keep her busy. When she wrote to me, she said that she felt she should dedicate her life to dealing with Mary's estate. Her one aim was to do exactly as Mary would have wished, and to this end, she gave generously to the ballet, with bursaries to help Black and Coloured dancers. Other matters were less easily resolved, and for a long time she agonized over the unfinished novel. While she knew that Mary wanted her to destroy it, she hesitated, unwilling to do anything so irreversible. She did not want to consult Juliet O'Hea, the other literary executor, or John Guest, afraid they might pressure her into publishing something Mary would not have allowed. Fifteen months after the funeral, she burned it.

*

In 1985 Joyce had an accident, which left her with a badly crushed hip and, on a whim, Julie left for England for the first time since 1948 to care for her. So much had changed physically that places she had known were no longer familiar, but more disturbing was the gulf that existed between her own experience of the past thirty-eight years and that of the people she encountered on her visit. It was most obvious in the BBC news programmes, which portrayed an image of South Africa quite alien to the one she knew. As soon as Joyce was on the mend, Julie was glad to return home.

At the end of 1987 she resolved her final nagging problem by taking the urn with Mary's ashes to Ceres, where she scattered them in the place they had both loved so much. As she shook out the plastic bag, some blew back in her face. She was not unhappy. 'I always wanted to touch everything she touched.'

In 1988 I wrote to say that I was planning to leave the BBC and would like to write Mary's life. Julie agreed at once, arranging for me to visit South Africa to talk to friends and see things like the houses in Durban, which I had missed on my original trip. But by far the most interesting part was Julie's decision to come to England again, so that we could go to all the places she and Mary had known when they were young. We even managed a day across the Channel at Equihen and, though the Hôtel des Falaises had been bombed in the war, there was still an upturned boat as a reminder of the artists who had once lived there.

Back in England, we drove along the narrow Cotswold lanes where they had walked as young nurses, with Julie reciting snatches of the poems they had once chanted together. Dacre Lodge, Mary's birthplace in east London, had been bought by the local council's immigrants' welfare division to use as a refuge for battered Asian wives. The dilapidated stable in whose loft Mary had first begun to write still stood, though not for long by the look of it. The most imperishable souvenir was at the Radcliffe Infirmary Nurses' Home, where the windows still sported the wooden chocks put in when *Purposes of Love* revealed what went on in those cell-like rooms. Shortly before she died, Mary had been sent a celebratory volume produced by the hospital, in which she was listed as one of the famous alumnae who had brought the institution much honour. They had smiled when they thought of all that had gone on there a half-century before, but, despite everything, Julie could see that Mary was pleased to have been remembered.

Acknowledgements

This book could not have been written without the permission and wholehearted co-operation of Julie Mullard, to whom I am very grateful.

I wish to thank the following, listed alphabetically, for agreeing to be interviewed, for lending letters, photographs and other memorabilia, and for granting me permission to quote them and to include them in this book: Kasia Abbott, Theo Aronson, Michael Atkinson, Alan Beale, John Boulter, Lionel Bowman, Joyce Challans, Peter Elstob, Dennis Folbigge, Leslie French, Gerald Gordon, Nancy Gordon, John Guest, Phyllis Hartnol, Judy Henderson, Rowland Hilder, Robert Liddell, Cedric Messina, Joy Millar, Owen Murray, Patrick O'Brian, Juliet O'Hea, Ronnie Orrell, David Poole, Brian Roberts, Raymond Sands, Roy Sargeant, John Sonnenberg, Colin Spencer, Os Therou, David Tidboult, Peter Toerien, Michael Tuffin, Julia White, John Whiteley, Barbara Williams, Helen Wolff.

I am grateful to Dr Howard B. Gotlieb, Director Special Collections, Mugar Memorial Library, Boston University, for access to and permission to quote from the correspondence of Mary Renault and Jay Williams.

Longman Group UK Ltd granted permission for me to consult their publishing files now deposited in the Archives and Manuscript Division of Reading University Library, whose keeper, Mr Michael Bott, kindly arranged for me to have access to any material relating to Mary Renault.

I also thank Lisa Johnson, who transcribed my taped interviews and typed the final drafts. I have benefited enormously from the editorial advice of Carmen Callil, Alison Samuel, Anne Freedgood and Alex MacCormick.

Finally, my especial thanks are reserved for the subject of this book. When I first read Mary Renault as an awkward, insecure teenager, I was transported, like Laurie in *The Charioteer*, to 'the wild outpost of an unknown continent . . . the mountains of the moon, the burial-place of the elephants: white on the map'.

David Sweetman, Pittefaux,
France, 1993

Bibliography

NOVELS BY MARY RENAULT

Purposes of Love, London, Longmans, 1939; as *Promise of Love*, New York, Morrow, 1939.

Kind Are Her Answers, London, Longmans; New York, Morrow, 1940.

The Friendly Young Ladies, London, Longmans, 1944; as *The Middle Mist*, New York, Morrow, 1945.

Return to Night, London, Longmans; New York, Morrow, 1947.

North Face, New York, Morrow, 1948; London, Longmans, 1949.

The Charioteer, London, Longmans, 1953; New York, Pantheon, 1959.

The Last of the Wine, London, Longmans; New York, Pantheon, 1956.

The King Must Die, London, Longmans; New York, Pantheon, 1958.

The Bull from the Sea, London, Longmans; New York, Pantheon, 1962.

The Mask of Apollo, London, Longmans; New York, Pantheon, 1966.

Fire from Heaven, New York, Pantheon, 1969; London, Longman Group, 1970.

The Persian Boy, London, Longman Group; New York, Pantheon, 1972.

The Praise Singer, New York, Pantheon, 1978; London, John Murray, 1979.

Funeral Games, London, John Murray; New York, Pantheon, 1981.

OTHER WORKS BY MARY RENAULT

The Lion in the Gateway: The Heroic Battles of the Greeks and Persians at Marathon, Salamis, and Thermopylae (juvenile), London, Longmans; New York, Harper, 1964.
The Horse from Thessaly (short story), in *The Twelfth Man*, ed. M. Boddey, London, Cassell, 1971.
The Nature of Alexander, London, Allen Lane; New York, Pantheon, 1975.
Introduction to *Sir Nigel* by Sir Arthur Conan Doyle, London, Cape, 1975.
'The Fiction of History' (article), *London Magazine*, London, 1979.
According to Celsus (short story), in *Tales of History*, ed. Herbert van Thal, London, Barker, 1976, reprinted in *Women Writing 3*, ed. Denys Val Baker, London, Sidgwick & Jackson, 1980.
'Murder in Macedon' (article), *Museum Magazine*, New York, 1980.
Introduction to 'A Letter From Pliny the Younger' in *Whales: A Celebration*, ed. Greg Gatenby, Toronto, Prentice-Hall Canada, 1983.
Afterword to reprint of *The Friendly Young Ladies*, London, Virago, 1985.

CRITICAL STUDIES

Men Are Only Men: The Novels of Mary Renault, Landon C. Burns Jnr., Minneapolis, Critique, 1963.
Mary Renault, Peter Wolfe, New York, Twayne, 1969.
The Hellenism of Mary Renault, Bernard F. Dick, Carbondale, Southern Illinois University Press, 1972.
Reinventing Womanhood, Carolyn G. Heilbrun, London, Victor Gollancz, 1979.

CRITICAL REFERENCES

Sex Variant Women in Literature, Jeanette H. Foster, New York, Vantage Press, 1956; London, Muller, 1958.

The Homosexual as Hero in Contemporary Fiction, Stephen Adams, London, Vision, 1980.

Gay Fictions: Wilde to Stonewall: Studies in a Male Homosexual Literary Tradition, Claude J. Summers, New York, Continuum, 1990.

SOURCES

Greece and the Hellenistic World, John Boardman, Jaspar Griffin and Oswyn Murray, Oxford, OUP, 1986.

Interpretations of Greek Mythology, Jan Bremmer, London, Croom Helm, 1987.

A History of Greece, J. B. Bury and Russell Meiggs, London, Macmillan, 1975.

Letters of J. R. R. Tolkien, ed. Humphrey Carpenter, London, Allen & Unwin, 1981.

J. R. R. Tolkien, Humphrey Carpenter, London, Allen & Unwin, 1977.

South Africa: A Modern History, T. R. H. Davenport, South Africa, Macmillan, 1977.

Prelude and Fugue: An Autobiography, Joan Evans, London, Museum Press, 1964.

Alexander the Great, Robin Lane Fox, London, Allen Lane, 1973.

Clifton High School 1877–1977, Nonita Glenday and Mary Price, Clifton High School, 1977.

A Sport of Nature, Nadine Gordimer, London, Cape, 1987.

The Essential Gesture: Writing, Politics, Places, Nadine Gordimer, London, Cape, 1988.

St Hugh's: One Hundred Years of Women's Education in Oxford, ed. Penny Griffin, London, Macmillan, 1986.

The Well of Loneliness, Radclyffe Hall, London, Cape, 1928.

Oxford in the Twenties, Christopher Hollis, London, Heinemann, 1976.

Apartheid: A History, Brian Lapping, London, Paladin, 1987.

Extraordinary Women, Compton Mackenzie, London, Secker, 1928.

South Africa: From Vorster to De Klerk, Keith Maguire, Edinburgh, Chambers, 1991.

If I Were King, Justin Huntly McCarthy, London, Samuel French, 1922.

Selected Poems, John Masefield (with a preface by John Betjeman), London, Heinemann, 1978.

An Adventure, C. A. E. Moberly and E. F. Jourdain, London, Faber, 1924.

Through Greek Eyes, Roger Nichols and Kenneth McLeish, Cambridge, CUP, 1974.

A Very Private Eye, Barbara Pym, London, Macmillan, 1984.

The History of the Radcliffe Infirmary, Jenny Selby-Green, Banbury, Image Publications, 1990.

John Masefield, Muriel Spark, London, Peter Nevill, 1953.

Secrets of a Woman's Heart: The Life of Ivy Compton-Burnett, 1920–1969, Hilary Spurling, Hodder & Stoughton, 1984.

Evelyn Waugh: The Early Years 1903–1939, Martin Stannard, London, Dent, 1986.

Evelyn Waugh, Christopher Sykes, London, Collins, 1975.

The City and the Pillar, Gore Vidal, New York, Dutton, 1948

Gilbert Murray OM 1866–1957, Duncan Wilson, Oxford, Clarendon Press, 1987.

Index

See under author for individual titles